Jolson

The Story of Al Jolson

Michael Freedland

First published as *Al Jolson* in 1972 by
W.H. Allen & Co. Ltd

This edition first published in Great Britain in 1995 by
Virgin Books
an imprint of Virgin Publishing Ltd
332 Ladbroke Grove
London W10 5AH

A catalogue record for this book is available from the
British Library.

ISBN 0 86369 972 3

Printed and bound in Great Britain by
Cox & Wyman Ltd, Reading, Berks

Contents

Foreword

There has to be a reason to justify republishing a book more than twenty years after it was first produced – a seventh edition, in fact.

Actually, there are two reasons: the birth of the musical show *Jolson* for which this biography was the starting point, and the sheer power and influence of Al Jolson on the century now drawing to its close.

It is surely amazing that a singer who died 45 years before who first trod the boards on Broadway no less than 84 years earlier and whose life story on film was produced almost 50 years ago, should not only still be remembered but should still prove to be a huge influence on the business of which he was king – and on the enthusiasts who can still go into a record store and buy CDs bearing his name and offering his songs.

The book begins with the way 'his' street, Broadway, marked his death in 1950. It was a unique commemoration of a unique performer – to say nothing of a unique life. But no one then could imagine that people would be paying him tribute and honour practically half a century later. To have done so would have meant reserving a place on the studio couch of one of show business's favourite psychiatrists.

That the name Al Jolson still means anything at all in the second half of the 1990s is uncanny, to say the least. That it is considered to be worth millions of pounds to invest in a major West End musical commemorating his life is practically unheard of. Perhaps only his contemporary Chaplin measures up to such a test. Who knows? Possibly Sinatra will be remembered in a similar way 50 years from now. Surely, his is the only name which comes to mind in these terms.

Jolson did more than just survive his contemporaries. His great rivals, both during his Broadway heyday and in his 'comeback' years (the short period between the première of *The Jolson Story* in 1946 and his death four years later) were men and women with names few even remember today.

Occasionally, you will see some of them in the record stores under the generic heading 'Nostalgia'. You still see those produced by the man who called himself 'The World's Greatest Entertainer' listed under 'Al Jolson'.

So why should anyone even remember his name? Simply because in his way he was just that, the greatest entertainer the world had ever known up to the time of his death – and for some, *since* his death too, a period that now exceeds that of his career. A sobering thought of sorts.

I originally wrote this book when the memory of Jolson was still fresh – if 21 years could be called a fresh memory. But more than that number of years have passed since then and virtually all the people who knew him and who spoke to me so graphically about him for this book have long gone themselves. The few who are still around to recall working with Jolson were very young then and are very old now.

Talk to them today and his is the one name which makes eyes light up and tongues wag. Not because Al Jolson was such a nice fellow. As you will see when reading these pages, he wasn't. He was too complicated for that; the factors which made him The World's Greatest Entertainer too important to be dismissed in such simplistic terms. Which is why it was worth writing a book about him in the first place, why it is worth republishing it now and why a new theatrical production needs to be called nothing more or less than just *Jolson*. Even now the name still rings resonant bells with people who were not only not around to see him live, but even to have bought his records while he was still among us.

So, then, Jolson was a phenomenon. They said in 1950 that there would never be anyone like him. Then they started throwing out names of people who could take on his mantle. The most popular choice was Danny Kaye. Or Judy Garland. Then they said it had to be Sammy Davis Jnr. Or Barbra Streisand.

The case is ready to be rested. Proof? There is none. There *can* be none. Except perhaps that the reader ought to ask him or herself a question: Will these other 'sensational' performers be remembered half a century from now?

Al Jolson will not be the top entertainer of the twenty-first century, but the twentieth is still his for the grabbing.

Michael Freedland
London, 1995

Acknowledgements

IT IS A HUNDRED YEARS since a child named Asa Yoelson was born in a tiny Russian town. The centenary of his birth is reason enough to recall the man he became – Al Jolson, the greatest all-round performer of the century.

Like thousands of others, I came under the Jolson spell as a small child, watching the two films of his life from a seat in a provincial cinema. I was a schoolboy when he died – an event that affected me deeply and was the start of this book.

That it eventually came to be written was largely due to a man whose knowledge of Al Jolson is matched only by his encyclopaedic familiarity with the cinema – Dennis Sykes. It was Dennis Sykes who made useful and constructive suggestions regarding source material and who provided so much background knowledge, and it can be fairly said that without his help this book would never have been. His colleague in the International Al Jolson Society, Leslie Kaye, who can recite dates and events in show business history with the ease of the learned student he is, was invaluable too. To those who provided the interviews on which the book was based, I give my thanks, too – Larry Adler, George Burns, Sammy Cahn, Saul Chaplin, Julius Epstein, Barbara Hale, Bob Hope, Fred Kelly, Evelyn Keyes, Abe Lastfogel, Stephen Longstreet, Bessie Love, Irving Rapper, Walter Scharf, Milton Sperling, Joni Taps, Harry Wayne, Hal Wallis and Jack Warner, Jnr. There were also memorable conversations with men who were part of the Jolson generation and, alas, no longer with us – like Jack Benny, Maurice Chevalier, George Jessel,

Ben Lyon, Ralph Reader, Morris Stoloff and Sidney Skolsky.

I must also thank those wonderful veterans of the world of show business in the Friars and the old Lambs Club of New York and the Hillcrest Country Club, Los Angeles, and the librarians of the Lincoln Center, New York, the Academy of Motion Picture Arts and Sciences in Beverly Hills, and of the British Library and the British Film Institute in London.

Nor can I forget, as I recall my early fascination with the subject of this work, my dearest mother who, with my late father of blessed memory, bought me my first Al Jolson record, 'I'm Just Wild About Harry' and who fired my imagination not only for this book but indeed for my whole career.

And finally, to my wife, Sara, who has been the greatest inspiration of all.

MICHAEL FREEDLAND
1984

We would acknowledge permission from Chappell & Co. for permission to quote from the lyrics of 'April Showers' and 'Liza', and from B. Feldman & Co. for permission to quote the lyrics of 'Rockabye Your Baby With A Dixie Melody' and 'When I Leave The World Behind' (Irving Berlin). Also the permission to reproduce the sheet music covers for 'Toot-Toot-Tootsie Goodbye' and 'Looking At You' from Francis, Day & Hunter Ltd, is acknowledged with thanks.

List of Illustrations

Al Jolson as Sinbad on Broadway
Jolson in 1911, newly arrived at the Winter Garden
Not only did Jolson have his own show but his own theatre too . . .
Jolson in 1913, showing off his fur coat
Jolson fooling around at home in 1912 with Louis Rosenberg
One of the Winter Garden leaflets which were distributed all over
New York
'Toot-Toot-Tootsie' – Jolson's tunes became the popular songs of the
day
Jolson singing 'Kol Nidre' in *Hollywood Cavalcade*
Al on honeymoon in 1928 with Ruby Keeler
Jolson the politician, at Marion, Ohio, with President Warren G.
Harding
Two 'greats' together – Jolson with Charles Chaplin
Jolson with Jack Dempsey
Al with Harry Langdon
Al with third wife Ruby Keeler, a big star in her own right
Successfully hiding the fear that Bing Crosby was grabbing at the
Jolson throne
Down Mexico way in *Go Into Your Dance*
Al with Peggy Lee
The two Jolsons: Al 'Larry Parks' Jolson and Al 'Asa Yeolson' Jolson
Larry Parks made up for the title role in *The Jolson Story*
Al with the son he and Erle adopted, Asa Junior
Painting the town red with Erle soon after their marriage
Jolson in Korea in 1950, where the GIs loved him
Al calling the tune again just like in the old days
Jolson the racegoer, the great love of his life after the theatre
Al showing Larry Parks how every movement in every song had to
be done for *Jolson Sings Again*

To SARA
who has the gift of making
music out of a marriage

One

Let Me Sing and I'm Happy

On the night of 23 October 1950 they turned out the lights of Broadway and the traffic that normally thunders in and out of Times Square was brought to a halt.

At the Friars Club in Los Angeles Harry Cohn, the iron dictator of Columbia Pictures, burst into tears. In a restaurant nearby Barnie Dean, one of the principal gag writers for Bing Crosby and Bob Hope, couldn't control his weeping on reading the telegram he had just received.

The news was that Al Jolson was dead. Not just a singer. Not just an entertainer. Not just a friend. But Al Jolson.

When people talk about the giants of the entertainment industry, the name Al Jolson can't merely be included as just one of them — it towers above any list. He was the all-time colossus of show business, an egomaniac who frequently referred to himself as the World's Greatest Entertainer. And nobody argued. Jolson wasn't everyone's favourite person. Many of his contemporaries disliked him. Many more were jealous of him. But no one has ever challenged his supremacy.

He was a man who could turn a tired, hungry audience of New Yorkers into a congregation of worshippers with him as their god. It has been said that he didn't play to an audience, he made love to it. He did more than that. For forty years he consummated that love openly, demanding as much in return as he gave. For his songs and his jokes he demanded applause — and was rarely disappointed.

When his star appeared to fall in middle-age, he went

[1]

searching for a magic ingredient that would hoist him to the top again. He found it in a picture called *The Jolson Story* and thus died with his popularity as high as it had ever been before. This picture became his memorial as others in his business knew it would and as he had hoped it would be.

Could a man like Jolson ever be happy when he was not singing? The answer lies in the 'other woman' cited by three wives in divorce actions against him – his audience. And that was because Jolson was only happy when he had a song to sing and someone to listen to him singing it.

George Burns said of him: 'It was easy enough to make Jolson happy at home. You just had to cheer him for breakfast, applaud wildly for lunch and give him a standing ovation for dinner.'

To Jack Benny only one entertainer came near Jolson, 'And that was Judy Garland. But Jolson was still the greatest.' George Jessel, who did not like Jolson as a man, had no doubt as to his status. 'There's only one other man who approaches Jolson – and that's Frank Sinatra. But he's twenty-five points below him.' Jonie Taps, an executive at Columbia Pictures, who crossed many swords with the man who insisted on calling him 'Knucklehead', looks back on Jolson with the trained ear of a musician, 'Jolson has been equalled by one man only – Frank Sinatra.' The same words and the same name crop up constantly in any conversation about Jolson.

Ralph Reader, the creator of the world-famous 'Gang Show' for Boy Scouts, began his professional life in a Jolson musical and needed only one word to describe the man, 'Electricity'.

Bessie Love, who was in Hollywood during the traumatic period when Jolson was responsible for making the movies talk, says of him, 'Oh – he was like a cyclone.' The cyclone called Jolson could be said to be the biggest single influence in entertainment history. Even Larry Adler says he plays the mouth organ as he does because of Jolson's influence.

Even today, young unknowns still make their débuts singing Jolson songs or saying that Al Jolson was the one entertainer they admired above all others.

His records are still avidly bought. His films still attract audiences. His songs are still played on the radio. He was the man who gave George Gershwin his first big break and who sang the first songs by an ambitious youngster called Irving Berlin.

He did everything that other show people have done since – sang in small towns as well as on Broadway, sang on the screen, on radio, on television and on long-playing records and sang to troops – only he did it first.

As Jessel said in his eulogy at the entertainer's funeral: 'Not only has the entertainment world lost its king, but we cannot say, "The King is dead, long live the King" – for there is no one to hold his sceptre. And we that are left behind are mere imitators, mere princelings.'

Jolson was the great Jewish entertainer. He wasn't observant, rarely went to a synagogue, but there was something specifically Jewish about the way he put his heart, his soul and his ambitions into his songs.

'In 1910,' said Jessel in that eulogy, 'the Jews who had emigrated from Europe were a sad lot. Their humour came out of their own troubles. Men of thirty-five seemed to take on the attitude of their fathers and grandfathers and were old before their time, and when they sang they sang with lament in their hearts. But then there finally came on the stage a man vibrant and pulsating with youth, authority and courage, who marched on the stage, head held high and with the look of a Roman emperor. He had a gaiety that was militant, uninhibited and unafraid.'

That man was Jolson – born in Russia but who sang of Dixie and a Swanee River he never saw until he was forty. A man who once said 'I've got so much dough that fourteen guys couldn't spend it in their lifetimes. But I'd rather die than quit this business.'

This, then, is his story.

Two

A Cantor for the Sabbath

THERE IS AN OLD tale in Jewish folklore about the cantor in the synagogue who yearned to be an opera singer; the man who spent his days singing to God, who really wanted to chant different melodies to an altogether different audience.

In Srednicke, a tiny cluster of wooden buildings in Russian Lithuania, Cantor Moses Yoelson stood before the Holy Ark in the little synagogue where he led prayers and occasionally allowed his mind to wander in that direction.

His ancestors for four generations had been cantors in places like Srednicke, little Fiddler-on-the-Roof hamlets which the villagers knew as 'schtetels', where everyone knew every other person's business and where the biggest scandal imaginable would be for one of their number to move away to places unknown, or worse still – marry a stranger of a strange religion. But in those days when the Czars ruled with arms of iron and where there was the constant fear of the sound of horses' hooves heralding Cossacks about to pillage and rape in a new pogrom, it did not happen very often.

It was even rarer for a cantor in a synagogue, the poor but always respected functionary who was never out of work, to even think of another calling. But Moses Yoelson loved music and sang the traditional melodies with a splendid baritone – and he did think. Occasionally, someone would return to the Pale of Settlement, the band of schtetels like Srednicke, which were the only places in which Jews were usually allowed to live, with tales of what they heard at the St Petersburg Opera.

Moses would listen spellbound and wonder what it would

[4]

be like to sing in the company that was next to present Boris Gudinov. Could he contemplate chancing his luck in that foreign world? The irony of that question took just one more generation to become fully apparent.

He thought – and then dismissed the idea from his mind. And as he did so, he knew that his father, grandfather, great grandfather, and great-great grandfather were resting a little easier in their graves.

On the throne of the Russias was Czar Alexander, a tyrant who dearly would have loved to find a solution to the 'Jewish problem'. He did not like his Jews but realised that they were a useful scapegoat for the ills in which his country constantly found itself steeped.

When there were financial problems or when the country was in political turmoil, there were conveniently Jews to beat, rape and murder. It was amazing how good that made Alexander feel. And there were also Jews to call up into the armed forces. With a country the size of Russia to control, this was one of their greatest assets.

But strangely for a Government system so autocratic, so heartless and so cruel, there was, nevertheless, one streak of humanity. The law insisted on every fourteen-year-old boy serving twenty years in the Army. All, that is, except the eldest son in the family. It was that escape clause that led to the mass emigration that was soon to take millions of Jews to the United States and to England, too.

The Jews had been trained from time immemorial to honour the laws of the countries in which they lived. Old, yellowed Hebrew prayer books are still in use with prayers in Russian script for the health and well-being of the same Czar whom they feared so much. But the religious among them – and few were not religious in those days because it was all they had to cling to – had to weigh any sense of national loyalty with the realities of the situation. The Ten Commandments, so precisely outlawing the taking of life, were infringed by soldiers every day of the week.

They also knew that once a young man went into uniform, there was a very real risk that he would never be seen again.

[5]

So families would scrape together a purse of rubles with which to bribe the local petty officials, and so formally disown their children. They gave them new names, and there were new phoney families to which their younger sons could belong – just so that these children would escape the draft.

Rabbis' families did it, too. So did that of a certain Hirsch Hesselson, a cantor – or chazan as the Yiddish-speaking people of his village knew him. He managed to scrape together enough money with which to bribe two separate officials – for two of his sons. Without using too much imagination, the two Hesselson boys took the name Yoelson. For them both were new papers and new families. They became sons of fathers who had met mysterious deaths.

The boys could not stay at home. But that was no great problem. It was time for them to start thinking of earning a living and it was quite usual for boys to leave home when their first jobs beckoned.

Moses Yoelson went to stay with an uncle in what then seemed the large town of Keidani. It was so big that it contained 500 houses! But it was near Kovna, the state capital, and that to the country folk seemed great in size and standing.

The uncle was impressed with his voice and suggested that the youngster should take part in the High Festival services at the local synagogue. But first, there had to be auditions.

Young Moses was looked at sternly by the elders of the congregation. One noticed the way he wore his hat – for the orthodox Jews never went without head covering. Another examined his beard – for the length of facial growth was in itself an indication of piety. But the decision on the strength of his voice was left to the synagogue's President. He was the man who sat next to the Ark containing the Holy Scrolls of the Law, the only one with real power in a community where the synagogue was the central pivot around which all else revolved. His name was Reb Asa Cantor.

As he heard the young chazan sing the Kol Nidre, the dirge recited in synagogues at the holiest service of the year – on the eve of the Day of Atonement – his mind wandered to other things.

He admired the way this man, who so desperately seemed to want the job, reached the high notes and held on to them. He wondered how he managed to switch keys almost without warning and make his voice plunge to his badly-worn leather boots. But more than that, he looked approvingly at his straight back and the fine features of his face.

Yes, he could have the job, Reb Cantor told him, but only on a short trial basis. However his main task would be to kill chickens according to traditional kosher dietary laws. Later, he would have to know how to circumcise baby boys to initiate them into the faith of their fathers and grandfathers. As he wrapped his prayer shawl and placed it neatly in its red velvet bag, he realised that singing in the synagogue was merely the 'glamorous' part of the job. Reb Cantor patted the young man on the back and invited him home to lunch.

Moses had never seen such a spread. On a white table cloth was hot soup. From the oven came the smell of chollent, the meat and potato mixture which had been simmering since sundown the previous evening so as not to offend the injunction against cooking on the Sabbath. But most exciting of all, there, in a neatly ironed white dress was Reb Cantor's daughter Naomi.

Her face had a fresh natural look that set Moses' pulse racing. Her silky brunette hair enhanced her and made her the prettiest girl he had ever seen. Within two weeks of that meeting. Moses and Naomi were standing under a canopy outside the synagogue. A glass broken under the young man's left foot symbolised the fact that they were now man and wife.

Everyone in the town came to congratulate the young bride and bridegroom. The men danced together. The women, all in their best clothes and their Sabbath wigs, stood behind rope barriers and clapped.

The elders of Keidani clapped loudest of all. For they knew that written into the marriage contract was that Moses and his bride had to live in Reb Cantor's house for one year – and that meant that for that year they would have a chazan to be proud of.

Before that year was up, the Yoelsons' first baby was born – a girl they called Rose. It was this that finally persuaded Moses to abandon his ambition to sing in the opera. With a family to support, his duty was to find security. So he decided to try to become a rabbi – a position with much more respect owing to it than a mere cantor or chazan attracted. The local rabbi heard him study, examined him on some of the sacred religious tractates of the Talmud, and awarded him his diploma.

But these diplomas – semicha – varied according to the respect in which the man awarding it was held. And the Keidani rabbi could not have had too good a reputation. In years to come, Moses Yoelson was lucky when he could be accepted as a chazan with a beautiful voice. More often, he was the singing shochet – the ritual animal slaughterer; or the mohel – the man who performed circumcisions.

But in Srednicke there was only one synagogue and it could afford only one officiant. A man who was both rabbi and cantor – as well as a shochet and mohel – was just what they were looking for. Word spread to Keidani of Srednicke's need.

Moses was asked to attend for an audition. But although they liked his voice, the community's leaders – the local butcher, the tailor and the milkman – thought he was too young. And, of course not eligible for the hand of any of their daughters. Indeed, he had a baby daughter to support – as well as a wife who appeared to be developing another bulky stomach.

Asa Cantor clinched the deal on his son-in-law's behalf with the donation of 100 rubles to the local mikvah – the communal bath house which Jewish Law dictates all married women should visit once a month to purify themselves.

In Srednicke, in a tiny wooden house, Naomi gave birth to another daughter, but the child was not strong enough to survive the cold Lithuanian winter. Within a few months, however, Naomi realised she was again pregnant. This time, their third daughter, Etta, was strong and robust.

When their fourth child was born a year later, Chazan

Yoelson seemed finally content. He now had the son who was to carry on the family tradition and be the sixth of the line to conduct services in the synagogue. They called the child Hirsch.

Life was hard in Srednicke. Without Naomi's father to provide for their needs, they had to learn how to run a home the tough way – by bitter experience. When the community was prosperous Moses and his family prospered – there were chickens to kill. When the villagers were poor, the Yoelsons went hungry with them.

Five years after Moses' marriage to Naomi, came a blow to the Yoelson household. Word reached the family that Asa Cantor had died, and for seven days Naomi sat on a low stool in the living room of their tiny house while neighbours visited her with words of consolation. It was a particularly hard time. For Naomi was going to have another child.

However, when the baby turned out to be another boy both Naomi and Moses were delighted. Not only was there to be another chazan in the family, but this one could be named after his grandfather. He was the new Asa. When the birth actually occurred no one now knows. It could have been any time between 1880 and 1888. It could have been in January or July. In the Russian Pale of Settlement in the 1880s no one thought of birth certificates. As we shall see, the most likely date seems to be 1885.

Years later that baby Asa was to decide that the year was 1886 and the day 26 May. But he simply liked the idea of a spring birthday and a year that made him seem a little younger.

The Yoelsons were a happy family. In those days, most religious Jewish families were. They never asked for wealth – because they realised they were unlikely to get any. The wealth that they did have was in their children, and they were content enough.

What is more, they felt they had a double bonus. A double religion, almost. They had Judaism, which they hallowed with a deep, sincere sanctity, and they had their music, which for the Yoelsons was inextricably linked with prayer.

As soon as his sons could utter their first sounds, Moses Yoelson set about the task of training their voices so that one day they would be the great cantors he was determined they should become. He propped open their mouths with little matchsticks so that they made the right sounds, and at home they practised their singing as much as they did the blessings they were required to recite before eating a piece of bread or drinking a cup of milk.

Moses's proudest moment was when they joined him in the synagogue for the first time. A little later on, the two boys stood at his side on the dais from which the congregation's prayers were led.

To the people of Srednicke, the Yoelsons became a family choir. From the ladies' gallery above the high voices of Naomi and her daughters Rose and Etta could be heard distinctly joining in the familiar melodies.

Judaism is by its very nature a family religion and religious practices were carried on in the home as much as part of the ritual as those in the synagogue. Everything the Yoelsons did seemed to have a religious purpose behind it. And for that purpose, there was music, too.

Sabbath lunches were punctuated with the singing of joyous family table hymns. For on that day the poorest shack became a palace.

No work was ever done from dusk on Friday until nightfall on Saturday. And for that day, the children were scrubbed, the tiny wooden home made as clean as Naomi's physical strength would allow, and hemlock was strewn on the floor to give an aromatic fresh scent – all to make the day seem special. As the hours went by, the scent would become mixed with the cosy aroma of the chicken soup. There was also the beautifully polished Sabbath samovar – in which was prepared the tea they would drink with a slice of lemon. But no one objected. It had to remain heated all day, lest the strict prohibition against making fire was breached.

At the New Year, the family went to the crowded synagogue, expectantly waiting for Moses to sound the shofar – the ritual blowing of the ram's horn, intended as a

[10]

clarion call to the faithful to spend the next twelve months in devotion to God.

Nine days later, on Yom Kippur, the day-long fast of Atonement, they watched admiringly as the handsome figure of Moses Yoelson, dressed completely in white, sang the traditional mournful melodies of his prayers.

Passover was the happiest time of the year. All the family sat around the long table laden with unleavened bread – matzoh – bitter herbs, eggs and saltwater, all of which symbolised the departure of the Children of Israel from Egypt, and they all sang the happy songs of freedom and read the allegorical tales which demonstrated the plight of a people always running away from some new calamity.

At Chanuka, the eight-day festival of the Maccabees, they all gathered round the eight-branch 'menorah' candelabra to sing the happy songs of the season. On ordinary week-days, there were the traditional foods that they all took for granted – the rich horseradish sauce mixed with beetroot, and the gefilte fish made from the carp which the day before had been swimming around the tin sink in the Yoelson kitchen.

The Yoelsons' home was their strength. Naomi, in particular, was the heart within that strength. Psychologists, both amateur and professional, have tried to see in this woman the root of all the Mammy songs that Al Jolson was to perform in the years to come. In reality, he probably did no more than find the right vehicle for his own talents at just the right moment. Mama Yoelson had little in common with the little old Negro lady who used to sing 'My Old Kentucky Home' and 'Old Black Joe' – except that she represented the Family.

When Asa was no more than about five or six that strength and that family leadership were put to their strongest test.

Cossacks rampaged through neighbouring villages in the Pale of Settlement, and the Jews of Srednicke quaked in their small houses. They were in the majority in the shtetl. They had a synagogue, whereas the local Russians had to use a room over the tavern for their Orthodox Church. They had a whole street of shops, whereas all the Russian trade

[11]

seemed to centre in that one tavern. But if the Jews were in the majority, it was the Christians who had the power.

For one thing, the town was owned by a local nobleman, for whom the whole population would turn out whenever his carriage passed by. And for another, there was the priest, who was believed to be influential with the local constable and, rumour had it, the constable had friends in high places in St Petersburg.

Young Jewish men vanished overnight. Some of them turned up in Siberia. But others it was learned later, had arrived in America.

The Yoelsons talked about this too. When the children were tucked up at night Moses and Naomi went over and over the same question: dare they risk trying this new life? Moses had an uncle in America and by all accounts the pavements in this new land really were covered in gold and everyone did live in a palace.

It was Naomi who made the decision. Jewish law rules that it is the mother who has the power to influence her children more than the father and, in the Yoelson family, she was the strong one. It was her word that counted.

She decided that Moses should go on to this brave new world they had heard so much about and that he should prepare the way for the rest of the family to follow. She did not admit to her husband that there were times when she felt so ill that she had no idea whether she would live to see him again.

Once the decision that he should leave for America was made, the question of how he was to get there had to be faced. The Russians were no happier about Jewish men leaving their country than they were about having them there in the first place.

It was left to Hayim Yossi, their neighbour and closest friend, to provide the answer. Yossi was a local wood-merchant who loved children. Because he had none of his own, he particularly loved the Yoelson youngsters and it was because of the children that he had let out half his house to the family. Since he was in the wood business, it was the best wooden house in the town. And because he respected religion and loved its music, he had taken the Yoelsons very much under his wing.

When Moses told him of his decision to emigrate, he promised to take care of the family while he was away. He also devised a plan to get the chazan out of Russia. He blackened the younger man's face, gave him a bundle of old clothes to put on and pointed to the raft lying on the shores of the river Neiman.

The river separated Srednicke – and with it Lithuania – from East Prussia. With Moses Yoelson acting as one of his workmen, they could float together across the river. No questions would be asked because wood was Yossi's business. And no questions were asked when Moses, having kissed Naomi and the children, made his way to the river bank.

When Yossi returned he simply told the customs men that his workman had got drunk and fallen overboard. For the second time in his life a false declaration was made in the name of Moses Yoelson.

For four years letters trickled into the Yoelsons' home. For some strange reason, no attempt was made to hide the fact that the Russian guards had been tricked and that Moses was really still alive and in America. Perhaps the Yoelsons never thought about such things as censorship.

For these four years, life went on. Naomi was ill and grew weaker but told no one. The children continued to play, to talk in Yiddish to each other – for they knew no other language – and to go to school at the local 'cheder', or Hebrew School.

From his letters they gathered that Moses was finding life hard; America was not the promised land he had been led to expect. But finally from New York they received a letter inviting the rest of the family to join him. He had a job as cantor at a synagogue at Newburg and enclosed in the envelope was enough money for their journey.

The first stage of the trip was to England – and to a city that had never heard their kind of music, but ironically one that three or more generations later was to symbolise another kind of show business not so different from the one of which Al Jolson was the master – Liverpool.

By the time the Yoelson family arrived in New York, Chazan Yoelson had a new job – in a synagogue in the nation's capital, Washington DC.

For Moses Yoelson Washington was little different from Srednicke. He had adjusted himself to being in a minority in a big city instead of one of a majority in a tiny hamlet. But life went on.

He was delighted to have his family around him. But his life was his work and he regarded the little domestic upsets that were becoming crucial as his wife's responsibility. For him the important things were his books and his singing in the synagogue. The girls were growing up now and seemed to be enjoying taking their places in running the home. But the boys were restless.

America was a bustling, exciting place the like of which the children had never seen before. The streets were not paved with gold – but they were paved, and that was remarkable. They saw men and women walking arm in arm with each other – something orthodox followers of their faith in Srednicke and the other towns of the Pale would no more think of doing than they would of eating a plate of ham.

They came face to face with the first blacks they had ever seen and heard their singing. When Hirsch and Asa came home singing about the Swanee River, Chazan Yoelson felt as though he had been struck by a bolt of lightning. But Naomi was there to pacify him. If the boys wanted to sing, she told him, it meant they were strengthening their voices ready for the day when they would join him as synagogue cantors.

She didn't always tell him of the times she spanked their behinds when they were late for her ready-made hot chicken soup or when they failed to wash their hands before sampling the Sabbath chalah – the home-baked loaf that played such a large part in the home religious ritual. They took their punishments bravely. They were mischievous, but somehow they knew they were usually no naughtier than other boys of their age. And they certainly loved her none the less for her chastisements. She had the knack of being a good mother.

She made sure that the boys had violin lessons – to which Asa seemed to take very well. But their father believed it was a mere frippery. He told them they had a God-given talent which they must never forsake for any other kind of music – their voices. So he gave them singing lessons when they were supposed to be practising their violins. The cantor pointed out how each note was a praise to the Lord.

Harry sang pleasantly, but not especially well, However, with little Asa, Moses realised there *was* something special. He knew how to breathe properly, he realised instinctively that singing came from his stomach – not simply from his throat.

Moses was delighted with his younger son's progress, and in their music there seemed for a time to be an instant rapport between father and boy. The youngster seemed to understand why his father made strange faces, why he lifted up his hands to indicate fluctuations of the voice and dropped them to show that another tone was needed.

Moses still grew angry when Asa wanted to rush out to play, but he put it down to the new surroundings which he was sure they would soon settle into. The Yoelsons, he liked to feel, were a happy family.

It was shortly after Hirsch's barmitzvah – the confirmation ceremony that spiritually marks the coming-of-age of the thirteen-year-old Jewish boy – that everything changed.

Naomi's continuing illness struck again. The children were taken by their father into her bedroom. Only the day before, she had been playing with them, helping the little girls with their cookery experiments, checking the boys' Hebrew grammar and learning with them the mysteries of this strange new English language.

But now her face was deathly pale. Chazan Yoelson walked desolately to his synagogue office in E. Street West just before the doctor arrived. He had no real idea of how ill his wife was. Hirsch was told to fetch his father. Together, they walked into her bedroom just as the sheet was being lifted over Naomi's face.

Al Jolson always remembered his mother's funeral as the time that he first had to think of being an individual and not simply one of a group. He was probably only nine or ten as he stood in a bitterly cold wind by her graveside. There had been no time to buy him any gloves, so he stood on the pathway, by the open grave at the Washington cemetery, with a pair of grey woollen socks shielding his hands from the frost.

Somehow, that frightening abrupt confrontation with reality was for this small boy the beginning of it all. If his mother had lived, he might now be remembered in some circles as one of America's most interesting cantors. Not a great one – but one with a joy in his singing. It is fair to assume that had she not died when they were so young, neither he nor Hirsch would have seriously thought of going into show business.

Because their father had been away from them for four long years, he was inevitably more distant than the mother they had loved and admired and who had always been with them. If he had had a little more understanding of the traumatic experience through which they were going, perhaps life would have been happier. As it was, he shouted at the boys and – for all his stern, rabbinical countenance –they tended merely to accept punishment as a tax to be paid for the fun they sought from life.

They joined a street gang – after Asa had proved he could knock down any kid bold enough to call him 'greenhorn'. They sold papers on street corners – in opposition to each other.

Hirsch was the first to discover the magic of money jingling in his pocket after selling the latest news from a street corner. Asa thought it was such a good idea that he got his own pitch – on the corner opposite, and any news that Hirsch called out, Asa magnified. If Hirsch shouted: 'Read all about it: Ten people killed in shipwreck', Asa would answer back by announcing: 'Twenty people lost in wreck. Read all about it'.

They had a flat above a shop that sold hay for horses. When he heard them whistling up the stairs, Moses Yoelson knew his boys and returned. Whistling, to him, was foreign – and he hated it. But even this he was powerless to stop.

In the local public school, Asa and Hirsch were known as bright pupils. But even though he was three years younger, Asa would try to find ways of getting his brother to take him home. He would say he didn't feel well, or that he had left their father ill in their flat and had to get back to his bedside.

Once in the street, the younger boy would egg on the older one to stand on the pavement and sing the ballads of the day for the odd cent or two. They must have looked a fine pair, two young immigrants still wearing the fringes of the ritual shawl all Jewish boys were supposed to have, and singing 'My Old Kentucky Home'.

When their father heard about this, it meant another swipe across the ears. But it made no difference. His boys were just 'loafers' – one of the few American words Cantor Yoelson had picked up from his surroundings.

Rose had by now taken on the mantle of the little mother. She cooked for them the way her mother had taught her – but the boys complained that the 'lockshen' – the home made noodles that even today are essential in all the best plates of chicken soup – was not as tasty as they had been used to.

When Etta chastised them for making their bedroom untidy, the boys just laughed – and went out to fight with the other boys on the block.

Meanwhile, their father grew more uncompromisingly orthodox in his ways and spent more time in his synagogue work or wrapped up in his books – when he was not killing more chickens or circumcising more babies. He no longer dreamed of being an opera singer, but he would have liked to have become a great rabbi. He now knew this was not to be either. Neither could he pride himself on being a successful father.

Perhaps, he thought, it would be better if I married again? He remembered the daughter of Perri Yoels, his wife's cousin back in the old country. Would she marry him? She wrote back accepting by return of post.

Her name was Hessi – or Ida as she later Americanised it to. But instead of acting as a bridge between their new life and the old family traditions, Hessi only served to make an even bigger wedge between father and sons.

In later years, they were both to grow very fond of her – because Hessi was not very much older than themselves and because she was good and kind. But when she first joined the household the boys simply resented her as an intruder.

At the age of fifteen, Hirsch gave himself a new name. He was to be called Harry. He convinced Asa that, unless he changed his name too, he would not be able to hold his head up high, so Asa became Al – Al Yoelson.

The signal for the real change in their lives came when Harry was walking near the Capitol building, singing one of the latest vaudeville tunes. A politician, who was sitting on a park bench, told him he did not feel well and asked the youngster to call him a cab. As he helped the elderly gentleman to the seat of the horse-drawn vehicle, Harry felt a coin being pressed into his hand. A gold ten-dollar piece.

To Harry it represented riches beyond all his dreams – and he used the money for the train fare to New York. Meanwhile, Al paced up and down at home, quarrelling with his father, shouted at his sisters, and brushed aside the kindly advice that Hessi tried to offer.

He was determined to join the brother he considered brave, adventurous – and totally sensible. He had no idea where he could find Harry, but he did have enough sense to find out where most of the newspaper sellers hung out – on the Bowery. In New York Al, too, sold papers, shined shoes, did anything that could raise a cent or two. He was probably about twelve and, as he said many years later, 'you get awfully hungry when you're twelve years old'.

He was walking along Broadway one day and for the first time in his life he saw a theatre. He could not afford the price of a ticket. Neither had he learned the tricks of sneaking in through the side entrance. But there was a magic about the colourful marquees, the posters and the theatre people he saw walking up and down the district that made an immediate

[18]

impact on him he could not really understand.

All he did know was that he was being drawn to the theatres by a powerful force. As he walked down Broadway, he heard the sound of singing coming from the alleyway at the side of one of the big show-places in that street of entertainment.

If he were very quiet, he thought, he could edge his way towards the stage and hear a little more. What he did hear led to an event that was to affect the future of show business for half a century.

The tall, stately blonde singer was rehearsing a new song. A stage hand came by and without seeming to worry about his gatecrashing told Al her name: Fay Templeton. The song had a gay, throbbing lilt to it. It was, 'Ma Blushin' Rosie'.

'Funny,' Al thought, 'that should be a song for a man, not a girl.' And, when Miss Templeton had finished singing, and had told the rehearsal pianist to pack away his music, Al couldn't get out of his mind the breath-taking sight of a real theatre.

When he did eventually leave, and walked back to the Bowery, the song still remained in his mind. He couldn't forget it . . . 'Rosie, you are ma posie . . . you are ma heart's bouquet . . . come out, here in the moonlight . . . ma blushin' Rosie . . . ma posie sweet. . .'

He walked and he walked. And, as he said long afterwards, he got hungrier and hungrier. When he reached a small grimy-looking restaurant on the Bowery called McGirks, he couldn't take his eyes from the window. There, inside, were plates of steaming hot food being handed over the heads of the patrons.

Eventually, he plucked up courage to approach the owner of the joint. 'Would you give me something to eat if I sing for you?' he asked.

The proprietor was a kindly man who had seen hungry boys before. He knew the pain of seeing food without being able to afford to eat it. He smiled and agreed. And through the noisy, smoke-laden atmosphere of McGirks came the sound of Al Yoelson singing 'Rosie, You Are Ma Posie. . .'

[19]

By the time he had finished a hush had descended on the diners. It was the first indoor public performance by a boy who was to become a show business legend, singing what was to become one of his best-loved songs.

Al got his dinner, the first food he had ever eaten that was not kosher. But it didn't bother him. What mattered now was that he was getting into show business.

On the Bowery he bumped into Harry, who was living in a home for newsboys. A kind Jewish woman had given Al a pair of worn, over-large shoes and the two youngsters felt sure they were on the crest of a great career. However, they continued to grow hungry. Eventually, they plucked up enough courage to visit an uncle living in Yonkers. They were not alone. Their elder sister, Etta, had beaten them to it and was living and working there after a row with Hessi.

Etta put Al on the train back to Washington – she did not trust him to take the fare and go by himself – even so, he still got off at Baltimore. There he was arrested by the Gerry Society – a group who regarded it as their solemn duty to keep children at school and not in the theatre or worse – who had a description of Harry and picked him up in mistaking him for his brother.

The events that followed turned into Jolson legends. The police took him, still mistaking him for Harry to the St Mary's Industrial Home for Boys in Baltimore's city centre, run by Roman Catholic monks.

The idea of a boy from a strictly Orthodox Jewish background suddenly thrust in the midst of a Catholic institution like St Mary's makes the mind boggle, and in later years this was to become fully developed and embroidered, not least of all by Al himself.

There have been stories of him being chosen to sing in the church choir – indeed *The Jolson Story* made a great play of this – but it seems unlikely. He was not at the home long enough to learn the Latin hymns he would have been required to sing.

Babe Ruth, who meant to American baseball roughly what Jolson meant to show business, spoke often of meeting Al there for the first time. A gangling coloured dancer called Bill 'Bojangles' Robinson, another of the Broadway sensations of the twenties, said the same thing. St Mary's was the only home those two ever had as boys. But it was never home to Jolson.

Al, himself, complicated history still further with one of the stories he liked to embroider around himself – so much so that he almost believed it. He told an interviewer in 1930. 'I ran away again and Papa caught me. I ran away again. He caught me. I could go on saying that for five minutes and it would be true.' Of that part of the story there can be little doubt.

But he went on, 'One day he told me I was just a bummer and he was going to lock me up. He took me to Baltimore and put me in St Mary's. My good Papa – and I like to kid him about it now and he likes it – told the priests what a low-lifer I had turned out to be and asked that Catholic lickings be tried where Jewish lickings had failed.'

It seems hardly likely that a man whose own religious outlook would have prevented him from ever entering a church would consider allowing his son to live in that sort of environment.

But there is another part of Al's own account of those days that seems likely to be true. The young Al misbehaved so frequently at the home that he was placed in solitary confinement in a monk's cell – where he stayed until Cantor Yoelson came to collect him. That was probably just long enough for word to reach Washington that Harry had been caught and for the cantor to realise that his younger son was the one in custody.

In later years Al was to tease Harry by telling him, 'Remember I did time for you once, son.'

In 1948 Al took his wife to see St Mary's. 'The gate's open,' he told her. 'It was always shut when I was here. I remember bars all round. Once I hit a boy on the stairs, coming down from chapel. They put me in solitary. That's bad enough. But to look out the window – and watch the others playing – well, honey, I screamed and hollered until I ran a temperature. So they had to let me out.'

Harry joined Al back in Washington for a while. They sold

[21]

water melons in the streets of the capital – and kept on singing in the streets. This time they sang outside the burlesque theatres their father hated so much. To him, they were dens of evil and sin, places with names like Kernans and the Raleigh.

At the age of seventeen, Harry left Washington again, vowing never to return. Al stayed at home for a while, but he felt that even if he wanted to remain, it was not the life he felt he needed. Hessi was kind to him, all the more so because she felt Moses Yoelson was doubly strict to his son. But her hands were full with children of her own now. She and Al's father were well on the way to having a complete new family – three sons and a daughter. Hessi affectionately called her predecessor's youngest child Asekla, but conditions were just too hard to give him the kind of love that might have persuaded so headstrong a child not to run away any more.

Not even bouts of coughing – early stages of tuberculosis were diagnosed when Al was at St Mary's, but he recovered as soon as he left the institution – could persuade Al to stay at home. Singing made him feel better, he'd tell his father. But not through the magic panacea of the Hebrew prayers.

It was hearing a band play 'Goodbye Dolly Gray' that really set the future entertainer on the trail of show business success. It also gave him a first introduction to singing to men in uniform.

It was 1898 – Al was probably thirteen or fourteen – and the fife and drum bands marched, one after the other, down Washington's Pennsylvania Avenue on their way to Cuba.

The battleship *Maine* had been sunk in the dispute over whether America or Spain had territorial rights in Cuba and the two countries were at war.

Al was spellbound as he heard the bands playing and, like many another small boy, eagerly joined the marching ranks. The bandmaster took a liking to the small curly-haired youngster with the big eyes and, when he heard him singing to the rhythm of the marches, made Al his first theatrical proposition: 'Why not become our mascot? You'll be able to sing.'

[22]

To Al it was manna from heaven. To be actually asked to sing . . . such joys had never come his way before.

He went all the way to Florida with the fifteenth Pennsylvania Volunteers. But at the camp the commanding officer decided the boy was much too young to be taken to a battle zone – and ordered Al home before his men sailed for Havana and the charge of St Juan Hill.

He may have lost one battle, but from that moment on, the sight of a flag waving or of men with dust of battle on their faces was an invitation to be mesmerised – and to take others under the spell with him.

For a brief moment Al was home again. But his feet itched once more – and for the first and only time in his life there was the smell of sawdust in his nostrils.

He saw a poster advertising the arrival in Washington of 'The Greatest Show on Earth – Walter L. Main's Travelling Circus'. Never much of an animal lover – unless there was money to be made from a piece of moving flesh – the magic of the circus for him was in that one word 'Show'. There was the colour of the bandsmen's uniforms and the sound of the ringmaster shouting act after glorious act under the Big Top.

Asa talked his way into a job in a circus – as an usher. But his fascination did not last for long. The uniforms were tatty, the animals were mangy and the people didn't pay the price of admission. The circus folded – and Al went home once more.

At Washington's Bijou Theatre, he sneaked into the gallery just as Eddie Leonard, one of America's great vaudevillians, was on stage singing his speciality – 'Ida – Sweet As Apple Cider'.

'Come on everybody,' shouted Leonard from the gas-lit stage, 'join in.' The customers did so – but not too enthusiastically, except for one young boy soprano up there in 'the gods'. For the first time, the voice of Al Yoelson could be heard *inside* a real theatre.

Leonard was so impressed that he made young Asa sing the song as a solo. He also insisted that the boy meet him backstage. The next day, Al was at the Bijou again – singing with Eddie Leonard just as spontaneously and just as well. The act was repeated day after day.

The old trooper asked the young beginner to join him permanently and make it an act. But Al Yoelson had no ambitions to sing from a mere balcony. He wanted to be down there on the stage – with the spotlight shining on *him*.

Harry, meanwhile, had got himself a job as an usher at the Bijou and tried to persuade his brother to take up Leonard's offer. But it wasn't easy. Besides, Cantor Yoelson had heard about it all – and had presented Al with a few more cuffs about the ear than the boy felt happy to take. He regretfully said farewell to Eddie Leonard – but the memory of that experience of singing inside a real theatre, a theatre full of that warm, stale but so inviting smell, lingered on.

He ran away from home again and ended up with a troupe called Rich and Hoppe's Big Company of Fun Makers. This didn't last long, either – the company was so prosperous that it gave Al Yoelson, as he was now being billed, a table cloth to wrap around him for a cummerbund. In fact, he lasted a mere week with Rich and Hoppe. But they inched him just very slightly nearer fame. By the end of that week Al Yoelson had become Al Joelson – it sounded more American that way.

When he came back to Washington, Al spent most of his time walking the streets of the capital, wondering where the next break was coming from. It came unexpectedly quickly.

Harry had gone up in the world by now. He was selling peanuts and popcorn at the Bijou – instead of merely showing the customers to their seats. He managed to sneak Al into the balcony once more, in time for him to watch one of the most daring acts that the Naughty Nineties had yet developed – the bump and grind of Miss Aggie Beeler, burlesque queen.

Taking an ample leaf from the book of the British King Edward VII's mistress, Lillie Langtry, she billed herself as Jersey Lil and, in feathers and rouge, the busty Miss Beeler held the Washington men in the palm of her well manicured hands. She, too, called for help from the audience and, once more, the only real sound from the customers was that of the soprano Al Joelson – this time crooning for all he was worth 'You Are My Jersey Lily'.

Aggie Beeler succeeded where the famous minstrel man Eddie Leonard had failed. Al decided to defy his father once more and agreed to 'sign' with Aggie and join the act – singing alone with her from the balcony whenever her own voice needed a rest.

Al was really in show business now. He was a member of the Villa-Nova Touring Burlesque Company.

He proved a great attraction. She realised that the fourteen-year-old Al was being talked about. Today, he'd be called a gimmick. At that time, he was just a sprat to catch a mackerel – the big audience. Strange to think that a stage sex symbol should require a boy soprano to help out. But she did – and help he certainly did.

When Cantor Yoelson got to hear about it, he was so angry that he forcibly prevented Harry from leaving the apartment to go to work at the burlesque theatre. But to some people being forbidden to do a thing is all the encouragement they need to go ahead and do it. Once his father's word became obviously final, Harry left home for good and he went to New York, where he got a job as a singing waiter. But Al was in no position to argue when Cantor Yoelson got around to him. There had been a row with Aggie because she would not give him the billing he felt he was entitled to expect. Nor would she let him join her on the stage.

So the businessman in Al that was to become increasingly in evidence emerged for the first time – and he resigned. He decided to join Harry. He was back again, walking the streets, and humming songs that he could not get out of his mind. It was while trudging through New York's Orchard Street market, where the Jewish pedlars sold anything from oranges to prayer shawls, that Al had the break that finally launched him into show business once and for all. He was spotted by a talent scout who was looking for youngsters to play in a crowd scene . . . on a real stage.

Three

Is It True What They Say About Dixie?

IT WAS PROBABLY THE luckiest thing that had ever happened to him. The scout was looking for a youngster with noticeably Jewish features – and the lad born Asa Yoelson had those all right. His hair was curly and jet black; his eyes were big. He was just the sort of healthy specimen the man from the Herald Square Theatre was looking for.

For this was to be the American première of the play that had drawn the crowds from the East End of London for years – Israel Zangwill's *Children of the Ghetto*. It was about life in a Jewish quarter very much like the one in which Al had been wandering the day he was discovered.

To the scout, Al had the right background, and the right appearance. But to Al Joelson it was something more – a special feeling about appearing before hundreds of people. Just what, he wasn't yet able to put into words. Certainly, it was nice to have a dollar or two at the end of the week with which to buy food and to pay for a room on the top of a tenement building. But the money was only a part of it.

He could feel a magnet drawing him closer to the audience every time he glanced over the footlights. When the extras in the crowd scene were supposed to disperse, to allow the leading performers to stand in the spotlight, he lingered behind. The stage was as magical as his expectation had led him to believe it would be.

The date was 16 October 1899. *Children of the Ghetto* ran for a mere three performances. But it was enough to infect him with the germ. Just a single sneeze is necessary to give someone a cold, and Al Joelson had just been subjected to a veritable barrage of show business virus.

For three months, Al was out of work. He jogged along with Harry, but for him being a singing waiter didn't offer much in the way of compensation. He was now a man of the theatre and nothing was going to drag him away from the ultimate ambition – to find his public.

A man called Fred E. Moore helped him find it. Fred was a stage electrician in the Dewey Theatre on New York's 14th Street when Al had played there with Aggie Beeler. He had always wanted to be a performer, but the money came in more regularly at the wrong side of the lights and, because he was a family man, he had little alternative but to take any financial opportunities which presented themselves, whatever they were.

Fred and Al were walking aimlessly down The Bowery early in 1900 when they bumped into each other again. Al was little more than a child, but Fred, having heard his story, was astute enough to recognise that he could help the boy break into the sort of show business he yearned for.

'Why not join me in an act?' asked Fred. 'We'll be the best song illustrators in the business.'

The idea appealed to Al. So did another part of Fred's idea – his wife, who cooked the best Irish stew this side of Killarney, could build him up in the process.

But Fred didn't think the name Al Joelson did anything for the lad. 'Call yourself Harry,' he said.

And so as 'Fred E. Moore and Harry Joelson, Introducers and Promoters of High Class Ballads and Popular Songs', they caught a train out of Grand Central Station and made for the big beyond. Fred's buxom wife cooked the stew, Fred and 'Harry' grabbed what work they could find. In fact, once they were seen in Baltimore, the offers came in thick and fast. They never got beyond the bottom of the bill – but there was always work.

The fine Irish tenor of Mr Moore and the light Jewish choir-boy soprano of Master Joelson set the women rummaging for their handkerchiefs and the men to swill their beer with a jaunty touch.

Al thought this was real success. And it was – until the day his soprano voice started to change. Suddenly there were just no notes up high where he had expected them to be. And when he tried to go down for a more comfortable sound, all he got was a croak. Al Joelson's voice was never to sound the same again – it had broken.

And so, he feared, had the Al Joelson career. Al had pride –but only when he knew how to control it. When those notes seemed as distant to him as the chances of making a real fortune, he fell into one of those deep depressions that in later years were to haunt him constantly.

How was he now going to live? Certainly not by singing. For nights he slept on park benches. Day after day he trudged around the New York theatre district, hoping against hope that, when he next opened his mouth, there would be a voice to offer to the managements.

But his voice had gone – seemingly forever. It was while walking along the Brooklyn freight yards in despair that he jumped a lift on a Washington-bound train and sped home. There were tears in his eyes – both from utter remorse and from the smuts flying up from the track.

When the train arrived in Washington, he managed to jump clear just before it reached the station. With head down to his chest, he softly crept up the stairs over the feed store and knocked on the door that had once been his home.

Hessi was there with her own young children, but she gave her Asekla a warm hug and made him a glass of tea. When his father walked in from the synagogue a little later, his words were sharp, but the boy noticed a twinkle in the now greying man's eyes.

'No more with the loafers?' asked the cantor. 'Now, your place is in shool with me.'

But Cantor Yoelson knew in his heart that this was not to be. And his son Al knew it, too. When Harry arrived at the apartment shortly after this – his own attempt at finding jobs singing in saloons had fallen as flat as his younger brother's voice – it was the end of the happy family reunion.

The boys' father couldn't stand their blasphemous talk about the theatre, and they couldn't tolerate the old life. The boys decided to run away again. But not before they had planned what they were going to do. They decided to form an act. Always with an eye for faces, and an ear for the language those faces spoke, they now had an idea that seemed to contrast the two worlds in which they were living.

They called themselves 'The Hebrew and the Cadet'. Harry was the 'Hebrew' – a cross between Fagin and a Hasidic gentleman just off the boat from Poland, and Al was the cadet – smart in West Point uniform, with his hair brushed back neatly, his face sparkling clean and to them representing all that was wholesome about America. Now, this could seem to symbolise Al's determination to rid himself of his orthodox, foreign background – but this is not an altogether fair judgment.

The problem of Al's singing voice didn't arise. Harry did all the singing the act needed and Al whistled. That in itself was to be the beginnig of a staple part of the Jolson theatrical diet.

The two were billed as the Joelson Brothers. They stole most of the dialogue they 'wrote' for the act.

'You're a monkey,' said Al.

'Vot – you call me a monkey?'

'Sure. You know what a monkey is? A monkey is a very fine person.'

And Harry the Hebrew replied:

'I know dat. Mine father, mine mother and mine brothers and sisters are all monkeys, too.'

Apparently, it went down well enough. The act was booked for the theatres just off Union Square – then the centre of the vaudeville business. They went on tour, too.

But, as had happened in the past and was to be in the future, show business always reflected the world around it, and in September 1901 the people who paid for admission to vaudeville theatres weren't spending their money. President William McKinley had been assassinated and was succeeded by Teddy Roosevelt.

This was one time when the show did not go on. And the people who came off first and came back last were the newcomers like the Joelson Brothers.

It was back to the park bench – and haunting Tin Pan Alley – in the hope that someone would hear them. And someone did. Al's voice was coming back.

The boy soprano was gradually turning into a mature but high tenor. In a country that went crazy over Count John McCormack, that was no great hardship.

An agent booking a new burlesque show called The Mayflowers heard the boys and gave them a chance. They were undoubtedly the best part of the bill – playing the Hebrew and the Cadet routine one minute and Harry blacking his face as a minstrel another. Al had decided not to play around with burnt cork. It didn't seem to go with his Cadet routine, he said. An ironical decision when years later Harry was to be accused of imitating Al as a black-face artist.

The Mayflowers lasted a couple of weeks. Next, came *The Little Egypt Burlesque Show* – when they were only as good as their jokes were dirty. The two boys had been around a bit now – but Al was still probably only sixteen and the two of them were little more than greenhorns in that kind of territory. The sort of jokes they knew hardly turned a hair – but they were strong enough for the Gerry Society to be on their tails and to frighten managements away from the boys.

But when the panic lifted, the boys were asked back and given a contract. It was worth $17.50 a week – between them. Between acts they sold song books – usually containing naughty pictures of women wearing Eastern costume. Any man lucky enough to have a box of matches in his pockets had to strike one behind the semi-transparent paper to see the ladies wearing rather less.

When *Little Egypt* folded it wasn't as difficult for the two Joelsons to get work as it had been before. People were beginning to notice them. A line had even appeared in the showbiz papers.

For Al, at least, it was to be the first of thousands of entries.

In the world of burlesque, a gentleman called Billy B. Van

had a reputation for providing a good couple of hours' entertainment – and for being shrewd enough to pick up the best acts for the smallest financial outlay on his part. He heard about the Joelsons and booked them for his *Patsy Bolivar Revue*. They were to get $40 a week each.

But they weren't due to start for a few weeks. They filled in the spare time by crossing the border into Canada and getting on the bill at the Royal Theatre in Montreal.

But they never got further than the wings of that theatre. Harry had fallen in love with a chorus girl – much to the disgust of one of the stagehands who had taken her out before the 'American bigshot' had appeared on the scene. He pounced on Harry and seemed likely to break his neck with a giant-sized grip, so Al joined in the mêlée, too.

The Joelsons were immediately struck off the bill. But this incident had created a brotherly love for each other that somehow had never been there before. Certainly, they had not felt that way a few hours earlier – when they had the kind of row over a small inconsequential matter that later was to recur time and again.

They didn't mind that they had lost the Montreal job. They had the big Patsy Bolivar contract to fulfil. But that was not to be, either. Soon after arriving at his theatre, the boys had a row with Van, because he ordered them to stay behind with the chorus after rehearsals while the stars went home. They told him that as the real stars of his show they were disgusted at being so insulted. He replied by firing the pair and demanding the return of the $20 advance they had been given. Van didn't get his $20 and they didn't find anywhere to sleep – except, once more, the park benches.

Dixon and Bernstein's Turkey Burlesque Show booked them next – despite a succession of rows in which Harry demanded advances on salary and Bernstein refused. Before long the boys bought a typewriter on the instalment plan, sold it for $20 – and disappeared.

They felt dishonest, it is true. But they had also felt hungry, and that was the more pressing of the two emotions.

Their next job, with a man called Dan Casey, was to play a

couple of Irishmen in a show called *The Brigadiers*. Neither of the two had ever played anything but Jews before – and Americans, which to some of the melting pot audiences of Union Square, was much the same thing.

The accents – particularly Harry's – were none too successful. When Casey chided him for this, Harry replied, 'What's the matter, haven't you been to Ireland?' Casey had to admit that, despite his name, he had not.

'Well I have,' said Harry, 'and they have Jews in Ireland, too. I'm an Irish Jew.'

It was enough to sustain the pair for another few weeks – this time at a $50 a week salary, already a reasonably big advance on what they had earned before.

When they got an offer to open at the Odeon theatre in Baltimore they really thought they had made it big. It was modern and in the world of burlesque had something of a reputation as a nursery for Broadway. As far as the Joelson Brothers were concerned, it remained a mere reputation. The Odeon burned down the day before they arrived.

Baltimore was near Washington. Once more, they pocketed their pride and went home in an effort to fill their stomachs. They had the usual kisses from Hessi, the same sarcastic comments from Rose and Etta, who had now married but had returned home, too, for a visit and more chastisement from Cantor Yoelson, although even he now did not bother to talk about their following him in the religious life.

His son Hirsch always seemed a downright no-good and now he has even worse than that – for he had led Asa astray. What he never seemed to realise was that when things were going badly for the boys, it was usually Al who had persuaded Harry to try again and not give up. Certainly Al was the one who found it harder to leave the theatre atmosphere and who got depressed at any prospect of having to do so.

Again, it was the same old story. Father and sons couldn't live under the same roof with each other – and just as soon as the two youngsters had saved enough money from the jobs they picked up singing in Washington cafés and saloons, they were off again. Their destination was New York once more.

When they arrived, they had enough between them for a room on 14th Street. It was across the road from Lew Schrafts' Restaurant which Al in later years was to describe as the 'Stork Club of the nineties'.

It wasn't so much a room, he observed. 'More like a broom closet. But I was able to see the fancy people going into the restaurant – people like Diamond Jim Brady and Lillian Russell. And I could smell the fancy food. I suppose it was that sort of thing that persuaded me to want to make it big myself one day.

'Most important, though, I could hear the music. I'll never forget the thrill one rainy night when I first heard Jim Thornton play for them his song 'When You Were Sweet Sixteen'. All the years in between haven't dimmed the thrill of that moment, because whenever I sing that song, I'm a young kid again staring out there on 14th Street in the rain.'

But the thrills were few and far between. When there was no more money to pay the rent for that 'broom closet', the boys were back sleeping on the park benches and knocking on the doors of the agents' offices.

Then came the break they had been looking for – they bumped into a man called Ren Shields on a summer afternoon in 1903.

Shields was none too successfully trying to write vaudeville acts and one of the people he had been trying to write for was Joe Palmer, a man who in his day had headlined a reasonably prospering act. But he had been struck down with multiple sclerosis – and in those days there was little but sympathy for an actor in a wheelchair.

As for Shields, himself, he needed a break as badly as Palmer. He had had his moments – notably when he had written the lyrics of 'In The Good Old Summertime' – but the royalty cheques were small and didn't come in very often.

The Joelson boys seemed to be the answer to his problem. He would team up with Palmer in a new musical comedy act.

[33]

What's more, he would tailor the act around the old trouper's wheelchair. Palmer would play the patient in a nursing home, Harry would be the doctor and Al the bell-boy.

For once it meant that Al would have all the punch lines in the comedy skits and Harry would be the straight man. Palmer was the 'feed' for them both.

The first thing for any new vaudeville act to do was to advertise – if they could afford it – in the theatrical Press. If not, they certainly had to have cards printed. But that presented problems. They couldn't find a printer who would prepare the sort of cards they had in mind – their names engraved over little oval pictures of each of the partners, and above the portraits the names 'Joelson, Palmer and Joelson.'

'The names are too long for the card,' said one printer. 'How about shortening them?' Palmer's name wouldn't make much difference he said, but the boys' were different. They both had the same name – and a long, foreign-sounding name it was at that. 'Take the "e" out,' he said.

The boys decided to give it a try. Their act was to be called Jolson, Palmer and Jolson. When they got a booking, it meant that for the very first time an audience saw a performer called Al Jolson. The audiences loved the act. It made them laugh until they were dry – which pleased the vaudeville houses, because it meant they sold more beer.

It was while playing in Brooklyn that the Al Jolson of the future was really launched.

Only eight years later Al was to describe it like this, 'I had a Negro dresser who told me, "You'd be much, much funnier, boss, if you blacked your face like mine. People always laugh at the black man."' No one in 1912 thought that was in the least offensive and, when Al told it, he had the audiences in fits.

It was a good, colourful story of those times. Much more likely, however, was the other legend about a decision that made Al Jolson the most successful minstrel man of all time.

On the bill with him was a blackface comedian and monologue man called James Francis Dooley. 'Why don't you try some of the burnt cork yourself?' he asked the youngster. 'It'd go perfectly with that Southern accent of yours – and you'd make a much better bell-boy.'

From that moment on, the act was better than it had been before. Al's confidence had been sagging, but from the moment he blacked up he felt he owned the whole of show business – and before very long show business owned him.

In later years, Jolson's blackface routine was to be condemned as an insult to the Negro. It's fair to say that he never considered it to be that. Only very late in his career was it even mentioned – by which time he could parry comments with the speed and effort of a world tennis champion's volley.

Blackening up at the turn of the century was just another vaudeville convention. No one believed that minstrels with burnt cork on their faces were really Negroes. In a way they were a race of their own. They were rarely as insulting as the non-Jewish actors playing characters like Fagin or Shylock, or a stack of other long-nosed anti-Semitic studies.

To Al Jolson, it was the passport to a completely new world. When the makeup was on his face he never seemed to worry. It was as though he had a mask, behind which he could shelter and hide his problems. It also seemed to make him twice the personality he had been before.

The act toured the country – billed as *A Little of Everything*. As far as they were concerned, 'Everything' meant a salary cheque and a reference from the management to go with it.

In April 1905 came what they thought was the biggest big break they had a right to expect. They were offered a contract by the famous Tony Pastor to play at his 'Music Hall'. Second only to the Palace on Broadway, Tony Pastor's has gone down in history as the top spot in vaudeville. It was there that Irving Berlin worked as a singing waiter when he wrote 'Sadie Salome Go Home' – his very first hit.

With the offer went a fee of $40 a week each – the sort of money no one sneered at in those days. The Jolson Brothers took it in turns to carry the contract so precious a document was it.

By the time they got to New York to cash in on the contract, the paper was ragged and dog-eared. However, it was never to be more than just a piece of paper. Just before the act was due to go on at Tony Pastor's, Harry and Al had their first really big row and one that was big enough to drive their careers apart for all time. In retrospect, it is fair to speculate that this was probably the one single step that put Al Jolson firmly on the road to his future fortune.

The two had quarrelled over who was to look after Joe Palmer – whose illness was growing more and more debilitating every day. In the end they had to take it in turns to wash and dress their crippled partner. Finally, they came near to blows when both decided they wanted the evening off at the same time.

The row ended with Harry walking out and Al and Joe going it as a twosome at another theatre. But it didn't work out. Al, who was growing increasingly restless every time he felt the lure of the audience, thought he could do better still on his own. As for Joe, he found another partner, who shortly afterwards managed to stop the crippled performer driving his wheelchair over a window ledge.

To Al the desperate need was to make a success of his career. On his own now, he placed an advertisement in *Variety* – declaring 'Watch me – I'm a wow'.

Harry, meanwhile, temporarily discarded his black face makeup and worked up a routine as a Jewish juvenile. In brown 'Derby', and striped frock coat and trousers, he billed himself as *The Ghetto Sport*. He got bookings – but nothing like those that were suddenly coming Al's way as fast as he wanted them.

Al had split up from Joe in California, and from the moment he pranced around the boards for his first solo audition, he got the work he wanted, on the West Coast.

He arrived in San Francisco in 1906 a week after the earthquake. Within days of the 'quake and its fires, temporary theatres went up in the city – some of them just tents, some huts. The local administration decided that entertainment was vital for morale – and to be sure that there would be enough workmen to build up 'Frisco' again.

To play in one of those makeshift theatres Al Jolson was paid $75 a week. Within weeks that fee had been doubled. Harry Jolson wrote many years later that San Francisco was the town that loved Al the best – and the one for which he had the softest spot himself. An ironical thought when one considers that it was here that Al was to die in 1950.

What is surely true is the impact made on San Francisco in 1906. To the people watching him it was as though another earthquake had hit the city. No one had ever seen a single performer who was so dynamic. He only had to open his mouth and it seemed the crowds flooded in to the box office. The only thing comparable to his pull were Revival meetings – and in many ways that's just what these were. Al Jolson was responsible now for a completely new kind of adoration and worship.

By the time he left San Francisco at the end of 1906 he was earning $200 a week. He had also begun to perfect the act that was soon to make him famous. As for his personality, it was there already.

It was while standing on a makeshift stage in one of those temporary San Francisco theatres that he first made the statement that has gone down as his own epitaph.

One didn't have to be in show business to see what the crowd was doing to the young man of about twenty-one that night. They were shouting at him, demanding one new song after the other. Hard-bitten labourers with the grime of rubble on their hands and faces together with men in evening dress and women in fashionable long dresses were as brothers and sisters in this near-religious frenzy.

Al, with collar undone now to allow the sweat to escape below his chocolate makeup, saw what was happening and felt an elation greater than he had ever felt before. He stood up, pushed his hands across the footlights in what could be described as the response from a Messiah to his apostles, and called back. 'All right, all right folks – you ain't heard nothing yet.'

For the next forty-four years, there was never to be a Jolson performance where that phrase was not uttered, and when it

[37]

did not evoke just the same sort of response that greeted it that night. The audience screamed and shouted for more.

Enrico Caruso was in town at the same time. Al liked to joke that the Italian tenor didn't receive the same sort of response as he was getting.

None liked the handsome young singer more than the girls of the city. Whether they knew it or not, they were fostering the Jolson ego which was always to play such an important part in his story – and few had better opportunities to show just how much they admired him than the curvy girls who were working on the same bill as Al. They flattered him by rolling their eyes and by pushing out their well-padded fronts every time he got near them. They even asked him for dates.

And they got them, too. All, that is, except one of the chorus girls who held back while the others pushed. And because of her apparent disinterest, she was the one he wanted most. Her name was Henrietta Keller, a tall, blonde, breathtakingly pretty girl, whose Norwegian father had ruled her with a rod of iron before she left home in Oakland, California.

Mr Keller did not like the idea of show business. But he became reconciled to his daughter going on the stage on one condition – that she did not develop too close an attachment to show people. As a dutiful daughter, who accepted that she must never fall in love with a man in the business, she didn't allow herself to be tempted. She just turned down all the offers of dates that came her way – including those from Al Jolson.

It hurt his pride deeply. He even told her it was harming his image. But she said that her own happiness was the most important thing that she had to be concerned about. Nevertheless, there were signs that Henrietta was weakening.

There were shy smiles when he rolled his eyes on stage in her direction. When he sang directly at her she felt a peculiar sensation in her stomach. Soon, she was not only agreeing to go out with the young star, she was also accepting his proposal of marriage.

The ceremony before a justice of the peace in New Jersey

was the climax of the first romance Al had ever had. The only person he had confided in about the marriage was his old friend and mentor Fred Moore.

He only hinted at it in letters to Harry, who himself was doing well now with the leading Keith Circuit – under the billing *The Operatic Blackface Comedian*. (He had now given up his Jewish act and was following his younger brother's lead – although he insisted he was merely continuing where he had left off in the *Turkey Burlesque Show* four years before.)

Harry found out about Al's plans to marry through Fred Moore and tried to stop him before it was too late. Marrying a gentile girl, Harry pointed out, was just about the most wicked thing a Jewish man could do. Wouldn't Al reconsider? If his younger brother had had any such thought, Harry's request was all he needed to fire his determination to go through with the idea.

When the news filtered through to Washington DC, Cantor Yoelson went through the ritual he had last performed after burying his first wife, Naomi. He sat on a low chair and recited Kaddish – the prayer for the dead.

Al, meanwhile, had a recurrence of his old tubercular trouble and with Henrietta went into the hills of Washington State to recuperate. As soon as he showed signs of improvement, he and his bride went south again – and back to work.

The months spent in idleness in the Hills had made Al restless. Far more so than he had ever been before. He wasn't like a normal man relaxing with a new wife. Instead, Henrietta felt she was just along for the trip – while his real love was thousands of miles away.

He showed her in those first weeks that she was no substitute for the raucous crowds who had filled his life for the past year. When an offer came from the Sullivan and Consadine Circuit to join them in tours of the Middle West and West, he jumped for joy. They paid him $250 a week – and he placed more advertisements in the trade papers. This time they read, 'Perhaps you've never heard of me – but you will.'

He never made a truer prediction. He didn't predict, however, what his brother might say about his billing. While Harry had chosen the label of *The Operatic Blackface Comedian,* Al called himself *The Blackface with the Grand Opera Voice.*

Harry saw red – and threatened to report his brother to the theatrical profession's disciplinary body – The White Rats. Al made a few choice comments about Harry and carried on just the same. He played in the West, Harry in the East – and deliberately the twain ne'er met.

Between bookings, however, there was the indignity of being asked by agents if he and Harry Jolson were related. One after the other they told him, 'He does a similar routine to you.' One critic wrote, 'It's going to be a toss-up as to who has the better act of the two, Harry Jolson or his brother Al. Harry accomplished something at the American last week at nearly every performance which I have often read about and heard talked about, and that was to stop the performance.'

And he went on, 'If it had been a pre-arranged affair it might have been understood, but the applause was so insistent, and so enthusiastic were the demands that he returned and began all over again and it was absolutely useless for the act following him even to start.

'Jolson was some hit and already the Broadway managers are squabbling for him.'

Alas for Harry, the managers were to squabble over him on very few occasions – although for a while he was riding high.

He was playing the William Morris Circuit when it went bankrupt. It collapsed leaving Harry and a thousand other artists completely stranded. He couldn't get work anywhere. When Eddie Leonard – the man who had first realised the potential of Harry's brother Al – heard about this, he offered Harry the chance of joining the new minstrel troupe he was planning.

But Leonard had a row with his 'angels' and that was the end of the show. Harry went off to England to find work on the music halls there.

He now had a bride of his own to take with him. The man

[40]

who had scolded his brother for marrying a gentile now did the same thing – and eloped. He later told his father that the cantor's brother, a Rabbi Julius Hess, had given him his blessing. But in England, he said, what he needed most of all was luck.

Al, meanwhile, was getting noticed and drawing rave reviews from the Press, wherever he went. And, what was more important at the time, people in the profession were noticing him, too.

It was in 1907 that a dapper young agent called Arthur Klein saw Al at work in one of the country's earliest cinemas. It was in El Paso, Texas. Later he recalled, 'Black face, white socks, straw hat – the man electrified me. I followed him through Texas and Mexico, travelling by train to catch his act.' He tried to persuade Al to let him sign him up as his agent and make him a big name – but Jolson was convinced he could do it on his own.

He was playing at the Pantages Vaudeville House at Little Rock, Arkansas, the same week as another blackface outfit – Lew Dockstader's Minstrels. They were the biggest name in minstreldom. The biggest since the days of E. P. Christie and Stephen Foster.

An entertainer called Will Oakland had advised Dockstader to go to see Jolson. He watched young Jolson from the wings and then convinced him that he could do better as part of his firm than trying to make it on his own. He could play as a single within the framework of the minstrel show – and that was nothing less than a golden key to success.

No longer would he have to hope to play in towns where his name would mean something. As part of the Dockstader show there were assurances that there would be standing room only wherever he went. Jolson's ego needed to hear no more. Besides, he was shrewd enough to gamble on the future – Dockstader promised him big billing, and the people who saw him at the end of the minstrel line would never be allowed to forget. He had the promise, too, that he could choose not only the songs he wanted to sing – but the way the orchestra played the accompaniment, too.

[41]

In America at the turn of the century, the minstrel show was reaching the apex of its success. It had been a nation-wide institution for fifty years, with a never-changing pattern. Like the minstrels in Tudor England who went from house to house with a song and a tale, troupes like Dockstader's went from town to town forming their own kind of folk art.

Like the circus they were, they'd march from the railway station to the theatre, dressed in top hats and tail coats, but at that stage without their black face makeup. At city hall, they'd stop surrounded by swarms of people, while the leader of the minstrel company would recite platitudes about the 'fair town' they were visiting.

There were always precise rules on how the minstrels dressed – striped trousers, big floppy bows, tall hats – and particularly how they wore their burnt cork. The big circles around their eyes and the oval border to their lips may be considered a cruel caricature of the Negro – but no one has ever suggested that Negroes look like minstrels. It would have been difficult to mistake one of Dockstader's men for the genuine article.

Their routine on the platform – whether in a tin hut or an ornate theatre – never varied. In the centre was the one man in the company with a white face – Mister Interlocutor who would be to the minstrel company what the conductor is to the symphony orchestra. When he took his place, a rattle of tambourines would greet his instruction – 'Gentlemen be-ee-ee seated.'

The leading performers would be the 'end' men in the front row of the company. They would trade insults with each other, and be the butt of the interlocutor's jokes.

By the time Jolson joined Dockstader, the first warning shots had been fired across the theatre's bows to show that the day of the big minstrel show might be ending. Vaudeville was drawing youngsters away from the old traditions and had progressed to theatres, leaving the beer parlour and saloon far behind in its history. What is more, the motion picture had proved that it was plainly here to stay. Short comedy reels, dramas and early science fiction had come to the nickelodeon.

Movies were no longer just peep shows. The first cinemas were being built. And in the home, the parlour piano was now elbowing for room with the phonograph – from which resounded the first sounds of what was soon to be called ragtime.

Dockstader gave Jolson his head because he thought this obviously powerful young man would help him bridge what today would be called the generation gap.

When, forty years later, *The Jolson Story* showed the young Al's constant battle with the frustrations of the minstrel show –a never changing routine with little opportunity to branch out on his own – it was only telling half the story. What Dockstader did was to present Jolson with an almost God-given opportunity to develop a style that he was never totally to abandon.

If he was able to hide the constant battle with his nerves behind his black face, he was able, too, to prove to himself that when he was alone on the stage he could hold the audience in the palm of his outstretched hands. He exaggerated a southern accent because it helped him cover up what vestiges still remained of the Lithuanian-Yiddish sounds he had brought over from Srednicke.

Unlike his ancestors. Al had not been content merely to sing. For him singing meant using every movement of his body. He discovered that a small on-the-spot dance helped him while he sang to attract that part of the audience whose mind seemed to be wandering. By opening out his arms at the same time, he could feel the audience being enveloped to his bosom. By shaking his head, he showed that he was firmly in control.

The days with Dockstader also proved that success on stage was a two-way affair. Sometimes he played in halls where the house lights couldn't be dimmed. But he revelled in that situation. Not merely was there no spotlight to blind him, but he could see the faces of the people out front. If they were smiling at him, he smiled underneath his makeup and his heart beat more quickly.

[43]

It was in 1908 that he first went to work with Dockstader. By 1909, it was evident that he had eclipsed Dockstader himself and his other star Neil O'Brien.

Dockstader led his men in old minstrel numbers like 'And He Played To Her His Fiddle-e-dee'. Jolson sang the current hit songs like 'Sweet Sixteen' – and his very first Mammy number 'It's A Long Way Back To Dear Old Mammy's Knee'. Before very long Dockstader had to face the fact that the customers were coming to see the young – he was twenty-four or twenty-five at the time – Al Jolson, and not simply his minstrel show.

But Dockstader was happy so long as the cash flowed in. Amid a crescendo of bones and tambourines he would proclaim the entry of 'Our premeer end man – Mistah Al Jolson'. Al received the same salary as Dockstader claimed to be paying himself – $75 a week.

In 1909 the troupe came to New York and played at its famous Fifth Avenue Theatre. For the first time, *Variety* opened a Jolson file. Their columnist Sime noted, 'Haven't seen a demonstration for a single act, or any act for that matter, as was given Al Jolson.'

Al left Dockstader for a brief time. He said he was fed up with the routine in which he had to join forces with Dockstader and O'Brien for what was called the *Possum Club Picnic*. The big star no longer felt happy in the bell-boy's uniform the act demanded. He felt he had left that life behind when he said goodbye to Harry and Joe Palmer.

In 1912 he told *Variety*, 'I have never regretted becoming an end man and was very happily situated when we reached the Grand Opera House, New York.'

Just how 'happily situated' can be imagined – for at the Grand Opera House he was spotted by a pack of vaudeville talent scouts.

It was just part of the job. The agents and talent scouts were constantly in theatres like the Opera House – hoping to spot new artists. When they saw Jolson, heads went together, whispers were exchanged and there was an immediate rush round to the stage door.

For the young singer, it was an opportune moment. Dockstader felt the need to rest, and closed the show in mid-season. So Al was open to offers. The one he accepted was to open at Oscar Hammerstein's new theatre, the Victoria.

On his first night there, he introduced a new Jolson ritual. He walked straight to the front of the stage and shouted to the electricians, 'Bring on the houselights. Ya know, folks – this is the happiest night of my life. Yes siree. I'm so happy. Ya wanna listen. . .' And he then went into all the most cheerful songs in his repertoire.

Jolson was successful – but not as fantastically so as he had hoped. He went on circuit around the Orpheum chain in the East. The most satisfactory feature of this to Jolson at the time was that he was becoming so well known that he could call the stage-door keepers by their nicknames. Such was fame indeed.

What he described as 'this delightful tour' folded when he became ill with the throat infections that were continually to dog him during his career.

It was Louisville, Kentucky, and for the first time in his life Al Jolson was claiming on an insurance policy. 'I shall never forget the agile interne who was sent by the accident insurance company to examine me,' he told the Variety reporter for that 1912 interview.

'He was to make sure that I was actually sick enough so as to get the $12.50 a week they were good enough to allow. From the way the young doctor-to-be went about his work, I felt that he was afraid that I was shamming illness for the $12.50.'

In December 1909 he was back in New York – at the Colonial Theatre, singing 'Hello, My Baby', one of the first big ragtime hits, when one of the billed stars refused to work during the Christmas holidays. This time, he was the sort of hit he wished he had been on opening night at the Victoria.

There were cheers from the audience and tears rolling down his cheeks as he stood on the stage that night – the building resounding with the vibrations of the audience's applause.

A party was thrown for him after the show that night and he

rushed back to the hotel where he and Henrietta were living to tell her about his success. Instead of being ecstatic in the way he thought she should be, she managed a faint smile and turned to the bedroom. Somehow, the excitement on her husband's face seemed to confirm her worst fears – the more successful he was to become, the harder they would find it to live a normal sort of married life.

Because Al was working in the heart of New York, that's where they had to live. And because the heart of New York meant one of two things – a luxury apartment or a poor tenement – the only sensible place for home was a hotel suite. That, at least, was how Al worked it out.

Henrietta had other ideas. Her means of showing what she felt was to tell Al to go to the party without her. She had a headache, she said. In fact, she confessed later that the pain was a little lower down.

Early in the following year of 1910 he went back to Dockstader – again singing the hits of the hour, but never having the chance to introduce a brand new song. Nevertheless, Tin Pan Alley was already courting him. A young man in a music publisher's office persuaded him to try a number that he predicted would be very big.

Jolson sang it in the show's olio that night. It was called 'Alexander's Ragtime Band'. At one end of New York, Al Jolson and the minstrels were singing the number to the sort of syncopated beat Dockstader himself detested. At the other end of the city, the song's composer Irving Berlin was making a fortune, playing the same tune on his own one-key piano.

The publisher's fifteen-year-old song plugger, meanwhile, was busy searching out more potential hits for Jolson. It would be a job he would do with loving care for the next forty years. His name – Harry Akst.

Dockstader didn't like the ragtime tunes, but he had to admit that they drew the customers. And he watched what was drawing them in at other theatres, too. When he found out what other headliners like Nora Bayes and Jack Norworth were singing, he made sure Al sang them, too – 'Come Along My Mandy', which Bayes and Norworth had written for their

[46]

show, and 'The Jolly Bachelors' which became an established hit of the Dockstader Minstrels, too.

Jolson sang the Bert Williams speciality 'Why Adam Sinned'. He also perfected a new routine – by whistling some of the passages. What had previously been a substitute for his broken voice was now becoming a trade mark.

It was then that Art Klein appeared on the scene again. He decided that Jolson was underselling himself. And that, Klein said, he could not allow. 'I'd like to sign as your manager,' Klein told him. 'I think you ought to go back to vaudeville. I know a lot of people have got their eyes on you. But I think you're such a great artist that there should be really great things in store. And now for the first time, you're really going to get a chance.'

In a café on Columbus Circle, Jolson and Klein signed a ten-year contract.

Klein, as always dressed immaculately in trousers with razor sharp creases, smoothly pressed jacket over a white shirt and black necktie, booked his new protégé for $250 a week into two theatres simultaneously. Jolson had enough energy in him to commute from one theatre to the other in the course of an evening.

Al continued successfully for a year. So successfully in fact that he was able to cock a snook at the great Florenz Ziegfeld. Ziegfeld asked Klein to bring Al down for an audition. In what the showman regarded as the supreme folly of youth, Klein told him, 'Jolie doesn't audition for anyone.' It was a gamble, but he confessed to his shattered client that he did not want Al to be lost in the midst of the big Ziegfeld production extravaganzas with their beautiful semi-naked girls. He said he had bigger plans for him. But it was a chancy decision. 'What I was determined to do was get Al on Broadway,' Klein said years later.

When he saw demolition teams move into the old Horse Exchange in the midst of what was already the street of dreams and disasters, he saw his opportunity.

The place had been taken over by the ruthless Shubert Brothers, who were experts in creating the sort of magic Klein knew Al could help weave for them. Jake and Lee Shubert were on site every day, watching the last remnants of the straw and the smells of the Horse Exchange being consigned to oblivion for ever.

When Klein approached them to use Jolson in their first show they weren't interested. 'He's from vaudeville, Art,' they told him. 'We're legit. This is going to be the classiest musical theatre on Broadway.'

With that neither he nor Jolson ever quarrelled. The theatre was going to be called the Winter Garden.

Four

Give My Regards to Broadway

IN 1911 THE LIGHTS of Broadway were still partly fed by gas. The roadway echoed to the sound of clattering horses' hooves and of the streetcars trundling their way to and from the Bowery.

There was straw on the pavements everywhere and, when theatregoers in their finery crossed the road, they had to be wary of what their feet might pick up. But there were signs that the old order was changing.

The car had arrived – although even on Broadway people still turned their heads to look when they heard the sound of a horn heralding one of the vehicles on its way. And the Horse Exchange had become the Winter Garden.

The Shubert Brothers, who had by now established themselves as the biggest names in the musical theatre business, had built a tasteful gold-encrusted palace. The Winter Garden symbolised the new golden age into which that business was now entering and it was appropriately just where the streetcars turned round.

A young song writer called Jerome Kern had been asked to produce most of the score for the theatre's first production *La Belle Paree.*

It would be nice to think the Shuberts had the foresight to decide that a theatre of such magnificence with such a brilliant composer providing the music also needed a bright new star called Al Jolson. They didn't. He was merely part of a package the Shuberts had bought when they took over Dockstader's Minstrels. Klein simply persuaded them to change his role.

Even so, they didn't think Jolson was right for a Broadway musical – and to prove it, he was only allowed on in the very last scene. When they saw Jolson perform the Shuberts believed their worst fears had been justified.

No one seemed to be taking any notice of him. *The Cook's Tour through Vaudeville with a Parisian Landscape,* as the show was subtitled, seemed to take second place to the landscape of the theatre itself.

Eyes were wandering throughout the long evening and the newspaper writers seemed as impressed with the décor as were the audience. After all, they had heard that one man had paid $19 for a $2.50 seat – just to be there on what he was sure was an historic occasion.

One columnist wrote: 'Crowds began to arrive at the Winter Garden long before 8 o'clock until the sidewalk was almost blocked and the lobby filled to overflowing. The line of carriages and automobiles extended for two blocks when the first nighters were coming more plentifully. . .

'Once inside the theatre, the people seemed disinclined to go at once to their seats, but filled all of the wide promenade space back of the orchestra seats until the overture began.

'Large baskets of flowers, bouquets and elaborate floral designs were banked in the rear until the walls were hidden. Garlands of flowers were draped around the box fronts and the side of the proscenium arch. Not the least attractive part of the Winter Garden is the simplicity and harmony of the decorations of the auditorium. The walls and balcony front are in old ivory and gold and the ceiling marked off in latticed squares in old ivory behind which is an artificial sky of blue. . .

'The audience last night found the seats wide and comfortably spaced, with a receptacle for cigar ashes attached to the back of each chair.'

The writer did not record that they were equally enthusiastic about Al Jolson.

The show had been running more than three and a half hours when the little blackfaced figure walked on stage and

[50]

announced he was Erastus Sparkler – 'an aristocrat of San Juan Hill cutting a wide swathe in Paris'.

'Paris Is A Paradise For Coons', he sang, but few took much notice. The audience was noisy after listening to what had proved a pretty nondescript score. Many hand already gone home – for they had not only suffered the earlier scenes of *La Belle Paree*, but had endured, too, a Spanish ballet performed by 'Sixteen Moorish dancing girls' and *Bow Sing* which was described as a 'one-act Chinese fantasy opera'.

They believed in giving value for money in those days, but second and third features only really served to dull the mind for the main production of the evening.

Al was a knotful of butterflies by the time his music struck up and he had forced himself to dance out on to the stage apron. Most of the people out front realised this – they were kind but largely indifferent. Blackface had never been featured in a 'legitimate' show before and the men and women who had paid to come along to the Winter Garden on 20 March were clearly not in a mood to be impressed.

Most of the critics had gone, too – to make sure their reviews were in the next morning's papers. But there was one who did stay – Adolph Klauber. Writing in *The New York Times*, he said: 'Among the very best features were those provided by two unctuous ragtime comedians, Miss Stella Mayhew and Mr Al Jolson, both of whom had good songs and the dialects and the acting ability to deliver every bit of good that was in them.'

The number that took Mr Klauber's fancy was the one in which Al – still in blackface – joined with curly-haired Miss Mayhew, to play a clown.

It was Klauber who saved Jolson for Broadway. Art Klein who claimed it was his own persistence that had got the singer on the Winter Garden stage in the first place, recalled: 'Jolson was very, very sad about this. He told me I had no right to sign him for such a big place. He was happy in vaudeville – and making more money there, too.

'That night, he was an absolute failure – because he really didn't have faith in his work. I was disappointed but he felt vindicated.' Jolson himself wrote: 'I felt so nervous that night that I walked to 95th Street instead of 53rd where I was living before I realised what I was doing. So you can understand how I felt.'

But after reading Klauber's review, the Shuberts understood, too – and gave Al a new position on the bill for the second performance – the Thursday afternoon matinée. They thought his reputation as a showman meant he was big enough to cope with the sort of traumatic experience that opening had been. And he proved them right.

He came out on stage and poked his head through the still-closed curtain. With that one gesture, he began the job of not merely entertaining the people out front, but spellbinding them. And he used a number that symbolised this new age in which people were buying automobiles to impress their neighbours – particularly their sweethearts.

In the middle of the song, 'He'd Have To Get Under', Jolson pulled out of the air the trick that once more gave them there and then his full attention. The huge ornate Broadway stage bounced with the sound of his whistling between choruses. The audience opened up to him in the sort of frenzy that he was later to demand as his right.

As Art Klein said: 'In those days you must remember there were no microphones. But this man had the most resonant voice of any human being I ever knew. I stood at the back of the theatre with my hands on the wall – and I could feel the bricks vibrate. The bricks shook with this one voice – and with no microphone to help him.' But the way those bricks were arranged had helped Al in this feat. There was one spot on the exceptionally wide stage from which a whisper could carry to the top balcony. Jolson, nevertheless, would have been a sensation in the old Horse Exchange before it was converted.

Variety saw the way the tickets were being bought and billed *La Belle Paree* – 'Double Sockeroo'. In the show business Bible's own language that meant a sell out on all fronts. And Jake and Lee Shubert appreciated what they had bought when the signed on the dotted line for Dockstader's troupe of Minstrels.

[52]

Jolson's fame got around. The critics came to see what they had missed the first night and wrote about this magnetic new singer Al Jolson. The Social Register people, who previously would have been reluctant to be noticed anywhere less than in the Metropolitan Opera House's Diamond Horseshoe, realised that it was now the fashionable thing to go to the Winter Garden.

They came from Park Avenue and from Brooklyn and The Bronx. And they came from out of town, too. Some people even took a train from Chicago just to catch this new stage-struck marvel in blackface.

What they came to catch, too, was the ever-changing Jolson personality – and routine. Right from the word go, he showed he wasn't going to be like the other characters in a Broadway show, the ones who simply read their lines or sang the songs the composer had written for them. From the moment Jolson introduced 'He'd Have To Get Under', he showed he was going to sing his own songs – despite what poor Mr Kern had hoped. So he sang 'That Lovin' Traumerei', which had been adapted from the original by Robert Schumann and another called 'That Develin' Rag', by Billee Taylor. The big stars of the age – George M. Cohan, Irving Berlin, Al's idol Fay Templeton came to pay him homage. To them all, he had a special name – 'Jolie'.

The people who came to hear him once, came again and again. For not only was there the incredible novelty of seeing what this dynamic fireball was going to sing next – but there was also the anticipation of discovering *how* he was going to sing his songs. For even when he repeated songs in subsequent performances, he changed the way he delivered them. The Winter Garden regulars played games with each other – spotting the changed lyric, the different treatment of a chorus, the substituted phrase.

Oscar Radin, who conducted the Winter Garden Orchestra – he was an uncle of Oscar Levant, the pianist who a couple of generations later was to become Jolson's foil on his post World War 2 radio shows – was completely thrown from one performance to the next.

Al revelled in these games he played with the musicians and, because it made people talk and the talking made more people buy tickets, the Shuberts revelled along with him. They let him decide which numbers to use for the show. Right from the early days of *La Belle Paree* his own part got bigger and bigger while the other more experienced performers found their lines declining in significance, and their songs suddenly disappearing from the orchestra's sheets.

For a time, Jolson joined the cast of *Bow Sing* as well as *La Belle Paree* itself. But largely through his pressure, the second feature was removed from the bill and the other artists from the payroll — after a mere thirty-two performances. *La Belle Paree* was to go on for another seventy-two.

When the show came to an end for the traditional summer break Al was filled with an urge to continue working. The sound of the audience's applause was too strong for him to want to return to the hotel room where he and Henrietta were living.

Henrietta thought differently. To her this was the perfect opportunity to start the family she had planned — although nothing had yet happened to indicate that this would be accomplished either. Her doctors had said that Al was probably too tired.

Henrietta was becoming increasingly aware that her husband was happier going to the racetracks than staying with her. He certainly found it more convivial to spend the after-show hours at one of those floating crap games Damon Runyan later immortalised in his Broadway stories. The games floated from one location to another, to keep the police at bay.

Henrietta begged Al to spend some time with her, but all he could really think about, even when playing the dice, was his own career.

He gave Jake Shubert the idea straight, 'Why not take the show on the road?' he asked. 'You know, just like we did with Dockstader? We'll take the same scenery and casts and use all the same songs. It won't cost very much.'

Lee and Jake Shubert had intended to concentrate on the new show they were planning for the Winter Garden the next Fall. But now the thought came to them that Jolson could be on to something big – the proposition was irresistible.

So the people far away, who had read about Jolson in their newspapers, now had a chance to see and hear what all the fuss had been about. More important for the history of the theatre, they were for the first time being given the chance to see a complete Broadway show – and right in their own backyard, to coin the sort of phrase Jolson later immortalised in a song.

A former haberdasher from Missouri confessed to Al nearly forty years later that a ticket for *La Belle Paree* somewhere in the sticks had been his first opportunity to see a Broadway import. His name: Harry S. Truman.

By October the cast was back on Broadway. Gaby Deslys, the sensation of the Paris music halls, had been booked by the Shuberts for their next Winter Garden performance and Al Jolson was there, too, to take second billing.

On 20 November 1911 – five days later than originally planned, because the Shuberts didn't think Mlle Deslys knew her lines and songs well enough – the curtain went up on *Vera Violetta*. Al Jolson played Claude – once again a blackface role in a European setting.

Also in the cast was the darling of London's Gaiety Theatre, Josie Collins – who sang her famous Cockney number 'Tar-Rar-Rar-Boomdiay'. Jolson had a number with a similar title – 'Rum-Tum-Tiddle'.

Meanwhile, the first trappings of stardom were beginning to wrap themselves around Al. As a big Broadway hit, he felt he needed status symbols. So Klein bought him his first second-hand car, and a fur coat. It was mid-August when they negotiated the salary terms for *Vera Violetta*. The weather was oppressively hot but nothing would stop Jolson wearing the fur coat for this meeting with the Shuberts.

'I don't want any of your summer salaries here,' he told them, and as he said it, he pulled the collar of the fur coat tighter around his neck.

The Shuberts need not have worried about the money they paid Jolson. He was a fantastic hit in the new show on its first night. And in that microphoneless age, he developed for himself yet another new aide to success – he danced, marched and hopped up and down the Winter Garden aisles from the front of the stage right up to the back of the theatre.

He would launch himself into a number behind the footlights and then prance to the street doors singing and whistling as he went.

The *New York Times* were not slow to catch on to Jolson's effect. They wrote, 'There was Al Jolson in the role of a coloured waiter who succeeded in rousing the audience into its first enthusiasm in the early part of the evening and kept them enthusiastic much of the time afterwards.'

The main scene of the show was a skating rink. The name *Vera Violetta* came from a perfume constantly referred to in the production.

Gaby Deslys played the sweetheart of a professor and, as the *Times* said, she performed 'remarkably well'. Much more happily in fact than she performed off stage. Never before had she acted in English, and now she felt that the rest of the cast were making fun of her. Even worse, she sensed that though Jolson's name was billed below hers, it was he the audience wanted to see, and it was he the rest of the cast were interested in talking to.

One buxom eighteen-year-old chorus girl in the show made a constant play for his attentions – and more than once succeeded in having him walk her home. Her name was – Mae West.

Miss West got no notices for *Vera Violetta.* Indeed, every time the show was mentioned in the Press, it seemed to be Jolson's name that appeared more often than anyone else's – 'Stella Mayhew and Al Jolson made the two hits of the night,' said *Variety.* 'Gaby Deslys went big also with Al Jolson singing with her in a song "I Want Something New". Jolson just kidded while she sang. Al Jolson opened with "That Haunting Melody" and after he got through with that, the audience called for "Rum-Tum-Tiddle" and he certainly can sing that song.'

He certainly could. In *Vera Violetta*, Gaby Deslys' name was above Jolson's on all the credits, but it was clear that it was the young newcomer whom the people had paid to see, not the Parisienne star. On 23 November he placed another ad. in *Variety*. This time he knew people had heard of him. 'Everybody likes me,' he wrote. 'Those who don't are jealous. Anyhow, here's wishing those that do and those that don't, a Merry Christmas and a Happy New Year – Al Jolson.'

During that Christmas week he went to the Victor studios to stand for the first time before the big acoustic horn which in those pre-electric days served as a microphone. He sang 'Rum-Tum-Tiddle' and 'That Haunting Melody', both from *Vera Violetta*. What is more, he performed the two songs just as he had on stage – dancing from one end of the room to the other. The recording engineers went berserk at his antics. If they were to get their record, they insisted, the artist had to stand still – and right in front of the horn.

They told Al this and he promised to co-operate. But when he got to a particular part of 'That Haunting Melody', he himself became haunted – with the instinctive rhythm that told him it was time to dance a few steps. In the end they placed a coat around him, buttoning it at the back like a strait-jacket, sat him on the chair and told him to sing without moving. Surviving copies of that first recording – and there are now hundreds of pirated tapes of the record in circulation – show that he was none the worse for that experience.

In fact, the record made more people want all the more to go to the Winter Garden – and ensured *Vera Violetta* a run of 136 continuous performances. Jolson told *Variety*, 'When I look back and see how things have been made easy for me, I feel more than grateful to the Shuberts.'

On 5 March 1912 that gratitude was returned when Jolson starred in his own right in a Shubert vehicle at the Winter Garden. It was *The Whirl of Society*, in which Jolson appeared for the first time as Gus – a stock character he was to recreate in further Winter Garden extravaganzas and in filming. Again, he was teamed with Josie Collins and Stella Mayhew.

For *The Whirl of Society* – the second item in a three-part bill – Jolson sang early hits like 'My Sumurun Girl' and 'On The Mississippi'. He also introduced an early Irving Berlin piece called 'Ragtime Sextette'. It was the time when Berlin was being billed as 'The Ragtime King' – and when people thought he was the only one writing that kind of music. When Jolson sang it, some couldn't believe that any other performer had the right to try to do the same, either.

There were stories that the newly-crowned King of Broadway was forsaking his old haunts and his old friends completely. They were not true. Jolson, the poor boy who made good, still could be seen occasionally at the East Side home of his friend Louis Rosenberg.

He and Rosenberg had a fair amount in common: their humble Jewish origins, their love of show business and their deep, sincere commitment to gefilte fish. Long after Al had become a star and Louis was an advertising manager they would gather at the Rosenberg apartment, each eating healthy portions of Rosenberg's mother's speciality, her gefilte fish. One night, as Al was leaving to go, Mrs Rosenberg presented him with a plate of her delicacy to take to the theatre with him. Al said he could not think of a nicer gift.

Two weeks later, Mrs Rosenberg wondered why she had not heard from the young star. 'This friend of yours, Jolson,' she chided her son, 'he likes my gefilte fish so much that he ate the plate too?'

Louis gave Al the message. The next day, a delivery boy arrived with a huge parcel for Mrs Rosenberg, Inside was a $300 bone china dinner set and the following letter:

Dear Mother Rosenberg,
    Your gefilte fish was delicious. Sorry I misplaced your dish. Does this make us even?
            Love,
                Jolie

On 15 March 1912 he was back in the Victor studios again – this time with the threat of a real strait-jacket to keep him still enough to record numbers like 'Brass Band Ephraim Jones' and 'Snap Your Fingers' – which was what Jolson always did when he performed.

Every time a new Jolson disc hit the streets – with another artist on the reverse side – it meant more tickets for the Winter Garden. It didn't seem to matter any more who was on the bill with him or what the story was about. Now there was just one desire – to see Jolson perform.

It was early days yet – certainly the sort of fanatical dedication he would come to expect from fans was still some time off. However Jolson was already being admired as a great performer.

Many years later – it was in 1947 – Charles Hastings wrote in the magazine *Motion Picture*, 'Because of his tremendous vitality, Jolie never had a flop on Broadway and some of his shows were pretty bad. Some of them had little else but Jolson in them. But that was enough, because Al sang in a way that rattled your backbone and made you want to jump up and dance.'

Indeed, the way Al was able to manipulate his audience to move when he moved and mouth the words when he sang them was all and more than the Shuberts could ask for.

And the Jolson ego loved every aspect of the success his new-found fame brought him. But there was something more he wanted – even craved. He felt a need for his peers to know how good he was. And for him, this was the most important thing of all – certainly more important than the views of Henrietta, who was being shifted more and more into the background of his life. It was one thing for his close associates to see his success, and he was more than content that the general public were able to witness and respond to him in action. But it was quite another to feel that the people he had worked with in his first years in show business were equally convinced.

There was a desperate beat inside him that seemed to demand the applause of the people who had thumbed their noses at him a few years before. To hear them acknowledge his success and, more important, his talent, was what he really needed.

Jolson talked it over with the Shuberts. 'Why not Sunday performances – just for show folk?' he asked them. The two brothers, seeing more dollar signs before their eyes, realised that Jolson could be leading them to a new road to fortune. They jumped at the idea. And so did the show people.

They bought enough tickets to sit not just on both sides of the footlights, but also to stand in the promenade section at the back of the house, too. And they stayed on open-mouthed as this comparative newcomer to their old profession was able to keep things throbbing along in a one-man show for what was often four or more hours at a time.

Al was twenty-seven, but he was already holding court to the people double and treble his age. When they stood to cheer him at the end of that first Sunday concert, it was obvious that a new Jolson institution had been born. Already another show was booked for the following Sunday, and another for the next week and so it went on.

On 23 March 1912 Sime, *Variety*'s all-seeing columnist wrote, 'The Shuberts may run the Winter Garden, but Al Jolson owns it. That dandy performer does as he will with the audience, whether Sunday or on weekdays. He had to sing three songs with his ad lib stuff, thrown in for good measure, then close with the melodrama.'

A week later that same columnist wrote, 'Al Jolson had to put on extra steam to keep up with the demand. Jolson probably takes more chances at the Garden than anyone else would dare to. Sunday night, dressed in a tuxedo, he removed his collar and tie after the first few numbers, remaining necktieless thereafter. Al Jolson said, "This is just like playing pinochle."'

And on a Sunday in November that year Sime noted, 'Al Jolson arrived before that time (11 pm) and kicked up the usual riot in the theatre that always follows his appearances. It's marvellous what Jolson can do or say at the Garden and get away with. He thinks nothing of removing his coat, collar and tie after having been dragged to the stage. Sunday night he demonstrated his popularity in New York.'

The following March, Wynn, another *Variety* writer, noted,

'Jolson was the loud noise of the evening. He sang many songs, one or two new, and had Melville Ellis as accompanist for a couple. Jolson kidded so much, he broke himself up in "The Spaniard That Blighted My Life" and had to make a fresh start with it. When it comes to ad-libbing on the stage, Jolson makes some of the others look foolish.' And the writer noted something else. 'He appeared in white face.'

Blackface or any other theatrical rig was strictly banned on Sunday nights, but these concerts were all that was needed to prove how Jolson could dominate a theatre without the aid of props. He could do it, too, without the help of the sort of stories then being written for Broadway shows.

Again, in *The Whirl of Society*, he developed his technique of getting over to the people sitting in the auditorium. But the aisles were not big enough to contain him and all that he had to offer.

So he went to the Shuberts with yet another idea that would aid the adoration of audiences and at the same time bring more money flooding into the Winter Garden box office. Instead of simply running down the aisles he suggested a sensational alternative, why not perform on a runway right through the middle of the house, leading from stage to the promenade section?

That way, he told them, he could get close to his audience while remaining on stage – the whole theatre, in fact would become the one stage he believed it really was.

At first the Shuberts treated the idea with the typical disdain of businessmen. It would cost them money and not only that, the runway would take up valuable seat space, and if there were fewer seats to sell that meant less money coming in. Jolson's answer to that criticism was that the show would last that much longer.

They bowed to his psychology. Besides, it also gave the audience a chance to get near not only to Jolson, but also to the near-nude chorus girl who would follow him as he leapt from one end of the Winter Garden to the other. The Shuberts knew enough about the business to realise that the thought of male customers being only inches away from silk-encased pairs of girls' legs was worth two tickets for every one they had sold previously.

As far as Jolson was concerned, the runway was yet another path, another road to success. It brought him closer to the audience he adored, and with the houselights all turned up as he nightly instructed the theatre electricians to do, closer to their faces, too. When they smiled, he sang twice as confidently. And again the Winter Garden rocked.

When Jolson heard the response, he felt he had to top it. 'You ain't heard nothin' yet,' he called from the runway – which turned into a signal for more songs and more patter, none of it related to anything he was supposed to do in the script.

They thronged to the Winter Garden when the temperature outside the theatre was eleven degrees below freezing and when the pavements were smothered by snow from the blizzard that had swept New York for days.

When *The Whirl of Society* went on tour, Al made sure that there was a date for his old home town – Washington, DC. He had not seen his father for a couple of years and, with Harry trying his luck – not too successfully – in England, his personal links with his family were getting fewer as his success grew greater.

He kept two reserved seats for Cantor Yoelson and his wife on the opening Friday night in Washington. But they didn't come. Al had become so estranged from the once familiar pattern of life that he had forgotten what that meant. Nothing could possibly persuade the Orthodox Jew to venture outside his home or synagogue on the eve of his Sabbath – but somehow the significance of this had slipped his mind.

When, after the show, he went hurt to the old flat above the animal food shop, there was more chastisement from the man who had never been in a theatre at any time – let alone on a Friday night. 'A father doesn't call on a son, Asa', said the cantor. It was something Al was never to forget.

On future visits to Washington, Al made sure that he would call at the Yoelsons' flat before appearing on stage. Usually the cantor would find he was able to use the seats – although

[62]

the old man would never agree to meet Henrietta.

While he could accept, reluctantly, that his son had taken a path that was unholy in the extreme, he could never reconcile himself to a Yoelson breaking faith with his heritage and marrying someone who was not Jewish.

At first he never mentioned his 'shiksah' daughter-in-law. It seemed better to pretend that she never existed. Then, learning through curiosity, he ventured to ask why a man should be away from home so frequently without his wife. He couldn't resist asking whether perhaps she was pregnant. When he heard she was not, he shrugged his shoulders not knowing whether to be pleased that there was no member of his family born into a strange faith, or sorry that there was not a new generation on the way.

Very occasionally, the now grey-haired cantor would go to New York. On one occasion a newspaperman recognised him in a store and pointed out the rabbinical figure to the assistant. 'That's Al Jolson's father,' he said. 'Nonsense,' said the man behind the counter. 'Everyone knows Al Jolson is Italian.'

It was the nearest the old man ever got to blows with a stranger. Despite his bitter disappointment with the way his Asa's life had gone, there was still a tingle of pride to be felt when he heard the young man's name mentioned in public. But to call him an Italian – it seemed as bad as hearing that his daughter-in-law's parents were Norwegian.

Sometimes, Henrietta went on tour with Al. But, more often than not, she stayed in their New York apartment. Al was more concerned with his own show-business friends and the people with whom his career brought him into contact. By September 1912, for instance, he had his first Press agent – an attractive girl called Nellie. When he opened at the Lyric Theatre, Chicago, in *The Whirl of Society*, Nellie was constantly at his side. When she went into his dressing room, it was not always simply to help with interviews.

One evening, when she was acting in a purely professional capacity, the *Sunday Recorder-Herald* of Chicago reported a performance as amusing as anything on stage. It was the first occasion when a writer noticed Al's determination never to let the facts spoil a good story.

'Nellie is the greatest of the new tribe of women publicity artists,' Katherine Synon wrote in that paper. 'But she was operating the spotlight and dodging it whenever a stray beam caught a glint of her evening gown. "It's Al's show," she declared, "and I wouldn't necessarily be in it at all if he weren't so shy." But because he was shy she coached from the sidelines until the Jolson monologue finally was launched. For Al was really disinclined to unfold information about anything but his distaste for his dressing room.

'The dressing room was the scene of the informal production. Nellie had made a way from the stage door through ranks of chorus girls who greeted her with acclaim and flung after petitions to be exploited in airships.

'"I'll put you all together in a hydro and sink you off the pier," she threatened over her shoulder as she knocked at the door of the Jolson dressing room. The "come in" was not cordial, especially as it was followed by a sotto-voiced remark, 'If there's room to get a mosquito in here, I'd like to find it."

'But we went. Al Jolson. Blackface comedian, Atlas of the song revue whose weight falls from his slender shoulders, will never look any funnier on the stage than he did then. His close-fitting wig, pushed high from his head to give him air, left a Caucasian streak that endowed him with a zebra effect. He stopped his frantic search for a clean white tie, to roll startled eyes at Nellie as she explained the design of the rest of her party of two. 'She wants you to talk, Al,' she said soothingly.

'"Oh, Nellie, you won't leave me, will you?" he cried in panic – and Nellie stayed. . .

'"Al started his stage career in Chicago," said Nellie. Jolson rolled surprised eyes at her. "It was Chicago, wasn't it, Al?"

'"Oh, yes . . . it was Chicago."

'"And you were only six years old?"

'"Only six."

'''Where was it, Al?'

'''It was at a vaudeville theatre. It must have been the. . .''

'''The old Olympic, Al?'

'''Yes, the old Olympic.'''

And, so the paper reported, the interview went on. Nellie made up the lies, Jolson eyed her curvaceous form and approved. Apparently, though, he got impatient – even with Nellie.

As Miss Synon tells the story, Nellie said to him, '''Oh, Al! Do you remember the story about the baseball game you went to in New York?''

'He fidgeted nervously again at being thrust back to reminiscence. ''No, I don't,'' he finally made his declaration of independence. ''I don't remember one line about mah past. And it's time to go on.'''

Nellie apparently apologised to the local reporter. 'You won't hold it against him, will you,' she is reported to have pleaded.

And as the Chicago *Sunday Recorder-Herald* reported, 'When we elect comedians' presidents, Nellie will be Al's ambassador to the Court of St James's. ''If you had to be funny all the time,'' she entreated, ''you'd like a little joke of your own sometime, wouldn't you?'''

Less than two years after that flop opening night at the Winter Garden, reporters were writing of Jolson in terms of the White House. Yes, he had gone far.

On 6 February 1913, the hoardings outside the Winter Garden announced a new production. But this time 'Gus' was the star beyond all doubt.

Gaby Deslys was still the female lead, but now the name Al Jolson was billed above hers. *The Honeymoon Express* was a two-act 'spectacular farce', and Jolson made a great hit with one particular tune. 'My Yellow Jacket Girl' had been written for the show by the men who provided the score for the production – Jean Schwartz and Harold Atteridge. Jolson made an even greater hit with the song he had introduced at that Sunday concert – 'The Spaniard That Blighted My Life'.

It had been written by Billy Merson, an English music hall

star. But from *Honeymoon Express* on, it was to become the subject of a legal wrangle.

A decade and a half later, when he reached Hollywood stardom, Jolson recalled the days of *Honeymoon Express* and his Broadway triumphs. In an interview with *Theatre* magazine he reminisced, 'The big kick on the legitimate stage is the first night, the nearness of that audience and the realisation that you can play on their moods.'

Truth of the matter is that Jolson was never at his best on opening nights – certainly not until the last hour or so. His stomach was so knotted that he could neither think straight nor remember his lines. But he mastered the situation that opening night in 1913 by a device he was later to use to master Broadway itself.

Two thirds of the way through the evening it was obvious that the final curtain was going to be hours late. So he called to his audience, 'Do you want to hear the rest of the story – or do you want me?'

Once he was sure it was only he whom the people in the orchestra seats and in the gallery really wanted, Jolson let rip.

He sang not only the songs from the new show, but the numbers from his previous attraction, too. And he sang the song he had just recorded for his new label, Columbia Records, 'You Made Me Love You'. When a Winter Garden audience heard him sing that, they wouldn't let him sing anything else. He gave them one chorus after the other. And when he turned to another tune like 'That Little German Band', they made him return to 'You Made Me Love You' once more. It was a mutual declaration of nothing less than the truth – the audience had made him love them and they adored him in return.

If there were a comedy number in *Honeymoon Express* to rival 'The Spaniard That Blighted My Life', it was the one in which he was to play around with a whole succession of dialects, 'Who Paid The Rent For Mrs Rip Van Winkle?'

It soon became obvious, though, that whatever Al sang, the audience wanted him to go on and on singing. Gaby Deslys saw the way she had lost their attention to Jolson and sat and sulked between performances. Once, Jolson even dismissed the cast while she was still on stage. She walked out in a crashing crescendo of high heels. But the people out front didn't mind at all.

Nor did the Shuberts. When Jolson first got involved in a law suit in December 1913 they happily paid up. A writer named Junie McCree sued for $250 because she claimed an act of hers called 'Razor Jim' had been rewritten for Jolson without her consent. But Al Jolson was plainly worth the $250 to the Shuberts. In fact, they had just signed him for a new seven-year contract – at $2,000 a week, thirty-five weeks of the year. For good measure, they threw in a $10,000 lump sum bonus. The Jolson troupe was full of young talent. But Al outshone them all – including a Latin youngster called Rudolph Valentino.

Fanny Brice, the original 'Funny Girl', played one of her first roles in *Honeymoon Express*. So did a songwriter called Harry Fox, who later married one of the Dolly Sisters.

Fox was one of the earliest of what was to become almost a profession of Jolson imitators. They tried – and generally completely failed – to sound like him. To look like him, they blacked their faces and wore his kind of slim jacket and short trousers – and many of them succeeded thus far. They threw their arms out like he did, and often it was difficult to tell them from the real thing.

They also used to get down on one knee like he did. But probably few of them ever knew how Jolson devised the technique that he turned into yet another trade mark. It happened during the run of *Honeymoon Express* – when Al was plagued with an ingrowing toenail.

He tried hopping from one side of the stage to another, but Jolson couldn't relieve the pressure that way. In those days he couldn't sit on a stool either – audiences demanded to see their entertainers work for the money they received. So when it came to a poignant moment in 'Down Where The Tennessee Flows', when he was expected to beseech his black Mammy to allow him to go home, he got down on one knee. It not only

[67]

made his toe feel a lot easier, it also made sure that there was another Jolson mannerism for posterity.

Performers all over America heard about it and adopted the idea – so did Harry Jolson. Harry had been having a tough time ever since he first left for England in 1910. He had arrived in Britain to begin a theatrical tour just at the time when the country was in no mood to go to the music hall – King Edward VII had died.

Harry went back to England a year later and did moderately well. But he decided to go home again. He was convinced that he was underpaid. In fact, he had been lucky to earn the money he had. He couldn't get top bookings anywhere in America. Now, though, they were both working in New York. While Al Jolson was playing Broadway, Harry Jolson was playing Brooklyn.

Furthermore, he was being billed as 'AL JOLSON's brother – Harry'. He said it hurt him to be featured in that way – but he was plainly told that he either accepted that sort of billing or there would be no billing at all. It took the realisation that he had a wife to support to make him accept the situation.

But Al, who was galloping from one success to another, was not particularly concerned. Harry said Al ought to help him as he had done once before by talking things over with the Shuberts. A few weeks before Al signed his new contract with them, the scheming Shubert Brothers handed Harry a contract to look over, too. He was to star in a new production of theirs to be called the *Review of Revues*.

But Al objected. So his brother's routines dwindled one after the other as the day for signing his contract got nearer. It was not long before Harry realised why – the Shuberts were using the elder brother as the carrot to get the younger one. They knew that Al wouldn't tolerate having another Jolson under the famous and prestigious Shubert banner, and the less they offered Harry the more they were likely to get Al to agree terms.

Finally, when they agreed to cut Harry's routine down to one number at the end of the show, Al signed – and Harry walked out in disgust. He pleaded with managements to give him a chance on his own, but they insisted that he either agreed to capitalise on Al's name or forget about it.

His act was too similar to Al's, they pointed out. As for his high tenor voice, it might have been all right for England, but Broadway could do without it. Harry went on tour. Al stayed on Broadway – relishing the notices that the New York Press gave him. When he appeared as Gus in yet another Winter Garden hit called *Dancing Around* in 1914, the *New York Sun* wrote, 'Al Jolson had been too long absent from his public as its particular star. He was welcomed back with enthusiasm born of the hunger to see and hear him again.

'He was never more amusing, never acted with more evident enjoyment of the task for its own sake, never sang with more artless delight in the occupation. Nothing ever checks the wave of contagious magnetism that spreads through the theatre whenever he appears, and makes him and his audience the best of friends.

'He is the spirit of rough gaiety and his admirers sit in happy captivity under his irresistible ministrations.' The paper noted that Al was 'about the most refreshing characterisation in the world of stage humour. Almost any actor would give anything to be able to reproduce such a characterisation. But only one man can, and he happens to be Al Jolson – so he need not trouble about any other role.'

But Al did trouble. And the papers noted that, too. They remarked on the way he had 'mastered eccentric dancing'. They'd never said that about him before. But he knew he was great. When the Shuberts wanted him to play in one of their other theatres between the runs of *Honeymoon Express* and *Dancing Around,* they paid him $2,500 for the six-day run.

The only real loser was Henrietta. She went out for walks alone. She met friends for coffee. And she sat in her apartment. When Al came home, it was usually to sleep. If he stayed at home in the afternoon, barely a word passed between them. He was content to be indifferent towards her, while she had gradually become completely hardened to merely accepting her portion of his pay cheque. She had the clothes she wanted and all the jewellery she could wear. But Al was married to the sound of people queuing up at the box office, and hearing them mention his name as they did so.

And that was quite plainly also the only thing keeping Harry Jolson in business. He once stood on a stage and begged the audience to listen to him for his own sake – they just laughed.

Harry put it very poignantly in his own autobiography *Mistah Jolson,* 'There were two Jolson brothers appearing on stage' he wrote, 'and Al was both of them.'

It was a tough situation for a man to face. But whereas Al was quickly establishing a reputation as the most outstanding artist that this street of artists had ever known, Harry was no more than a mediocre also-ran.

At one time, when Art Klein and Al were having negotiating problems, Al suggested that his brother join him as manager. Harry turned him down, his pride deeply hurt. He did not want to face the inevitable truth.

For the third time, he went back to England and happily sent Al Press cuttings of his sensational success in Leeds – singing 'Put Your Arms Around Me Honey'. Three thousand miles away, Al was pleased that Harry was doing well. If it had been nearer home it would have been another matter entirely.

Dancing Around ran for 145 continuous Broadway performances – aided by a score from Sigmond Romberg. But again the hits of the show were the ones the composer didn't write. The really big Jolson hit was 'When The Grown-up Ladies Act Like Babies' by Joe Young, Edgar Leslie and Maurice Abrahams. There was also the first number Al sang by a husband-and-wife team he was to use time and time again, Gus Kahn and Grace Le Boy – 'Everybody Rag With Me'. He also sang 'It's A Long Way To Tipperary' – imported from England and the trenches of France – and 'I'm Glad My Wife's In Europe'. Friends in the know noted the wistfulness in Jolson's voice when he sang that. He quite plainly wished that she were.

When the run of *Dancing Around* finished, Jolson took it on tour. And again, one of the first ports of call was Washington, DC. But it was to be a very different visit from his last.

There were two messages waiting for him when he arrived at the stage door. One was the note he had been expecting – from his father, wondering when he would be going home. The other was on White House stationery. President Wilson had asked him to breakfast the next day.

The President greeted the young star and told him how much of a Jolson fan he was. 'I've heard some of your records,' said Wilson, 'and I've read all about your great success on Broadway, but I haven't been able to see you perform.'

It was the perfect cue to Jolson. 'Wait a minute,' he said with the twinkle the Winter Garden audiences had grown to expect from his rolling eyes, 'wait a minute – you ain't heard nothin' yet.' And he sang 'You Made Me Love You' as Woodrow Wilson sat with his aides.

When he left the White House, Jolson's chauffeur drove him direct to the feed store. After he climbed the stairs to the apartment above, Moses and Ida Yoelson were waiting to greet him. They still did not approve of show business, but if it meant their Asa being received at the White House, then who were they to object? Perhaps he was not quite the loafer they had imagined. Al spent the day with his father, stepmother and his three half brothers and their sister.

Accompanying himself on the parlour piano he sang 'I Didn't Raise My Boy To Be A Soldier' a strange pacifist number for the hawk he later proved himself to be. But Jolson was still very much mesmerised by the presence of Wilson – the man who won the following year's election on a 'No War' ticket.

The city papers were full of chat abut their 'local boy makes good' and when he pranced through his *Dancing Around* routines, the Washington audience showed themselves even more enthusiastic than those who paid to sit in front of the stage at the Winter Garden. It all put Jolson in a very good frame of mind. When the local Methodist church asked him to sing at their charity show, during his Washington run, he gladly accepted.

Moses and Ida equally gladly accepted Al's invitation to the next performance of *Dancing Around*. But they didn't go round to his dressing room after the show as he had expected. Al had to go to them as they sat in the empty orchestra. 'I told you, Asa,' said the old man. 'A father doesn't call on a son.' But he and his wife had plainly enjoyed their first taste of show business. What was good enough for Woodrow Wilson was all right by Moses Yoelson, too.

On 29 June 1915, Jolson and the show's company played at the Panama Pacific International Exhibition at San Francisco, which gave them a world-wide reputation, as any important event at a world's fair usually does. But Henrietta was no more impressed by this than she had been about his Broadway triumphs. She told friends that a wife did not enjoy being insulted by a husband who was a star any more than she did by a failure. Rumours were rife of his shouting at her and calling her names on the few occasions when they were seen together.

Not only did she not like his being away from her in the evenings and afternoons that he was on stage, but she also resented his constant restlessness. He had taken his car on the train to San Francisco with him – so that his chauffeur could drive them on a leisurely trip back East when the exhibition was over. But once in the city, he felt he couldn't get back to Broadway quickly enough. He left the chauffeur to drive the car back to New York. Jolson himself caught the train – while Henrietta stayed behind in Oakland.

He had, he felt, important business to discuss with the Shuberts and nothing could be allowed to interrupt the strategy he intended adopting when talking with them. For his next show he did not want to be merely co-starred. He was determined to be the only star – without any Gaby Deslys to even look like threatening his premier position.

His word was without doubt the Shuberts' command. For the opening of *Robinson Crusoe Junior*, Jolson was not just listed as the star. For the first time, he was described as 'America's Greatest Entertainer'. A decade later, he was to be called 'The World's Greatest Entertainer'.

Robinson Crusoe was the nearest Jolson had yet come to a show with a real plot, although from opening night on, it was quite plain that the story was not going to be allowed to interfere with his domination of everything else on stage.

He was the little native boy on the desert island who helped Robinson Crusoe find his destiny. In fact he was Man Friday. But in other scenes he changed back to the old familiar Gus and in one act he even allowed himself to be called Fatima.

There were three songs in the show that Jolson was to take into what became very much his own personal library of numbers, songs he would sing right up to his last radio shows and his final recording sessions. One of them was 'Where The Black-eyed Susans Grow', which was always to be one of his own favourites. It was to be recorded for *The Jolson Story* although it was never used. The other two were 'Yaaka Hula Hickey Dula', a Jolsonesque version of the 'Hawaiian Love Song' and the inevitable 'Where Did Robinson Crusoe Go With Friday on Saturday Night?' – a ridiculous piece of nonsense which Jolson somehow managed to turn into a reasonable ballad. The rest of the show was simply what Jolson made of it – himself.

One evening he told the Shuberts. 'This show's a lot of bunk. Let's get a Negro chorus to sing in the background and I'll do a couple of spirituals. I'd like that.' And who were the Shuberts to contradict their star? If Jolson said he'd like it, they'd have to like it, too. It was pretty certain the Winter Garden audience, who liked anything Jolson would offer, would regard it as their right to hear anything his voice could produce.

So, for no apparent reason, the scene on the desert island suddenly became a backdrop for a Negro choir – Al sang 'The Old Folks At Home' by Stephen Foster and spirituals like 'Swing Low, Sweet Chariot'. Both Sigmund Romberg and Harold Atteridge could be see pulling their hair out at the way the star was – they thought – ruining the show.

But the Shuberts stood in the wings, arms folded, wide smiles on their faces. And for 139 performances the customers queued to get into the Winter Garden. They could ask no more.

In 1916 Jolson was invited to go into a new medium – films. He did a short picture for the Vitagraph Co., but he didn't like the result. 'I'm no good if I can't sing' he said. But it was to be shown simply to aid the Traffic Police's Benefit Fund and he decided not to worry too much about it. Then, however, came word that the picture was getting a wider release. He was furious – and promptly ordered all the showings to cease and copies of the film to be confiscated.

Harry Jolson's career was hitting one of its frequent rough periods at this time. The Jolson name was by now becoming more of a handicap than an advantage. He was being compared more and more with his younger brother – and always unfavourably.

It became increasingly clear that Harry had little or no talent. Al was advised by Klein that his brother's lack of any ability to hold an audience could ricochet on himself. 'It's no good, Al, to have this guy held up as your brother. He's doing you a hell of a lot of harm.'

Al took Art's advice and went to see Harry at his run-down apartment. 'I'll give you $25 a week to get off the stage,' he told him. Since Harry had no work at all at that time, he accepted the offer.

But it was difficult, even in those days, to manage on $25 every week. Harry's wife Lillian eventually plucked up enough courage to go and see her brother-in-law. 'Al,' she told him, 'we just can't manage. Do you think you could make it $30?'

Al's reaction was immediate: 'Why you ungrateful. . .' he shouted at her. 'You won't even get your $25.' So Harry was forced to go back looking for work. Sometimes he got jobs that paid good money. Frequently, he did not.

Yet, when there was money for him to make, it was again his brother who was responsible. Georgie Price, the man whom Al once said could impersonate him better than anyone else, insisted that the singer was somehow ashamed of letting anyone know he could do a good deed, or give money to charity.

Al once went to the United Booking Office and asked them to book Harry. 'I'll give you all my arrangements and all my orchestrations – and whatever you pay him I'll pay half his salary. You can give him my songs and my jokes – but don't tell him I had anything to do with it.'

And Harry never did find out. What's more, recalled Price, 'Until the day he died, he went on saying that Al was holding him back. I happen to know of the many charitable things that Al did. But he never wanted anyone to know anything about it.'

It was early in 1917, when Al was in California, that he heard a young ukelele player in a six-piece Hawaiian band and liked what he heard. They were not the sort of tunes being played in Tin Pan Alley. They had a sort of freshness about them. Jolson, always on the look out for other people's talents which would help his own, was very impressed.

He introduced himself at the end of the show. The young musician told him his name was Buddy DeSylva. The tunes were his own and he wanted a chance to play them in the big time. Up till then, he had had to be content with writing music for college shows and band concerts – songs he had dreamed up on the Californian beaches where he was supposed to be working as a lifeguard. It is a fair bet that had there been any lives to save when he had a song to write, the songs would have won.

Jolson told DeSylva to come to New York and call round at his Park Avenue West apartment – and to bring along some of his music. DeSylva took him up on the offer. One of the songs he brought was called ''N' Everything'. Within six months it had earned the young songwriter $20,000. It was his very first royalty cheque and it had come to him because Jolson had interpolated the tune in his new Winter Garden show – *Sinbad*.

On 14 February 1918, the night that *Sinbad* opened, the Winter Garden public were yearning for something that would help them take their minds off the war their country had entered less than a year before. The Yanks were coming all right, but the war in France was going badly now that the Russian front had collapsed.

Jolson had volunteered for war service, but was told that his country needed him most to boost morale at home. So he sang for the troops before they left for France and at war bond rallies. And of course he still sang at the Winter Garden.

The two-act extravaganza had Al singing in flashback roles as Sinbad the Sailor, as the old familiar Gus and even as the front half of Emile – The Talking Mule. And he sang his best crop of numbers to date.

With this new collection of songs, the Jolson ego took new shape. He fancied himself as a song writer. So for each tune in which he found slight alterations necessary to the lyric or to the phrasing, the name Al Jolson appeared among the credits of the song writers. It was there, together with those of Buddy DeSylva and Gus Khan in ' 'N'Everything'. And it was featured on their song 'I'll Say She Does'. And again in 'Chloe'. Altogether Jolson's name appeared in the Sinbad song credits seventeen times.

But his name was not on the three other numbers he introduced in his show, songs that were to be among his greatest. On opening night the theatre was gripped by near hysteria as Jolson started to sing a tune that was quite obviously made to measure for him. Just how well it had been tailored for his needs became apparent from the way the audience started leaping over their seats in a mad rush for the stage and the runway when Al, their idol, had finished.

The song began conventionally enough for a Jolson tune, 'Mammy mine, your little rolling stone that rolled away, strolled away. . .' But it ended, 'Rockabye, your rockabye baby with a Dixie melody'. Al always said that it was his favourite song. He certainly put more punch and more enthusiasm into that number than even he had ever put into anything else.

The second song that became the sensation of *Sinbad* was

one that had been written for another show and with an altogether different kind of performance in mind. A nineteen-year-old song plugger had scribbled it on the back of a menu card over dinner – in about twenty minutes.

The song plugger and a young lyricist called Irving Caesar believed they had the answer to the current Tin Pan Alley sensation, *Hindustan*. The producer of the Capitol Theatre's Demitasse Revue thought so, too – and bought the tune.

He gave fifty chorus girls the opportunity to dance to it – each one with an electric light bulb glowing in her satin slipper. Everyone on stage sang it to the backing of the powerful theatre orchestra. But barely a copy of the song on view in the theatre lobby was sold. And it certainly wasn't being bought outside the theatre.

But it was to be fated for better things. The song was called 'Swanee'. The young song writer was George Gershwin. And through Al Jolson – and Buddy DeSylva – it became his biggest hit, the one that made more money than any other that Gershwin ever wrote.

It was DeSylva who suggested to Caesar that he should bring Gershwin along to a Jolson party. As at all Al's parties, it was to be an evening of him singing. Guests brought other guests and those people brought more complete strangers. There were so many unknown faces, it was impossible to tell who had been invited and who was simply gatecrashing.

When Al sang, it was only after a piercing series of shouts for 'Jolie' – a nickname at the time still mostly reserved for his intimates in the business. The shouts always came as loud and persistent as those vibrating the walls of the Winter Garden a few hours earlier.

The night Gershwin went to a Jolson party for the first time, he was determined to get to the piano in time to demonstrate what he had come for. He sat down to the keys and played – while Caesar sang the words: 'Swanee, how I love you, how I love you, my dear old Swanee. . .'

It had just the effect Gershwin desired. Four days later, Al Goodman, who led the Winter Garden orchestra, had dusted the number up, and within a fortnight Jolson himself was dancing up and down the runway to it – singing and whistling while the audience stamped their feet in accompaniment.

From the playing of a young musician and the crude singing of his lyricist, Al Jolson had found a hit that seemed to be the end of all hits. He had also shown his own genius for picking a good tune which he could make great – and thereby make himself even greater.

Sinbad opened and closed twice – when Al decided he wanted to take things easy. When it reopened in 1921, Jolson produced a new show stopper. Today, it is the one song that every mention of Jolson recalls. To some people, it is the only song he sang, 'My Mammy'.

Like 'Swanee', Jolson had not been the first to sing 'Mammy'. But also like 'Swanee', it was he who turned it into a hit that made money not only for himself, but for its writers – Sam Lewis, Joe Young and Walter Donaldson. Bill Frawley had tried to sing the song in vaudeville. But Al Jolson made it his theme song.

Indeed, by the time *Sinbad* first opened at the Winter Garden, Al Jolson could have turned Humpty Dumpty into a record breaker.

On 1 April 1918 came the supreme accolade for a man who desired the admiration of his peers more than he needed to eat a meal. The Friars – the band of show people who contemplated each other's navels as much to commiserate as to congratulate – honoured him at a special dinner at the Hotel Astor. They produced a special programme for the occasion. It showed cartoon figures lining up for a Jolson performance. One said to another, 'I've got a chance to see this show – if I don't die of old age'. Nevertheless, as the *New York Times* recorded, it was turned into a patriotic rally. For the guest speaker was Col. J. S. Dennis of the Canadian Expeditionary Force. As the *Times* recalled, 400 diners were brought to their feet by the man who had organised the British-American recruitment drives.

Jolson was notably chagrined at having the carpet taken away from under his feet by a colonel. But it inspired him to other things. With his chauffeur, he went to the nearest recruitment office and insisted on being called up. The chauffeur was rejected. Al was accepted – and was told he would be called that December. On 11 November 1918, the Armistice was signed.

The end of the war meant the job of raising money for the veterans who were going to need homes and work in the new peace. A mammoth concert was organised at the Metropolitan Opera House and Jolson was invited to take part. It was the sort of bill he had never been on before. His was just one among a whole pack of star names. When his turn came to go on stage, it was immediately after the hall had rocked with applause for another singer – a very different sort of singer.

Enrico Caruso had just finished 'Vesti La Giubba' when Al Jolson ran on to the stage. Before the applause for the world's greatest operatic tenor had died down, Jolson, in an immaculate blue suit with a rose in his buttonhole, threw out his arms and called, 'Folks, you ain't heard nothin' yet.'

He really didn't have to do much else. The sheer bravado, the – to use the sort of Yiddish word Al resorted to at moments like this – chutzpah of it, had the audience, stiff with their starched shirts and tight corsets, in the palm of his hand just as if it were the Winter Garden.

George Burns was in the audience that night. 'Imagine it,' he told me, 'this cute little Jew saying "You ain't heard nothin' yet" for Caruso – in Caruso's own house.' The opera critics were confounded. They used their most vitriolic pens to describe the Jolson 'insult' to Sig. Caruso. But the tenor himself confessed he was delighted. He sent word to the Winter Garden, inviting Al to join him in his hotel suite.

There he gave Caruso an impromptu private performance of 'Swanee' and 'Rockabye'. 'Come Al, and sing with me at the Met,' said Caruso. 'No, Rico,' Jolson answered. 'They couldn't have two of us on the same bill again. The critics would go daffy.'

But the box-office appeal of Jolson on a concert stage was not lost on the promoters. On 18 May 1919 Jolson gave a song recital at the Boston Opera House. It was the first time in history that an entertainer from Broadway – and certainly one who had grown to fame and fortune from the Russian ghetto via minstrel shows and vaudeville – had given his own soirée at an opera house. Jolson sang seventeen of his favourite songs – 'Rockabye', 'Where The Black-eyed Susans Grow' and 'Night Boat to Albany' among them – accompanied by the Boston Symphony Orchestra. More than $4,100 were taken that night – with $2 the price of the most expensive seats. More than 2,000 people were turned away. Art Klein arranged the Boston concert. But he did so in arrangement with a newcomer on the Jolson scene. His name was Louis Epstein. To him the sun shone out of Jolson's face and the stars gleamed in his eyes.

It was the beginning of a devoted friendship that was to die only when Jolson himself died. When Art Klein's contract with Jolson expired, Epstein stepped in as the star's manager. But he was more than that. 'Eppy', as Jolson now called him, was his friend, his father confessor. And the way his private life was now going, he needed that.

On 26 June 1919, Henrietta Keller divorced Al Jolson. The petite blonde had read lots of books during her thirteen years of marriage and she had taught herself French. But she never learned that to be married to someone like Al required super-human endeavour. She alleged that Al 'cannot stand success – because with that success his tastes ran far stronger – to wine, racehorses and other women'.

She also alleged that he deliberately arranged for her to go to California the previous March while he stayed on in New York. 'He said he loved me best when I was 3,400 miles away, because I'm only a small-town hick, anyway.'

She demanded and received $2,000 a month alimony. 'Why not?' she asked the judge. 'He's earning more than $3,400 a week.'

Al said he was dumbstruck by Henrietta's charges. 'Outside of my liking for wine, women and racehorses,' he said, 'I'm a regular husband.'

He tried for a reconciliation, and sent his secretary Frank Holmes to Oakland to try to get Henrietta to change her mind and cancel the decree. Holmes carried a note from Al, 'Come back to me and I'll give you all the money and clothes and motors you want.'

Henrietta told him, 'I don't want Mr Jolson's money and motors now. What I want is my freedom.'

Al gambled too much for her liking, she said. 'Recently, I heard that he was building a palatial home on the Pacific Coast. I wanted to know for whom he was building this castle, but I couldn't find out. It most certainly was not for me.'

But nothing more was heard of the Jolson castle.

Al repeatedly told reporters that he intended getting Henrietta back. 'It's all a surprise to me. I intend leaving in a day or so to spend the summer in California with my wife.' But the visit was no more real than was Henrietta's impression of her husband's palace.

Soon after the divorce, Henrietta went to stay with her former brother-in-law Harry and his wife Lillian. She told them the familiar story of his days and nights away from her, of how he only wanted to be out with his gang and to be worshipped by his public.

They seemed to sense that she desperately wanted to feel loved, and when Al called round to their old apartment to meet her, Harry and his wife felt they might after all that time effect a reconciliation. But it was not to be. She met someone else and was soon married again.

In private, Al joked with his friends about the girls he was now going to take out. And after he had done so, regaled them with the minutest details of the previous night's experience. The yellow papers loved the stories second-hand. Jolson equally liked telling them.

Henrietta faded away. But he couldn't completely forget her. He gave her a house and when they occasionally met there, he seemed to be more tender towards her than he had been during all their years of marriage. Meanwhile, Harry placed himself under Al's personal management. As for Al, he took on the rest of the profession.

Actors Equity called a strike and almost all Broadway's theatres were closed.

Two men held out against the strike more vociferously than anyone else. One was Al. The other, George M. Cohan – the Yankee Doodle Dandy who loved to go on stage trailing the Stars and Stripes behind him. He was the man who was once asked: 'Can't you write a show without a flag?' Cohan replied, 'I can write without anything but a pencil.'

But the strike was too much for George M. He said he'd rather never get out a pencil and write again than help the unions to change the face of Broadway. Jolson sided with him and for months it appeared that Al's career was in as much jeopardy as Cohan's. George M. retired to the country. But Al Jolson couldn't foresee that sort of fate for himself. It meant too much for him – and his principles didn't stretch to the thought of never putting on burnt cork again.

He was also too concerned about the way he behaved on stage. As he told one writer, 'If I don't get laughs and I don't get applause, the mirror will show me who is to blame.'

But he agreed that the audiences had something to do with the way he behaved on some occasions and was none too kind about them, either.

'I know of no other thing that is worse than the audience in New York,' he said. And then, as if ready to bite the hand that was feeding him, added, 'I often do not come on stage until half an hour after the curtain rises. While the play is actually going on, I sometimes stand in the rear of the orchestra seats to watch the people coming in.

'Well, I just can't describe the noise and confusion. People stop to shout hello to friends. They block the aisles in making engagements with friends for a month distant. They argue their seats and their programmes and do everything except recognise the fact that the curtain has gone up.'

Jolson was making a unique gesture of modesty. He might have been expected to state the obvious – that until he came on stage, there was nothing worth watching or listening to. With Jolson they knew they could expect the sort of performance no one else could give – the like of which even he had never given before.

As he had told *Green Book* magazine back in 1915, 'I've

never given the same performance twice for three reasons – I'm always trying something new, I'm a believer in spontaneous humour and I'd go insane if I had to do the same thing every night.'

Offstage he was the same performer. When he went to pay $7,600 in back income tax in 1918, he climbed six floors, patted the collector – called Big Bill Edwards – on the back and sang for thirty minutes while the tax office staff gathered round. There was so much bustle in the crowd that the pick-pockets did almost as well as the tax man – one man was relieved of a wallet containing $75 but said it had still been a good show.

Al still had his problems. For one thing, there was also another law suit to worry about. Giacomo Puccini sued Al for plagiarism – stealing the melody of his aria from 'Tosca' 'E Lucevan Le Stelle' – 'The Stars Are Brightly Shining' – and quickening the tempo to turn it into 'Avalon'.

Jolson and Vincent Rose each had to find $25,000. The singer learnt the hard way what being a song writer meant. But it was a good investment. He continued to sing 'Avalon' for the rest of his career and every time someone bought a copy of his record, there were double royalties for the Jolson coffers which he collected as singer and writer of the melody.

Not that money seemed to mean all that much to Jolson now. He was a free man with no wife to worry about. He had girls around him wherever he went, and the people who bought the tickets on Broadway regarded him as their king.

If he could hear people talking about Al Jolson in the street – and he always could – it was worth more to him than a thousand dollars. At the age of about thirty-five the world's riches were at his command and the world seemed to want it that way.

Five

I'm Sitting on Top of the World

THERE WAS NOTHING THAT made Al Jolson happier than standing on the terrace of a skyscraper overlooking New York's theatre district, watching the lights flickering below. He would smile and say to whoever was with him, 'Broadway – that's my street.'

With the birth of the twenties, when people first started talking about 'The Jazz Age', Broadway was indeed Jolson's street. He belonged to it from the top of his shiny black hair to the soles of his equally shiny black shoes.

If he had been born in a trunk in a theatre dressing room instead of in a poor Russian town, and if his ancestors had been acrobats instead of cantors, he couldn't have been more attached to the scene.

But if he belonged to Broadway, even more assuredly Broadway belonged to him. These were the days before mass communication, when top men in all walks of life could strut through the streets unrecognised. But not Jolson. He was so famous that he was mobbed wherever he went – when he left his dressing room, when he went to his own table at Lindy's and when he bought his newspaper from the boy near the Times Square subway.

Yet this adulation was no more than symbolic. As far as he was concerned, it was merely the audience's way of returning the love which he extended to them from across the footlights, seven nights a week.

The shouts of 'Al, Al, Al,' every time he entered or left a theatre were gestures that made it all seem very real. For the first time ever, the New York public were reacting to an entertainer in the same way they acclaimed a President or visiting royalty. And for Jolson, their acclaim was vital.

When attendances began to drop off for performances of *Sinbad,* the Winter Garden manager would go berserk with worry. He knew what Jolson's reaction would be at the sight of empty seats in the house.

As always, it was Eppy, the ever resourceful friend, who found the solution to the problem. He would run out into the street and accost the nearest passer-by. 'My wife's been taken ill,' he'd say. 'Would you like two tickets for the Winter Garden. It's Jolson – and he's great.'

Before the amazed pedestrian could say anything, Eppy would disappear into the crowd – knowing that the two empty seats would be filled.

Sometimes, Jolson himself got wind of his manager's game. If he were in the least suspicious of genuine ticket sales, he would sit in the theatre box office himself. With bowler hat firmly placed at the back of his head, he would find out for himself exactly how well the public were buying.

Sometimes, he would actually sell the tickets. Unless, that is, a potential customer asked where the seats were. To Jolson that was the supreme insult. You went to see a Jolson show because you wanted to see, to hear him, to join in the act of Jolson worship. Where that seat was, as far as he was concerned, was an irrelevance. God could see and hear His believers wherever they were. When a ticket buyer asked for a seating plan, Jolson told him all the seats were sold.

One night it became obvious to Jolson that *Sinbad* had little more to offer. He told Jake Shubert, 'Gotta terrible sore throat. Can't sing a note,' and slinked out of the theatre. His chauffeur drove him to Grand Central Station and he was on the next train to Florida. Shubert reacted by offering Jolson a new $2,000 contract for two Sunday concerts.

This was election year. The man who had sung for President Wilson had felt the mood of the public in the political sphere just as he always had in the theatre. And in 1920 his finger was right on the pulse.

He sensed that the post-war voters were going to call for a change. 'I like to be with the winner,' Jolson told reporters and promptly signed up to work for the Republicans' Warren G. Harding.

Al became President of the Harding-Coolidge Theatrical League and claimed to have written both the words and music of the party's campaign song – 'Harding You're The Man For Us', which was launched by him at a ceremony at the candidate's home at Marion, Ohio.

Newsreels showed him playing golf with the candidate and wearing a straw hat, silently mouthing the lyrics of his tune, 'We think the country's ready – for a man like Teddy.

'We need another Lincoln to do the nation's thinkin'.

'And Mr Harding we've selected you.'

History records this as one of Jolson's less enlightened judgments. But, when he appeared at the Harding in-auguration the following January, there was no hint of the scandal in the President's life which was responsible for his death in office two years later.

On the contrary, everybody was cheering – and Jolson along with them. He wrote special lyrics to his old song 'Down By The O-hio'.

He also sang, 'Take Away The Gun From Every Mother's Son'.

And Jolson had something else to be happy about – he had a new love. He first met dancer Ethel Delmar at a party – when she was having her face slapped by an inebriated gangster.

'Leave her alone,' said Al, throwing the drunk into a chair – and he took the girl home. He asked her about herself and found out that she was dancing in the chorus of the George White *Scandals* and her real name was Alma Osborne.

He proposed, and offered her a part in his next show – but she turned him down on both counts.

Jolson went back to work and to the race track and he dated other girls – but the memory of the tall brunette dancer haunted him. He saw her a couple of times walking up Broadway, leading a pair of dogs. But he couldn't pluck up the courage to talk to her. The ever extrovert Jolson was strangely shy with the girls whom he wanted to take him seriously. Eventually, he went up to the chorus dressing room at the theatre where the *Scandals* was playing, and waited.

The next day, they were sailing to Paris on their honeymoon. A local judge had performed a hurried ceremony and there was a new Mrs Jolson to compete with the Broadway audiences.

But it was tough competition, too tough for a twenty-two-year-old girl who never wished for anything more than marrying, settling down and having a family of children around her. However, it became increasingly obvious that she was as unlikely to have children by Al as her predecessor had been.

It was also obvious that nothing a wife could do could possibly satisfy Jolson as much as the roar of applause from a crowd of people sitting in a theatre. He yearned to be able to get back to work – and he figured he had good reason to do so.

The Shuberts had a new theatre for him, just off Seventh Avenue – and this one was going to named after him – Jolson's 59th Street Theatre. And for the opening, there was the most spectacular show in which he had yet appeared – *Bombo*.

On the opening night in October 1921 every one of the theatre's 1,645 seats was filled. *Bombo* had the same loose plot that all the previous shows had. But the crowds roared and shouted for more, just the same.

Jolson again played a character called Gus – this time a coloured slave brought over by Christopher Columbus who until that time seemed to have escaped mention in the history books.

The new score for the show had been written by Sigmund Romberg. But it was the tunes Romberg had not written, and the fact that Jolson substituted one wisecrack after the other for parts of the original script that earned the thirty-six curtain calls Al got on the first night. For *Bombo* had the greatest tunes that Al was ever to sing. He took the fabulously successful 'Mammy' from *Sinbad* and, with it, were another twenty or thirty songs. No one was ever sure how many. It depended entirely on the mood Jolson was in, and as before he always changed the numbers he sang from one performance to the next.

It was in this show that Jolson introduced a song that he was later to describe as his second favourite. It was also to prove to be the last he ever sang in public – 'April Showers'.

When he jumped on to the runway, pointed his right arm to the gallery and proclaimed 'Look, look, they're not clouds, no, no – they're crowds – crowds of daffodils', the packed auditorium was in a near frenzy.

Bombo was not only a means of Jolson winning over bigger audiences, but also a way of helping Buddy DeSylva again. He wrote 'April Showers' with the Jolson Theatre's orchestra leader, Lou Silvers. And with Jolson chiming in a chorus or two, he produced another *Bombo* showstopper 'California Here I Come'.

Gus Khan benefited from *Bombo,* too. He was assured of a successful and profitable future when he provided Jolson with a number that for the next twenty-five years was always to be heralded by an introduction of simulated train noises – 'Toot Toot Tootsie'.

George Jean Nathan saw Al at work around this time. 'The power of Jolson over an audience,' he wrote in the *American Mercury,* 'I have seldom seen equalled. There are actors who, backed by great dramatists, can clutch an audience in their hands and squeeze out its emotion as they choose.

'There are singers who, backed by great composers, can do the same. And there are performers who, aided by external means of one kind or another, can do the same.

'But I know of none like this Jolson – or at best very few – who, with lines of pre-war vintage and melodies of the cheapest tin piano variety, can lay hold of an audience the moment he comes on the stage and never let go for a second thereafter.

'Possessed of an immensely electric personality, a rare sense of comedy, considerable histrionic ability, a most

[88]

unusual music show versatility in the way of song and dance and, above all, a gift for delivering lines for the full of their effect, he so far outdistances his rivals that they seem like the wrong ends of so many opera glasses.'

Sigmund Romberg who wrote many of the tunes for *Bombo* described Jolson less charitably. 'Simon Legree in blackface,' he called him. For Jolson was unremitting in his quest for perfection from the people who were writing his songs.

'Work, children,' he called to Romberg, Buddy DeSylva and Harold Atteridge who would rather have gone drinking than sit by the piano on the empty rehearsal stage.

They had worked out a pact to drive to Montreal that night to escape Prohibition. 'Sorry, children,' said Al enjoying this strange new paternal air. 'I've got some friends coming from Washington tonight and I promised to let them hear your songs.' So the songsmiths stayed and Jolson had some new tunes to warble to his friends. Among those friends was Lillian Harris. She later became Mrs Sigmund Romberg.

It was while in *Bombo* that Al received the greatest plaudits that had come to any performer for their work in the First World War.

Al stopped a matinée to read a telegram that had just been received from the hero of the British Navy, Admiral Lord Beatty. 'All good wishes to you and the American theatre,' it said. 'The theatre and its people contributed a mighty part in winning the war. It helped to maintain the morale both at home and on the front.'

Jolson really had done that and throughout the run of *Bombo*, war veterans bombarded him with thanks for the things he had done. They had particularly liked one of Al's jokes which had sped along the front line in France, 'I'm looking for barbed wire – to knit a sweater for the Kaiser.'

The American Red Cross thanked him, too. After a big benefit show for the Red Cross, one journalist wrote, 'It was the most sensational performance ever given in the history of New York's theatrical benefits. . .

'Al Jolson outdid himself in his spectacular efforts to raise money. He alone occupied the stage for nearly an hour and a half.' During the performance, he asked all the soldiers and sailors in the audience to step on to the stage – and then auctioned them off.

The evening finished with Jolson conducting the orchestra for a rousing chorus of 'The Star Spangled Banner'.

A lachrymose piece from *Bombo* was to have another kind of audience steeped in a wave of nostalgia, six years later – *Dirty Hands, Dirty Face* – the first tear-jerker of talking pictures.

After more than 200 consecutive performances, *Bombo* closed – and Jolson turned his attentions to a different kind of show in a very different medium.

For years, David Wark Griffith, the acclaimed director of *Birth of a Nation* and *Intolerance* had been trying to persuade Al to try his luck on the screen. Jolson turned him down time and again. He had remembered his experience with the Vitagraph Film Company in 1916 and didn't like it.

'I'm no actor,' he protested every time Griffith asked him.

But the director was persistent. Eventually, over dinner one night, Jolson succumbed. He agreed to make a film in blackface. It was to be called either *Mammy's Boy* or *Black and White*. But Al insisted on one thing – there was to be no contract.

'I tell yer I'm no actor,' he repeated every time a lawyer suggested putting the deal in writing.

Meanwhile, the Griffith publicity machine got working. *Movie Weekly* devoted a full-page spread to 'Famous Black Face Comedian becomes Griffith Star'.

And Al was quoted as saying, 'Sure, I'm going into pictures. They won't let Valentino act, so I have to step into the breach.' Which wasn't exactly what he'd been telling Griffith. But he played along to the *Movie Weekly*'s writer Charles E. Dexter.

He told him that he never worked hard on Broadway – despite what other people thought. 'Going out on the stage and letting myself go – that isn't work. I'd rather crack jokes and sing songs than breathe or eat. It's all fun. . .

'You know, they say that picture making will be a vacation

for me – a rest in the out-of-doors and all that. But no jumping off the cliffs for me.'

Mr Dexter was quite astute, however. 'It's pretty hard to say how Jolson will get along without his tongue in pictures. The Jolson tongue wags faster than any other tongue in show business. Belonging to his company is like being with an animated joke book. . . But it is safe to say that D. W. Griffith will make Jolson forget that he can't tell jokes in pictures. In the first place Jolson is a talented actor. . .'

As the days shooting the picture in New York's Mamoroneck studios went by, Jolson felt more and more disillusioned with the whole operation. He was right about acting, he felt. Griffith and *Movie Weekly* were wrong.

He realised that he couldn't respond to a camera lens and worse still, the lens couldn't respond to him – not like the audiences at the Winter Garden. And if there were no songs to sing and no jokes to tell – well, what was the point of continuing? He demanded to see the rushes – and his worst fears were confirmed. As soon as the lights in the small studio theatre went up, he told Griffith he was not going to finish the picture – and walked out.

Griffith had meanwhile inserted an advertisement in the newspapers which proclaimed, 'Mr Jolson's wonderful personality registers on the screen as dynamically and delightfully as it does on stage.'

When reporters asked him whether the film would be finished, he told them, 'Certainly. It'll be ready for release this fall.'

Six reels of the film had been run off when Al decided he had had enough. He had already made that decision when an advertisement signed in Jolson's name appeared in *Exhibition Trade Review*. 'I'm in a new business now,' it said. 'I'm in good hands – and whatever I've got, I'm going to give it all to you.'

Jolson drove with Ethel to one of the New York piers and sailed for Europe. He was photographed giving his wife a big kiss of au revoir.

On the outward voyage, he telegraphed Griffith, CIRCUM-

STANCES OVER WHICH I HAVE NO CONTROL SUCH AS ILL HEALTH
MADE ME LEAVE STOP FEEL BETTER ALREADY AND WILL RETURN
NO LATER THAN AUGUST STOP ON MY RETURN WILL SIGN CON-
TRACT WITH PROPER CONDITIONS AND START WORK IF AGREE-
ABLE STOP

Griffith, who earlier had said he was so 'delighted' with Jolson's work, now stated he was not agreeable. 'I've invested $71,000 in this project and I'll sue,' he said. And he did.

Al was in Europe with Jake Shubert. For them, it marked the patching up of a quarrel almost as bitter as the one with Griffith. Jolson had complained that he was being made to pay 'extraordinary' sums towards the cost of his shows.

The Shubert brothers, who hated each other in almost every regard, had one thing in common – a desire to make as much money out of each other as possible. When they could not do that, they joined together to make as much money out of the public and their artists as they could.

Eddie Cantor found himself with a bill for $1,900 on one occasion for glue. He was told it was needed for all the elaborate sets the Shuberts were providing. Al was billed for $400 – for costumes for his supporting cast.

What was more, they were grooming Georgie Price to take over from Jolson at their Sunday concerts. It was, as they fairly reckoned, the one thing that would keep Jolson within their fold. They did a new deal with him, presented intolerable conditions to Georgie Price – making him report to the train as it waited in the freight yard eight hours before departure, and insisting that he stand around for four hours on stage without uttering a sound – and finally cancelling his contract for $25,000. Price went into Wall Street, Jolson went to Paris with the Shuberts.

Al was photographed next to the gargoyles of Notre Dame wearing a monocle and was reported complaining about the European weather. He was also quoted giving his own views on Americans travelling abroad.

'I'll never go abroad again,' he told *Billboard*. 'Unless that is with Mrs Jolson – and then I'll just go for the sea voyage.'

And he remarked, too, that many Americans went to Europe just to escape Prohibition. 'I don't think they should drink when they go abroad. They should have more respect for their own country's laws.' In Italy, he was received by Mussolini.

And Griffith? The *New York Tribune* reported 'Jolson's olive branches for Griffith wilt.' They quoted Al saying 'Now Mr Griffith will have nothing to do with me. Neither will any other film director – because I cut and bolted. Yes – it's true. I bolted.'

He tried to explain why. 'My doctor said, "For goodness sake, Al, go away – or you'll go crazy."'

The *Tribune* said Al was 'disgusted and disappointed' at the way the picture had gone – especially since he was not expecting Griffith to change camera crews halfway through production as he did.

Without knowing too much of the true story, they added, 'One of the ambitions of Mr Jolson's life has been to recreate his musical comedy success on the screen. "That was why I wanted Mr Griffith to direct me. I was afraid of being a failure. When they brought round a contract for me to sign and this provided for a second director to interfere I cut and bolted.'

When the Griffith affair came to court, the jury could not agree. Finally, in 1926, judgment was made against Jolson. He was ordered to pay $2,627. Griffith's demands had by then escalated to $500,000.

Ethel was as stunned as anyone by Al's sudden decision to break with Griffith and go to Europe. 'He was on the verge of a nervous breakdown,' she told the Press. And she denied that he had intended to stop work on the picture completely. However, it was obvious to his friends that she was anything but happy with the situation and she had begun to drink heavily.

When Al returned from Europe, he announced that he was going to work in *Bombo*. And once more, he triumphed – singing the same old songs as well as a lot of new ones.

He was frequently tired, however – which meant that he

spent the nights in hotels, instead of going home to Ethel. To try to relieve the strain this was having on their marriage, Jolson took Ethel with him to Chicago when *Bombo* went on tour. The audiences who greeted every Jolson visit with enthusiastic adoration welcomed his wife, too. But she found that she was no more a match for the Midwest public than she had been for the Broadway crowds.

Chicago was sensational for Jolson. Understandably so – because with *Bombo* Al refused to take to the road with anything but the best the Shuberts could offer. Whereas other performers were always content to take inferior companies on tour and rest very comfortably on their own laurels, Jolson insisted that the Chicago public see a show every bit as good as the one the Broadway audiences had been given. If *Bombo* were more spectacular than his Winter Garden shows had been, that was what Chicago should see, too.

This did, however, have an effect on business. Takings for the second house constantly dropped and yet the theatre remained full. It was, as always, because Jolson never sang the same songs twice in the same way, and the audiences who bought tickets for the first house stayed behind for the next performance, too.

They lingered even after the performance. On one occasion – Chicago still remembers it in its civic histories – Jolson filled the theatre until the early hours of the morning while he rehearsed with full orchestra the first performance of the Jack Yellin-Milton Ager song 'Who Cares?'

There were Chicago fans outside the theatres as well. But not the sort he was used to. It was early in the afternoon one day when he opened the door of his hotel suite to two men dressed almost entirely in black. They asked him to follow them.

Jolson wouldn't normally have accepted such an invitation but there was a sense of compulsion about these visitors. He followed them into the lift, out of the hotel into the street and went with them to their car. They didn't talk much on the journey – but the gun inside the car seemed to make conversation somewhat superfluous.

When they reached their destination, Jolson was politely told to go with his companions into a big house. He was shown into a palatial room and asked to sit down.

Before long, the big ornate doors opened and in walked two men who had driven him to the house – followed by a small pudgy third man, with a scar on his face.

'You sing to me,' said the stranger. 'What de yer want?' Al asked in understandable confusion.

'April Showers,' came the reply. 'My name's Al, too.' Jolson didn't need to be told that. The face of Al Capone was in the newspapers every day of the week. But for the next two hours an audience of Chicago hoods, sitting in the big house at Cicero, heard Jolson sing. It was the only recorded meeting of the two Als – but it was some time before Al Jolson had any further trouble from gangsters.

However, he did have other friends in the underworld. When he gave a Press conference during the Chicago tour, he introduced the reporters to a man called 'The Colonel'.

'My favourite gunman,' Al told them, as the man he insisted was named 'Colonel Gimp' grinned and shook hands with everyone in the room.

One thing at that particular conference intrigued the Pressmen – why he asked Frank Holmes to phone his wife in San Francisco when they knew that Ethel was right there in the theatre.

'Oh, I'm talkin' about the first Mrs Jolson,' he explained. 'We still keep in touch. I don't want her to sell our place in 'Frisco.'

Sensing that this could be a delicate interview topic, he called out to the 'Colonel', 'Did you see the Missus out there, tonight? Yes? Oh Ethel's lookin fine, ain't she? She's willing me to make good. And there's a regular seat out there just for her.'

When the reporters wanted to know more about the present wife, he told them, 'Oh, she's smart. But she ain't too darn smart, though.

'She thought she was a clever actress. Ho!'

After the show, Ethel joined him in the dressing room. 'How was I?' he asked.

'You were fine,' she said. 'You work awfully hard. I don't see how you can keep it up. But there's something I want to know – where did you get all those beautiful chorus girls?'

It was in Chicago that *Bombo* finished its run – in the midst of one of the strongest continuing feuds in show business history.

Jolson and Eddie Cantor were always close friends. But as close as their friendship was, so was their professional rivalry – and never had this been more intense than in December 1923 when Al fled to Florida with what he claimed to be an attack of laryngitis.

Jake Shubert knew exactly where to find him. As he thought, Jolson was lying in the Miami sun, by a swimming pool. There was a white silk scarf around his throat in case anyone got any wrong ideas.

'How are you feeling, Al?' asked Shubert.

Jolson reached for a pad. 'Terrible,' he scribbled. 'How's Broadway?'

It was the right question for the tactics and cunning Shubert had in mind. 'Not too exciting,' he answered. 'But Cantor's not doing badly. In fact, he's had his biggest ever week in *Kid Boots*. They took $45,000.'

It was a blood-red rag to a bull. 'It's a damned lie,' Jolson thundered in reply, forgetting his bad throat. 'We must get the next train back to New York. No – find out the first plane.'

After that he didn't miss a single Broadway performance of his show.

However in Chicago there could be no doubt that Jolson's throat really was bad. Cantor, meanwhile, was playing to equally packed houses in a neighbouring theatre – despite an attack of pleurisy. The doctors had strapped up his back and ordered him to rest. But he refused. Years later, Cantor confessed that he couldn't bear to imagine the newspaper headlines reading 'Jolson drives Cantor out of Chicago'. When he finally collapsed, the Cantor doctors saw their patient on to the train to New York.

Jolson came to see him off at the station. 'No show *has* to go on, Eddie,' Al told him. 'You're being wise.'

On arrival in New York, Cantor was greeted with the news of a second closure in Chicago. Jolson had folded his show, too. In fact, Cantor revealed, Jolson was more sick than he himself had been. But nothing would have persuaded him to close his show while Cantor was still packing them in with *Kid Boots*. Once his rival was out of the way, though, he was able to bring down the curtain on *Bombo*.

To Ethel, the show's closure was another chance to settle down. There were times when it seemed that married life was now offering the couple all that they could ask of it. One thing was apparent: Al was finding it difficult to father a child. He had never had any sexual inhibitions – the insecurity that frequently made him behave less than lovably didn't extend to his ability to get what he wanted from a girl. He had a reputation for being able to undress a woman and get her to bed in less time than it took him to sing 'Swanee'. There had even been the odd hushed-up paternity suits – indeed, long after his death, a singer was touring America and Europe under the name Al Jolson, Jnr., the result, he said, of one of Al's nights on tour. But, although he probably enjoyed the action, it is unlikely that the end result was as charged. He had singularly failed to make either Henrietta or Ethel pregnant. The assumption now, as far as Ethel and her doctors were concerned, was that Al was infertile. Then news leaked out that they were considering adopting a baby – Ethel was decidedly excited. They applied to the New York State Charities Board and went through a rigorous investigation procedure. Jolson told the officials, 'My wife and I have a splendid country home at Scarsdale. We have horses, dogs, cats, canaries. But there's always been something missing.'

But the void was not filled. The Jolsons never went ahead with their family plans. They did put on a brave front for outsiders, however. When they entertained Harry and his wife Lillian at the Scarsdale house, in New York state Al and Ethel really appeared to offer the perfect picture of domestic bliss. Not only were the couple getting on fine, but the two brothers appeared to be hitting it off well, too. The two men got round to talking business – and Al seemed to forget his old resentment at the way his brother's billing always seemed to read, 'Harry Jolson – Al Jolson's brother'. But on this occasion there was no acrimony. Harry heard that Al was to play a jockey in his next show *Big Boy*. 'And if you're a jockey, Al,' he suggested over drinks, 'what about the horse? You must have a horse to ride – so make it a big real one.'

When *Big Boy* opened at the Winter Garden on 7 January 1925 – the Jolson Theatre was occupied with the first performance of *The Student Prince* – the scene that stopped the show and had the audience gasping was when Al appeared – on horseback.

Harry was delighted. He phoned Al to congratulate him on the show's reception. The hit number was 'Keep Smiling At Trouble' and Harry told him that youngsters were already humming and singing it wherever they went. He knew Al deserved that sort of success. And wasn't the horse a good idea, too? 'I thought it would be,' said Harry.

'*You* thought so,' Al gasped. 'You thought so. It was *my* idea.' Another row between the brothers had broken out – and this one was not going to be any easier to patch up than the previous ones.

The horse turned out to be one of the great sensations of the show. For Al it brought together two of his greatest loves – the theatre and horses – and it was at the racetrack that he was sure to be found on most afternoons.

He had been known to cancel a matinée in order to see a horse he considered to be a certain winner – and treat all the cast of the show to free bets at the same time.

In 1921, Al had established his own stable, with a six-year-old called Snapdragon the Second. But he rarely had more than one or two horses at a time. He preferred to bet on other people's animals – usually noisily. When Al was calling encouragement from his box, his voice could be distinguished well above the rest of the crowd. The practice he had had at the Winter Garden stood him in good stead.

Al even had a piece of a prizefighter, much to his father's disgust at the idea of purchasing another human being – but boxing was never more than a diversion. Horses and racing were a most vital part of his life.

'A horse is a very good tonic,' he'd say. 'Mind you, I've had a few relapses in my time. There was once a horse in which I had every confidence. It betrayed me! For reasons of its own, it tried to pretend that it didn't know the right way round the course. It seemed to think that running backwards would win races.'

This was one of the rare occasions when Jolson admitted he'd lost a race.

George Jessel was with him at one meeting when just before the winner passed through the final stretch, Jolson called out, 'Come on, boy – come on.'

Jessel turned to him, 'But, Al – you bet on the other nag.' 'I know,' Jolson replied. 'But I changed my mind. I gotta winner. Ha! ha! I told you so. I got a winner.'

Jolson always bet big money at the races. Sometimes, however, the stories about his racing prowess were as big as his stake – and as exaggerated. One was that he and a member of the celebrated Vanderbilt family went to the track together and bet on the same horse. Vanderbilt, the American aristocrat, put $7 on the nose. Jolson put on $4,000 – and the horse romped home at forty to one.

Racing was Jolson's way of letting off steam – he sorted out many a personal crisis to the tune of horses' hooves – but more important, it gave him a chance to prove that he was everybody's top guy.

There were times when other animals fascinated Jolson. On one occasion, he was given a cat by an enthusiastic fan. Experts told him it was very valuable, one suggested that it could have been worth $5,000. Jolson was delighted and decided to capitalise on his investment. He walked into a pet shop and pranced out with a broad smile on his face.

'Did you get the $5,000?' a friend asked him. 'Sure did,' said the ever confident Jolie. 'I collected it in kind. The pet store man gave me two $2,500 dogs.' Even with a cat, Jolson couldn't admit defeat.

But no matter how seriously Jolson took other things, it was still his work on the stage that caused him most excitement.

Writing in *Life* – a pocket magazine of the period, not the photo-news glossy which was still fourteen years away – Robert Benchley said that to sit in on a Jolson performance in *Big Boy* was 'to know what the coiners of the word "personality" meant.'

He explained, 'The word "personality" isn't quite strong enough for the thing that Jolson has. Unimpressive as the comparison may be to Mr Jolson, we should say that John the Baptist was the last man to have such a power. There is something supernatural at the back of it, or we miss our guess.

'When Jolson enters, it is as if an electric current has been run along the wires under the seats where the hats are stuck. The house comes to a tumultuous attention. He speaks, rolls his eyes, compresses his lips, and it is all over. You are a member of the Al Jolson Association.

'He trembles his under lip, and your heart breaks with a loud snap. He sings a banal song and you totter out to send a night letter to your mother. Such a giving-off of vitality, personality, charm and whatever all those words are, results from a Jolson performance.

'We got enough vitamins out of being present that night to enable us to ride our bicycle at top speed all the way to Scarsdale, and we had enough left over to shingle the roof before going to bed.

'It may be that we were hypnotised by Jolson's eyes, but it seemed to us that, in addition to everything else, he had the funniest material that we ever heard him work with.

'It was so funny that we lost track of all the good ones we were going to quote and can remember none of them now.'

Big Boy was by any definition a sensation. Audiences were eating out of his hands just as they had always done. And Al was feeling generous – as he always did when things were going well.

There was one song in the show that he never really liked – so he gave it to Eddie Cantor. It was called 'If You Knew Susie' – and became Cantor's biggest ever hit. Some twenty-four years later, the two stars sang it as a duet on the radio – just to show that there were no hard feelings. But he told Cantor after the show, 'Eddie, if I knew it was that good, you dog, I'd never have given it to you.'

Of course, a song is a valuable showbiz 'prop'. But there is something that is worth even more to a young performer – encouragement. To a young actor from London, Jolson gave just that during the run of *Big Boy*.

Ralph Reader had come from England to try his luck on the American stage and was given a small part in the new Jolson show. The star took an instant liking to the youngster he always called 'English'. In his own biography, Reader said Jolson made him feel at ease as soon as he went out on the big Winter Garden stage and stood alone with him.

'Don't worry about me,' Jolson told him. 'Just look at me. No matter who might be watching, if you keep your eyes on me, they're bound to look at you. If you watch a searchlight, they'll nine times out of ten look back to where the light's coming from.

'Remember that your eyes are searchlights and if you keep them fixed on me, the audience will look back and see where those eyes are coming from.' Reader described this as the soundest advice he ever had. To him, Jolson was just 'electricity – entertainment in lights and yard-high capital letters'.

And he was to everyone else in the 'twenties, although the old insecurity would constantly raise its head. And once more, there was nothing like a few empty seats to make him think he was finished.

He saw there were seats unfilled and, before his dresser had the time to get out his make-up, Al was speeding to the station and on the way to Atlantic City. The Shuberts offered the audience their money back – for the brothers this was a unique gesture. But the people who had paid to see the world's greatest entertainer were not going to be so easily put off.

Lee Shubert rang the hotel in Atlantic City and stayed on the line until Jolson arrived there. 'Al, you can't let us down,' he pleaded. 'There may be a few empty seats – but that's because its so cold and there are people with coughs and flu. It doesn't mean they don't want you. I've got a thousand people out here who won't go away until you return.'

Jolson got the message. The people stayed in their seats for four hours – until Al returned to sing to them. Greater adoration had no man. By now, Jolson was not only established as an extraordinary entertainer, to many people he was superhuman.

The sophisticated *New York Times* – not usually overcome with ecstasy when discussing light comedians – shared those sentiments. 'According to common report,' they wrote on 6 September, 1925, 'Al Jolson has been discovered walking with a purely human tread the public pavements of Broadway and entering a purely vulgarian dining room where common folk seek their sustenance.

'Those who have seen him as Gus, the joyous blackface jockey in *Big Boy*, know how false these reports must be. . . At best it is only the shade of apparition of the astral body of the energetic Al. For the blackface Al himself never passes out of the theatre. His being is circumscribed by the stage. The gods cannot breathe the air of fleshly mortals. Al Jolson cannot leave the stage.'

And then as a final thinking point, the writer pondered, 'It would be interesting to know what his astral body seen walking in the streets would say about the way Al behaves on the stage.'

The truth of the matter was that Al Jolson behaved in any public place the way he behaved on the stage. If he were in a crowd, the people with him were his audience. He could even turn a courtroom into a theatre. Only a couple of months after the *Times* gushed about Jolson the god, his 'astral' body came before Judge Isaac N. Mills, who was hearing an application from wealthy Leonard Rhinelander for his marriage to be annulled.

Rhinelander had married a former housemaid called Alice Jones. In court, he produced letters from his wife that showed 'she was one of the most sought after girls in the world . . . Al Jolson had noticed her and so had Irving Berlin'.

She tried to get Rhinelander to marry her by telling him how many other men of substance wanted to take her out. In one letter she wrote, 'I was talking with Al Jolson today. He was swimming – but he's sure some flirt with the girls.'

The meeting, she alleged, had been at Paul Smith's resort in the Adirondack mountains. But the judge seemed unimpressed. 'Who is Al Jolson?' he asked – and the court dissolved into fits of laughter, with, apparently, the judge's own son Leroy laughing loudest of all.

The judge ordered Jolson to appear before him. And, when the singer arrived in court, he gave the sort of performance his public now expected of him.

'The comedian,' noted the *New York Times* who by now had obviously developed a great deal of affection for the Broadway star, 'smiling a broad smile, got into the box. After dusting down the chair on which Rhinelander had been seated, he carefully sat down.'

'No I've never seen Alice Jones or talked with her,' he told the judge. 'I have enough trouble with *my* wife. *She* won't talk with me or even have breakfast with me.' And to make the point about not being at the Smith resort, he added forcefully: 'I have hotel bills in my pocket which show I was in Atlantic City at the time.'

Nevertheless, he was plainly upset about being connected with Mrs Rhinelander. 'Every time I start for the dressing room at the Winter Garden, the orchestra plays "Alice, Where Art Thou?" This is no joke.'

This was just one way in which Jolson brushed with the law at the time. On other occasions, he proudly showed his public the badge which made him Deputy Sheriff of New York's Westchester County. 'I'm now allowed to arrest people whom I find committing a crime,' he quipped.

He had been deputised by his friend Sheriff Arthur Maudlin, and he took the position seriously, if somewhat tongue-in-cheek. 'You see, for a long time now, people have been passing my home in fast cars and I figure they have killed enough of my chickens. So I am out to stop them as well as anyone I find walking off with my property.'

There are no records, though, of his ever exercising a right that was undoubtedly his.

Big Boy closed down in the middle of what seemed destined to become a record run. He had never been better on any stage before and no audience had ever warmed to him – or indeed to anyone else – the way it was reacting to him now.

But Al's throat was troubling him again and his doctors advised a complete rest for a fortnight. It was a time that Jolson spent on one of his favourite relaxations, trying out medical remedies – although he claimed it was the racetrack that really cured him.

During the fortnight offstage, he sent away as many doctors as he called to see him, and discarded their medical theories at the same time.

One doctor insisted on wrapping him in an electric blanket all night. He lost weight, but not his cold. Another insisted on sticking electric needles into his neck. 'I was straddling on a chair when he put the needle inside me,' said Al. 'It was supposed to wander around and locate the pain. After it had wandered round for ten minutes I arranged to have the doctor thrown out – machine and all. . .

'Then there was the army doctor who cured two divisions in three weeks. He shoved a spoon down my throat and before I knew it, he had me black in the face. The scheme, I guess, was to cure the patient of his cold by diverting his attention to a broken neck.'

It didn't cure Jolson of his acute hypochondria, either. He continued to build up his fear of sore throats thinking that they might rob him of his voice for the rest of his life.

During the run of *Big Boy*, Al was true to form with another Jolson trade mark that no one but he would have dared to contemplate. He stopped dead again – right in the middle of the show, right in the middle of his lines. He walked down to the footlights and shouted, 'Do you want me – or do you want the show?'

From all over the packed Winter Gardens came the cry, 'We want Al. We want *you*.' The entire cast was dismissed. Al undid his collar so that the audience could see the line where the burnt cork ended and he sang until he had breath for no more. When he finally reached that point, he ordered all the houselights up and asked the people out front to sing to him.

On another occasion Orville Harold, then a famous tenor at the Metropolitan Opera, came round to the wings while the show was still in progress. It was Saturday night and he wanted to take his daughter Patti home before midnight.

'Sure you can,' said Al – completely unconcerned that Patti was the show's leading lady and on stage at that moment. Jolson went right on to the stage, gently held Patti's hand and told the audience, 'Listen folks – Orville is in the wings waiting for his little girl. You wouldn't like to keep an opera star waiting, would you? Would you mind if I send her home now and put her understudy on? I'll sing to you while she gets changed.' And for thirty minutes Al did just that.

Jolson's conceit, it would seem, knew no bounds. But Larry Adler, the harmonica player who says that Jolson influenced even his show business career, completely disagrees. 'You're conceited,' he asserts, 'when you *think* you are better than anyone else. Jolson *knew* that he was the best. It was, as far as he was concerned, an established fact.' It was certainly an established fact that when he dismissed his cast they'd stay on to see Jolson perform for the rest of the evening. He had the same sort of effect on audiences away from the theatre, too. At the end of a late show performance Jolson and a crowd of his associates – including Eppy and his new piano player Harry Akst – would usually go on to a nightclub.

Late one Saturday night, while Ethel stayed at home with the gin bottle, Jolson and the gang wound up at a smart hotel where the country's top bandleader Ben Bernie held court.

Bernie was famous for his catchphrase 'So help me'. On this occasion, he announced to an audience sozzled with illegal Prohibition booze, 'So help me – we have Al Jolson with us.' From the tables went up one continuous shout: 'Song. Al. Song.'

To this virtually uncontrollable crowd, Jolson called, 'Folks, this used to be my mother's birthday.' Suddenly, the place was hushed. He continued. 'Because this was my mother's day, I'm going to sing a song she loved.'

He told them that since the song was about a little village in Russia and he was going to sing it in Yiddish, he would explain the words to them first. It was, he said, about the small Jewish congregation who send three men to audition a new cantor – a tailor, a coach driver and a shoemaker. The tailor describes the man's singing as like a perfect stitch. The coachman said it was as elegant as a royal carriage and as strong as a horse. The shoemaker said it was like the best pair of boots he had ever made.

Recalling that evening, George Murray wrote in the *Chicago American,* 'Jolson made his audience live with him, momentarily, in that faraway ghetto in a tiny Russian village. Having told them what the song was, he sang it. Bernie, who knew the song, accompanied him on a fiddle. Did I say Jolson sang it? It was more than singing. He wept it. He laughed it. It played in his heart and the hearts of all responded to it.

For fifteen minutes or a half hour, Jolson sang the song of his mother's childhood. And in that Saturday night audience, not an eye was wholly dry. There was Jolson, no bigger than five foot six inches, slender, puckish, singing in a foreign tongue of a foreign place.'

And as he sang, he must have been aware of his own father still living a similar life in Washington to the one he had left behind all those years before in that 'foreign place'. Al decided he had to go see the old man. It had been a long time.

Ethel just continued to drink.

Six

April Showers

CALVIN COOLIDGE INVITED Al Jolson to help him launch his 1924 election campaign at a White House breakfast. When Jolson accepted and agreed to pose on the lawn outside the Presidential mansion, Coolidge and his staff breathed a sigh of relief.

The idea of Press cameras clicking as Jolson sang 'Keep Cool with Coolidge' was enough to win millions of votes.

'The race is now begun,' he sang.

'And Coolidge is the one

'The one to fill the Presidential chair

'Without a lot of fuss.

'He did a lot for us.'

It was probably the worst lyric Jolson ever sang. But Coolidge was delighted. When Al and Mrs Coolidge joked over the breakfast, the President laughed loudest – especially when his wife told her guest, 'The dog wouldn't lick your hand so much, Mr Jolson – if you'd used a table napkin.'

Word of the encounter spread and wags speculated as to who had been the more honoured – Jolson or the President. Others quietly suggested that Coolidge ought to visit Jolson. One was merely President, the other was king.

Coolidge wrote Al a letter thanking him for his efforts for the Republican ticket, 'With a very definite recollection of the service which the (Harding) League did in 1920, I want to thank you for your offer of help.'

Al was once more President of the Republicans' Theatrical

League. Once more, he saw his candidate win. Al was offered a Republican candidature himself in gratitude – as Scarsdale constable. But he turned it down because he said he was more concerned with his own business – although he left no one with any doubts how much he enjoyed the extra fame his political encounters brought him.

The Coolidges' near neighbours, the Yoelsons and the congregation of the synagogue at E Street West, revelled in it all. Moses and Ida walked proudly in the streets of the capital. But Al's half brothers George, Myer and Emil and their sister Gertrude, now growing up, took it all for granted. Asa was their celebrity brother and as far as they were concerned, he had never been anything else.

To other people, however, he produced nothing less than symptoms of shock. Maurice Chevalier, for one, who told reporters after seeing Jolson at work for the first time, 'I think I had better go back to the boat.'

Eddie Cantor felt the same, too, despite his own frequent outbursts of bravado.

Jolson in *Big Boy* had only a horse for competition – and a pretty mangy one, at that. Eddie Cantor had all the trappings of the big Ziegfeld productions, the most magnificent sets, the most gorgeous girls and a hundred and one lesser lights who any day could have topped a vaudeville bill on their own account. Cantor took $30,000 a performance and so did Jolson.

It was uncanny and Cantor and Ziegfeld together tried to work out the secret. Cantor thought a Winter Garden matinée might offer the key. So he bought his ticket for an orchestra seat and waited. He took five weeks to get over the experience. 'Something happened that afternoon,' he confessed privately to friends. 'For five weeks I just couldn't work properly again. I couldn't compete with Jolson.'

Looking back now one wonders why he even tried. Jolson could take many things – the occasional thumbs down from a girl whom he tried to date, the jealous comments from other performers. What he couldn't accept at any time was the idea of competition.

When he entered his star dressing room at the Winter Garden, he walked through the narrow whitewashed corridor backstage like a Roman emperor in procession. He didn't merely pass by, he triumphed through the few yards to the staircase. When he reached the top of the stairs, Louis Schreiber his dresser would be there to give the final royal welcome.

Wherever Jolson went, Schreiber went too – until he became an agent for the William Morris organisation. And then he represented Jolson. At the Winter Garden his job was to brush the king's clothes and to turn on the taps. For the sound of rushing water was Al's barrier separating him from the slightest notion that someone else would come along to claim his throne. If ever it seemed likely that another artist in the show was about to get a generous round of applause, Schreiber turned on the taps so that the water would drown the noise of the clapping hands.

On one occasion, Jolson had a team of performing elephants fired because he felt the audience liked them too much. He wanted people waiting for his own arrival on stage to be literally starving for his entry. He wouldn't allow anything that even partly satisfied them to appear before him.

In any case he had little to fear. When a man like Jolson could manipulate customers' emotions as surely as if he were a hypnotist, why did they need anything more? They didn't and he knew it.

He could walk on the stage, at 9.30 pm – an hour after he was due to appear – and prance along the runway with his overcoat over his arm and his hat still on his head and be met by a thunderclap of applause.

'Sorry I'm late folks,' he'd tell them. 'But it was cold and I stopped by for dinner at the little restaurant next door. It was such a good dinner that I just couldn't leave it. But now that I'm here, do you mind if I make up on the stage?'

The audience, of course, roared 'No'. So Schreiber and Eppy were instructed to bring his blackface kit on to the stage. The houselights would go up and, while Al joked and chatted, made the preliminary black ring around his mouth and painted on the burnt cork, they sat back expectantly.

When he finished, he sang his first song. 'Don't bring the horse on yet,' he shouted to the near frantic stage manager. 'I'm going to sing to the folks by myself tonight.' And for two hours or more he would do just that.

Comedian George Burns remembers that sort of evening as one of the milestones in the history of show business. 'He'd tell the ushers to buy half a dozen five-pound boxes of candy and, while he was singing, he'd pass the candy around to everyone in the audience.

'When it was all over, Al would say "I'm feeling hungry so I'm going back to that restaurant now. But there's a swell piano in there, and if any of you feel like it, why don't you wait till I've had something to eat and join me, then I'll sing a couple more songs for you." The entire Winter Garden seemed to empty and pour into that little restaurant. Jolson sang to them till 3 o'clock in the morning.'

The Sunday concerts were now as much an opportunity for Jolson to take control as they had been a few years back. And they were also usually death to anyone else on the bill.

However at one concert that Al gave, he retired to the back of the theatre for a drink and a smoke while another act filled in.

The act turned out to be the Ponselle Sisters. Rosa Ponselle sang 'My Buddy' at the top of her voice and Jolson shook with the theatre's chandeliers. It was the most powerful voice he'd heard and he didn't like it.

Without going back on stage, Al ordered the Shuberts to fire the Ponselles. They ended up at the Metropolitan Opera. But for months afterwards the theatre's talent scout was still looking for a new job.

About this time Jolson took one of his increasingly frequent vacations in Florida. To keep the money pouring in, the Shuberts hired comedian Jack Osterman to head the Sunday bill. Osterman did moderately well the first week and Jolson in an indulgent mood turned over in the sun and puffed his cigar. The second week, *Variety* reported Osterman as having received the cheers of the Winter Garden audience. Jolson was back on the next train into Grand Central Station.

He took *Big Boy* on the road and it did the sort of smash business a Jolson show was now assumed to do. Since Jolson always had a piece of the show now – the first star since the days of the great actor-managers ever to have a financial interest in one of his productions – the money coming into the box office now assumed as great an importance in his mind as the sight of the faces before him.

Takings were so good at Buffalo that Jolson insisted on an extra performance to keep the tickets rolling out. One Friday evening the Big Boy company were told there would be a special Saturday matinée – at ten o'clock the next morning.

But the following week, the Saturday matinée had to be cancelled – when Al again took everyone in the show to the racetrack.

In Philadelphia, the Shuberts always had a block of seats reserved for themselves and a few guests. At one performance, a fourteen-year-old boy was one of those guests. Jolson called for requests and the fourteen-year-old shouted 'Sing Swanee.' Jolson told him: 'I won't sing for you. You didn't pay to come in!'

Early in 1926, Al Jolson was billed to take over the star spot in the Winter Garden's revue, *Artists and Models.* The Shuberts, like Al, regarded the Winter Garden as Jolson's real home. Somehow, it seemed wrong that the theatre should feature any one but him, but for a long time now *Artists and Models* had been doing well – as the Shuberts' answer to Ziegfeld and his Follies.

There were completely nude girls on stage and always a leading personality to endeavour to take the audience's minds off the abundance of flesh being offered – a tough job for even the greatest stars.

The established pattern was that the star guest should fill in for about fifteen minutes towards the end of the show. But, of necessity, Jolson couldn't do what his predecessors had done. Because he was Jolson he *had* to be different.

When Al took over, he never got on stage much before ten

o'clock. He'd take a look at the mountains of white flesh around him, make an appropriate comment and allow them to exit with some semblance of decency.

Did anyone mind? His audience was as enthusiastic as it had ever been before – probably the only time in theatrical history that nude girls have been overshadowed by a balding man in his late thirties.

To the Shuberts, Jolson's return was a perfect way to celebrate the fifteenth anniversary of their theatre's opening. The *New York Times* reported, 'Mr Jolson with no sign of the recent illness which forced him to close *Big Boy*, gave of his utmost, as his custom, for nearly an hour. He sang and talked and talked and sang.'

Some evenings, he talked and sang for three hours.

The *Times* commented, 'How does he do it, year after year? How does he manage to alchemise these base metals of sentimentality and vulgarity into pure gold of entertainment?

'The pundits offer no satisfactory analysis. For although certain qualities of genius may be defined as they provide the eye and ear with recognisable elements, it's makeup, mannerism and sounds, the ultimate solvent remains an unknown quantity. . .

'He does not patronise an audience. By virtue of sincerity, he destroys the usual barriers (that) stand between audience and entertainer.'

Jolson and *Artists and Models* ran for four weeks. He couldn't commit himself to more. Later, he took the show to Chicago. There, it grossed more in its week than any other show in the history of the stage – $60,400.

The public who had never had an opportunity to see a Jolson show either on Broadway or on the road could always play him on their phonographs. Columbia Records had him signed up to an exclusive contract, due to come to an end in December 1923. But, by May of that year, there was still a chunk of that bargain unfulfilled. So for the Columbia label, Jolson filled in seven new discs – at $7,000 a side. A phenomenal fee for that time.

Even so, the Brunswick label were willing to pay even

more. Jolson signed a new contract with them – for $10,000 a side. It was a deal which made the Columbia executives bitterly angry with their star. They decided to stockpile the Jolson pressings they had just made and release them one by one at the same time as Brunswick released theirs.

Meanwhile this new label elected Jolson to their board of directors. 'We feel that anyone who can enjoy such widespread popularity as a singer can bring real ideas and help to our company,' said Brunswick's Vice-president Mr R. F. Besinger.

Columbia regarded Al's Brunswick deal as nothing less than disloyalty and defection. They felt that as they had nurtured his recording career for years, he should be loyal to them – and they told him so, but Jolson remained unimpressed.

He hadn't been any more co-operative during all the years that they had supplied him with a road manager – a man everyone knew as J. P. J. Kelly. He would follow all the Jolson shows on tour and plug Al's latest discs at the same time. On one occasion at Dayton, Ohio, Kelly was approached by a gentleman who called himself Bonesetter Reece. Reece was an osteopath who had been giving theatrical-type exhibitions of his skills and who had attracted a near-Revivalist following. Reece asked Kelly if he could get him a couple of tickets for the next Jolson show.

'Sure,' said Kelly. 'No,' said Jolson. 'I've got a piece of that show and if you think I'm going to give away tickets to some quack, you're mistaken.'

Kelly paid for the tickets himself. But he wasn't worried. He had a couple of sons of his own and one of them looked as though he was going to do very well in show business – a youngster called Gene Kelly.

But, although Al was hard to some people, he was remarkably generous to others. He passed the front door of the Winter Garden one day to hear an usher telling a boy of about eight to go away and not come back to Broadway until he had enough money to pay for a ticket.

'What's your name, son?' Al asked him. 'Al Cooper,' said

the boy. 'Well – we Als should stick together.' He ordered the usher to find young Master Cooper a seat in the front of the theatre and to show him around to the dressing room at the end of the show.

Jolson probably soon forgot the incident. But twenty-five years later, Al Cooper was among the mourners at his funeral.

Al's visits to his father in Washington were more frequent now than they had been for many years. The older man had forgotten his antagonism to show business in general and to his son's participation in it in particular. When Al offered to buy the Yoelsons a new house, the cantor accepted graciously.

What was more, he found he was able to talk to his Asa now. Over a glass of steaming tea, they could discuss the world's problems. Al enjoyed the sessions. They gave him a chance to slip into the old Yiddish vernacular, to hear some of the old stories which he embroidered into jokes for his act.

The Winter Garden audiences – always with a large Jewish element in them – liked the way Jolson inserted the odd Yiddish word into his dialogue, or rather his monologues. It was another bridge between the stage and the customers. He'd tell them about his father, too, 'I bought my dad a coat last week. It cost $200. A lovely coat. But I knew what my dad would say about that, so I persuaded the clerk to change the label for one that had a $12 price tag. Yesterday, I asked him how he liked the coat. "Fine," he said. "It was a wonderful coat for $12. So wonderful that I sold it to Uncle Moshe for $20. You didn't know your father was a businessman, did you?"' To his dying day, Al swore that was a true story.

Being Jewish to Jolson was something he took in his stride. Other entertainers like George Jessel have criticised him for not being Jewish enough. The truth of the matter is that Jolson's sleeve was too much in the public eye for him to wear his heart on it. But nevertheless, Big Time Show business was very much a Jewish affair in the twenties. Not only Jolson and Jessel, but Cantor and Georgie Price were Jewish. So were the Shuberts. So was Gershwin and Irving Berlin. So was Fanny Brice.

And so was Harry Richman, In May 1926, Al invited Richman

to join him at the Westchester Biltmore Country Club for a round of golf. The club trustees in a moment of thoughtless panic went green at the gills and refused.

'Sorry,' one of them told Jolson, 'but you see . . . he's Jewish.'

'So am I,' said Al. 'And you know what you can do with your club and its membership lists.' Later, when he finalised his resignation, he quipped, 'I shouldda told 'em Richman was only half Jewish – and please let him play nine holes.'

But Jolson had enough friends and enough places to go to without bothering about the Westchester Biltmore. Anyway he didn't have much time for golf, either. It was much more fun to go out with girls – girls who wouldn't demand his every attention, and particularly girls who didn't drink.

He and Ethel rarely even talked to each other now. She would arrange to be out with the dogs when he was at home – which wasn't very often.

However Al didn't like having to go out to get his own girls. As far as he was concerned, it was another chore he could safely leave to the ever-faithful Eppy – whose own wife had died following a fall from their apartment window.

Meanwhile, the papers showed Al in restaurants with brunettes, at the racetracks with blondes and getting into cars with redheads. To be seen with a pretty girl was almost as important to him now as being applauded by an audience.

There are still a few ageing matrons about today bearing the scars of their encounters with Jolson. Few of them talk about it. One, the Broadway star Fifi d'Orsay told me. 'He certainly knew how to use his hands.'

One of his dates, however, did get extensively reported at the time. It was while he was on tour in Billings, Montana, that he decided to take a member of the chorus out for dinner. After the meal, Jolson started paying the usual compliments and whispering the usual suggestions. He put his hand on his companion's knee – and had it sharply whisked away.

'Don't give me any of that business about loving me like a sister,' Al said angrily. 'No,' he was told. 'But I'll love you like

[115]

a brother.' At which point, his date pulled off a blonde wig to reveal what was very obviously a man's head underneath. Jolson ran from the restaurant as though he had a horde of creditors after him.

Years later, Al tried to convince Columbia to include the incident in *The Jolson Story*. They managed to talk him out of the notion.

At one stage he and Ethel did try to patch things up by sailing to Europe. They said they were going to Paris – 'for a second honeymoon'. They sailed in the *Leviathan* at the end of July 1926, occupying the Grand Suite – three bedrooms, three bathrooms and a sitting room.

But they weren't seen together very much once they reached the French capital. Indeed, on one particular occasion Ethel was very much alone. She secretly consulted a firm of French lawyers, went to court and obtained a divorce.

She returned to America the next day on the *Berengaria*. Al stayed behind in Paris for another week and returned alone in the same suite he had shared with Ethel on the outward trip on the *Leviathan*. His honeymoon had lasted just over three weeks – including the voyage each way.

Whether or not the pair *were* divorced was a matter for speculation. Ethel denied it when she arrived in New York on the *Berengaria*. Al shouted 'it ain't true,' when reporters questioned him in Paris.

But the Shuberts said they believed there had been a divorce. 'It's common gossip,' said an official working for the brothers. 'Everyone knew they had gone to Paris just to get divorced.'

Al, nevertheless, was still hotly denying any such thing. 'It started when a certain passenger on the *Leviathan* heard us having a little family tiff,' he said. 'I nailed him one night in the hotel and was going to wade into him for spreading malicious gossip when he called out that I must not strike him because he was muscle-bound. It made me laugh so much that I let him go.'

But wasn't he separated from Ethel? Again he denied it. 'I'm gonna rejoin my wife in New York tomorrow,' he said while still on the ship. 'But I've asked her not to meet me at the pier. I don't want to be surrounded by reporters.'

But reporters smelt smoke and believed there was fire. They were right – the divorce was made final later that year.

For days after his return from France, Al seemed morose. Not because he did not have Ethel around him any more – they hadn't been close to each other for years. But it was obvious that the Jolson ego had taken a battering. He sought her out and telephoned her day after day.

But she was having no more of him. He consoled himself with more days at the races, more orders to Eppy to find girls – only this time to be sure of their sex. But most important of all, there had to be the one thing he couldn't live without – his work, hard work and plenty of it.

He still had time to consider other business interests. He tried to buy a share of the St Louis Cardinals baseball team – but the deal never came to anything. Also he got involved in more of other people's law suits. In 1925, Earl Carrol, the man who had given Broadway the *Earl Carrol Vanities*, was involved in a perjury case.

Carrol was caught in the midst of a Prohibition scandal. During one of his parties a bathtub had been filled with liquor. Sitting in the middle of the full bath was a young dancer who had a part in the *Vanities*. When the police heard about the party, the tub had been emptied and Carrol denied all knowledge of the offence against the drink ban laws.

However he offended his young dancer – who happened to see next to her name in Carrol's diary the letters 'DD'. Repute had it that the letters meant 'Dumb Dora' – in other words, there was a lot that could be expected to go over her head and particularly her clothes.

Carrol protested it was not so. It just meant that the girl needed a little more work before she could shine on the Broadway stage. But the dancer was offended and went to the police. As a result, Carrol was pulled up on a perjury charge. 'Yes,' he confessed, 'There was a party. But the bathtub only contained ginger ale.'

And to prove what a decent guy he was, he got Al Jolson to

testify in court on his behalf.

'Earl's one of the finest men I ever knew,' Al told the judge. 'I'm proud to be his friend.'

Actually, Al had few friends who were anything like as big as he was himself. 'He was afraid to mix with anyone who was up to his standard,' George Burns told me, 'because he was frightened of them one day topping him.' And then Burns joked: 'I was one of his closest friends.' If he was and what he said was true, then a lot of Jolson's greatness rubbed off.

Carrol was fined and the case was finished. To Jolson, testifying was all part of show business. As for himself, he required perfection now even more than before. If he couldn't keep his wife, he had to prove to himself as much as anyone else that he could keep his audiences.

At Syracuse, he did the unheard of thing – at the end of the performance, he refused to give an encore. 'My throat's not up to it,' he told the startled manager back-stage. 'Why didn't you tell that to the customers?' he was asked. Jolson's answer was direct, 'I didn't want their sympathy.'

What he really wanted was a girl – and Eppy knew it. He regarded it as his principal function now – but he wasn't always able to deliver.

When Al wanted a 'special' girl, he thought of Ruby Stevens, a pretty blonde dancer whom he had met in Atlantic City.

He was in the New Jersey resort to judge a Charleston contest. When young Ruby came on the scene, he was immediately enamoured with her. At the end of the evening he sidled up to the winning dancer and said, 'You know, I've got $30 million in the bank. Why not help me spend it?'

It was a temptation to the young girl, a temptation she found hard to resist. He finally believed he had persuaded Ruby to go away for a weekend with him. A day or so before the planned rendezvous a telegram was sent to Jolson's suite at New York's Ritz Hotel. He had been living there since the break up of his marriage to Ethel.

Two doors away from Jolson's suite was another occupied

by Jimmy Walker, soon to be the flamboyant mayor of the city. In between them was a smaller room, rented by George Jessel. By mistake, Jolson's telegram went to Jessel. He opened it and saw it was from Ruby – calling off the affair. Jessel resealed the cable and gave it to Al.

When it came to the weekend, Jolson left for his destination as planned. He did not want anyone to know that he had been sent a 'Dear John' note. It took quite a time for Jolson to get over his infatuation for Ruby Stevens. As for the girl – she decided to stick to her career and become an actress. She also decided to change her name – to Barbara Stanwyck.

Jessel, who was making a name for himself now, starring in a Broadway play called *The Jazz Singer,* said nothing about the telegram. At that time, he and Jolson were close friends and he did not want anything to sour that friendship.

Meanwhile, Jolson's escapade with D.W. Griffith had at last reached the courts. Jolson told the judge that Griffith had assured him he was good in the picture although he himself knew that he was rotten.

And he added, 'Griffith told me he would show me a lot of people who are stars now, but who were flops at first.

'Then he showed me pictures of – a lot of cuckoos. I don't know who they were, but maybe they were all right. I told Griffith I would not be a flop and did not intend to go on.'

The judge asked him, 'You say that when you saw the first test you decided you were terrible and rotten?'

'Just let it go at rotten,' Jolson answered, now once more turning the witness stand into a stage.

The film, he insisted, made him look like a zebra.

'But I'm not a quitter and I'm not yellow,' he insisted.

At the centre of the action was writer Paul Kelly, who said Jolson had personally brought him in to write the film's screenplay. Griffith warned Kelly that Jolson was likely to be temperamental but the writer countered that he was sure he could get the singer to sign a contract.

But Jolson constantly refused. Kelly told the judge, 'Al said to me, "There's plenty of money in it for *you*. You'll be riding down Broadway in a pearl-studded Rolls Royce."'

[119]

The judge awarded Griffith $2,627 which affected Jolson just about as much as a request for a donation to help European refugees. When Kelly himself sued Jolson for his own lost earnings, the jury failed to agree and the matter was thrown out of court.

On 30 April 1927, a new but shaky dimension was added to Jolson's career. He sang 'What Does It Matter?' by Irving Berlin – on the radio. His début for NBC – in part of a programme appealing for funds for victims of the recent Mississippi flood disaster – was hailed by the entertainment industry as an inevitable but belated entry into this exciting new medium.

Almost everyone else in show business had been rushing to get to the microphone, but Jolson was deliberately being tardy. 'Why take the risks?' he asked. 'Besides, I like to see the people I'm singing to.'

The first radio critics noticed that Jolson felt uneasy when he sang over the air. However they welcomed his entry into the field, just the same. Not long afterwards, a picture of Al singing into the horn mike was featured on the cover of a radio enthusiast's magazine. 'Just think,' it said, 'you can hear Al Jolson just by turning a little knob, thirty miles away.'

Another kind of microphone was beckoning, however, and no one knew what was going to happen with that one. It was on 7 October 1926 that an audience sitting in the Colony Theatre in New York heard Al Jolson singing 'April Showers' – not on the stage but from the screen.

Sitting in a hut in the midst of a Deep South cotton plantation, he also sang 'Rockabye Your Baby With A Dixie Melody' and 'When The Red, Red, Robin Comes Bob Bob Bobbin' Along'. The audience saw the flickering on the screen and heard the voice just about synchronised with it.

The Warner Brothers' newly-acquired Vitaphone company were making an experiment with a one-reel shot. People came out of the theatre and chuckled at what they had seen. It was a good gag that no one was taking very seriously.

George Jessel made a similar short and no one bothered

with that, either. The other film studios took note of the films and quietly suggested to Harry and Jack Warner that it might be a good idea to show the pictures in fairgrounds.

Warners, meanwhile, were in financial trouble and it looked as though their fledgling studio was about as solvent as a shoeshine stand. Sam and Jack Warner needed something that could put them on their feet.

They thought of Vitaphone and shrugged their shoulders. It was all too easy to believe all that the opposition had been telling them about their sideshow productions. It was Sam Warner who persuaded his brothers to take the final step. He was the brother who constantly showed more imagination than the others. He was the one who had faith in what today would be called the new technology. Jack was the one who saw the excitement in what Sam was saying and persuaded Harry and Abe (Albert), the two brothers who were more concerned with balance sheets than film scripts, to go ahead.

They didn't want to invent a new story, so they would have to choose one they had already. The most likely to succeed was one that had also shown its worth on Broadway. Fitting the bill – George Jessel's *The Jazz Singer.*

It was a story that had an interesting pedigree. Before the war a student in the Illinois town of Champagne showed Al Jolson a story he had written called *Day of Atonement.* It was about a Jewish cantor who couldn't persuade his child to give up the theatre. It was very much like Jolson's own life story and young Samson Raphaelson asked the star to look at it. Jolson thought it was so much out of his field that he politely said 'No'.

A young actress called Vera Gordon heard about the story years later when she was starring in the Broadway show *Humoresque.* Raphaelson changed his story to allow a girl to play the main part, and changed the title to *The Jazz Singer.*

But before it got on the road, Jessel heard about the play. He persuaded Raphaelson that it would be much better to return the story to the lines of the old Jewish folktale, the story of the cantor's son who wanted to sing in grand opera.

It was a wise suggestion on Jessel's part. The play ran to

[121]

packed audiences for three years and it looked as though it would never end its run. What killed the play was Warner Brothers' Vitaphone – and Al Jolson.

When the studio finally decided on filming *The Jazz Singer,* Jessel was the obvious choice to star in the picture. But with a new invention like talkies to worry about and with the unknown effect it was likely to have on his career, a man like him wanted insurance – to the tune of $100,000.

Warners said 'No'. Eddie Cantor was approached – and he, too, said he was too worried about the effects of talking pictures on his career to contemplate the idea.

Warners took their minds back to the beginning of their discussions. Darryl Zanuck had said it half in jest, 'Jesus, for the sort of money Jessel wants we can get Jolson.'

Now that flippant idea was being seriously canvassed. For there was Jolson's renowned love of a gamble. 'What about asking Al Jolson to put money *into* the picture and draw stock from its takings?' Zanuck asked.

Jolson insisted on complete secrecy about the whole matter while he thought it over. He was staying at the Biltmore Hotel in New York at the same time as Jessel. The two had arranged to go out one Sunday for a game of golf when Al knocked at his friend's door and told him to go back to sleep. 'I'm going out for a walk,' he said – and disappeared.

Jessel turned over and went back to sleep. The next day he read in the papers that Jolson had signed with Warner Brothers to make *The Jazz Singer.*

'Is it any wonder I always felt bitter?' Jessel asked me. 'I felt sick. It was my part and partly my story. Jolson got the role because he put money into it. But he was better at it than I would have been!'

Seven

California Here I Come

WHETHER JOLSON COULD have imagined what *The Jazz Singer* would mean to show business, no one will ever know for sure. He certainly had an uncanny knack of breaking new ground, of being the first to do things which became the established practice of everyone who came after him, but no one seemed bothered about this new development.

No secret was made of his trip – or of what his mission was to be. But no one thought of getting in with sound films first. Without doubt, when he arrived in Hollywood for the first time on that day in 1927, the movie capital had no idea what was going to hit it.

Jolson was met at the railway station by Jack, Harry and Sam Warner, with Darryl Zanuck hovering behind. And he hadn't been in California very long before the other stars of the city came to pay homage. Charlie Chaplin and Douglas Fairbanks were happy enough to pose with him – without realising what this one man represented to their industry.

The King of Broadway was being fêted now as if he were the King of Hollywood – but only in a half-hearted sort of way. Hollywood felt flattered that the great Jolson, the man they had all read about who could turn mighty theatres into temples to his own deity, had come to join them. But they couldn't believe that he would really have any impact on their world.

If Jolson himself had any thoughts on the matter, it is doubtful that he realised that he might be creating a monster which, in time, would all but consume him.

To Jack Warner, making *The Jazz Singer* was, if nothing else, a one-man ego trip. He adored Jolson, he worshipped him. Having Al on the payroll was worth all the other stars on his books and all the money they might or might not make him – his biggest winner to date had been Rin Tin Tin, the Alsation dog who demanded no more than a bone as salary and a hamburger as a bonus.

Jolson was the only actor ever allowed access to his private office at any time – or to the private dining room which became the place where he held court. He even fancied himself as a Jolson carbon copy. He affected speech patterns like his idol. When he founded his own radio station, Jack – who had been a failed vaudevillian in his time – performed on the air himself, singing, so he believed, like Jolson. (His favourite tune was 'When The Red, Red Robin Comes Bob, Bob, Bobbin' Along'.)

Now that the studio was virtually broke – so much so that their staff salaries would be drawn on a New York bank so that they would have another four or five days before the cheques would be cashed – Jack saw a lifeline that also allowed him to indulge his greatest fancies.

Meanwhile, the fan magazines were writing about the new movie star-to-be and Jolson posed with the Warner Brothers for more pictures – among them a celebrated one in which the Warners between them carried the mouthpiece of a giant telephone while Jolson held the earpiece. There was something symbolic in the shot – without Jolson, Warners and the whole Vitaphone invention were useless.

The original idea was that *The Jazz Singer* would be a completely silent picture with just Jolson's songs and the occasional snatch of the background music. The Warner-Vitaphone film *Don Juan* the year before had proved that synchronised background music could be made to work.

If there had been anyone but Jolson starring in *The Jazz Singer*, exactly that would probably have happened. It is also conceivable that talking pictures would have remained a mere twinkle in an inventor's eye for a generation to come.

But with Jolson in charge – and that is precisely the way he saw things from the moment he first walked on to the set – nothing could possibly turn out the way it had been planned.

There were sub-titles for the picture – just as there always had been. So no one was terribly concerned when Jolson started ad-libbing in front of the cameras, disregarding the screenplay just as he had always abandoned the book on stage.

The orchestra was all tuned up, the cameras with their crews in a stiflingly hot sound-proof box were whirring and the microphones were all switched on. All was ready for Jolson to go into his first big featured number, 'Toot Toot Tootsie Goo'-bye'.

But Alan Crosland, the director, had never worked with Jolson before. Just as he gave the signal for everything to roll, Al got into the spirit of the thing. 'Wait a minute, wait a minute,' he cried. 'You ain't heard nothin' yet. Wait a minute I tell yer . . . you wanna hear "Toot Toot Tootsie". All right, hold on.' And then to Orchestra Leader Lou Silvers he called: 'Lou, listen. You play "Toot Toot Tootsie". Three choruses, you understand, and in the third chorus I whistle. Now give it to 'em hard and heavy. Go right ahead. . .'

No screen playwright could ever have put those words in a script and got away with it. But the mikes were switched on, the film and Jolson were in motion and those sentences were preserved for posterity. The film industry was never to be the same again.

Later when the rushes were run, Warners were astute enough to realise what they had on their hands. So an additional scene was written for the stars – in sound. Young Jakie Robin (Jolson) comes back to his aged mother (Eugenie Besserer) and fools around on the piano chirping 'Blue Skies'. The scene – and a happy incident in the film – comes to an abrupt end as Warner Oland, playing Jolson's father, storms into the room and shouts 'Stop!'

The novelty of sound made *The Jazz Singer* the success it was. But there was something more to it, something that managed to get beneath the maudlin sentimentality. For one thing, great efforts were made to ensure accuracy – greater efforts, in fact, than were usual for Hollywood, the town of make-believe, at the time.

To make sure that Cantor Rabinowitz really looked the stern father, Warner Oland – later to make his name as Charlie Chan – watched how the patriarchal Jews of the New York ghetto mastered their children. When he was ready to play the part himself, the camera crews moved from Hollywood to Orchard Street – in the heart of the Lower East Side of Manhatten.

He sat by the window of a restaurant and as Alan Crosland gave the word, walked into the street to get lost in the crowd. His beard was long – much longer than the one to be worn twenty years later in *The Jolson Story* by Ludwig Donath who played Papa Yoelson, and his skullcap was much taller too – and his whole appearance fitted in perfectly with the Orchard Street throng.

When he caught a young boy by the sideburns and pulled him into one of the street's mean little houses, no one took any notice. It happened there all the time. For days, too, camera teams studied the services at the old Orchard Street synagogue. Studio artists noted every detail of the architecture and created an exact replica weeks later on the Burbank stages.

The same devotion to detail was given to the Winter Garden scenes. The interior of the theatre was photographed and then rebuilt in the studios. But for some shots, only the real Winter Garden would do – and Jolson on the runway of his own theatre was what the filmgoers saw.

While the camera crews worked on Broadway in April 1927 a giant tarpaulin covered the usual flickering sign. The temporary fascia proclaimed 'Warner Brother Pictures Inc, will shoot scenes today of the New York Winter Garden for their forthcoming production – Al Jolson in *The Jazz Singer*. It pointed out that there would be no interruption of the current Shubert success, *The Circus Princess.*

At night the temporary sign was removed to reveal underneath a much more permanent looking one in the usual mammoth-size electric letters, spelling out the legend, 'Winter Garden – JACK ROBIN – The Jazz Singer'.

[126]

For the next twenty years Al Jolson would have to be content with the pseudonym. But with *The Jazz Singer* he already had his memorial. The world's first talking picture was really very much Jolson's own story.

Not that he particularly enjoyed the filming. 'I thought the picture would be a terrible flop,' he said soon after it was finished, 'because everything was new and strange to me. I would do a scene five times with tears in my eyes and then Alan Crosland would say "Do it again – and put some feeling into it!"'

It wasn't an easy film to shoot. There weren't the problems there would later be with the first all-talking, all-singing pictures, hiding microphones in anything from a leading lady's cleavage to a vase of flowers. But for the song segments, the cameraman had to place himself in a sound-proof box, so that the whirring of the camera wouldn't be heard by people sitting in the theatres. Huge carpets had to be hung on the walls of what had now become sound stages, to try to keep out the noise of passing traffic.

And then there was the problem of fitting in sound to match the pictures. Each reel of film had to be matched by a corresponding disc, and while it was easy enough to cut and edit a strip of film, you couldn't do that with a record. So once the film had been shot and the musical accompaniment added, that's how it had to stay. Alan Crosland, the director, had to shoot the non-singing scenes, edit and then assemble them and finally add the sound segments – which were each shot on adjoining sound stages.

Blank film was first inserted where the musical scenes would go. It was in this space that the precisely-timed sound sequences had to be placed. The silent scenes were projected on to a screen overhead, and when it was time for a song, or the piece of dialogue, work had to begin the very moment the blank piece of film came up on the screen – or the disc which had been playing the musical background to the silent scenes would be out of synchronisation.

But it wasn't a terrible flop. 'I wanted to go away and hide,' said Jolson. 'But the Warner Brothers got me by the collar, threw me on a train and packed me off to New York for the opening, which went over with a bang and made me very happy.'

It won a special award from the Academy of Motion Picture Arts and Sciences – largely for its novelty value. But it was a novelty that that was soon to smash the old Hollywood as though it had been hit by a combined tornado, earthquake and atomic bomb.

People queued for hours on the night of its première to glimpse the arrival of the stars and the other showbiz personalities. Those who managed to get into the Warners' Theatre for the film itself had no idea of what was going to hit them once the projectors started to roll. What they did see and hear made them screech and shout until they nearly went crazy.

Jolson was among the audience that night of 6 October 1927, experiencing from a seat in the circle what he had previously only known from the stage. The Warner brothers were not there, though.

Jack had been in New York, preparing for the première, when he had an SOS from his brother Harry. Sam had suddenly been struck with a severe mastoid inflammation and two operations had failed to get him better. He died the day before what should have been his greatest triumph.

But the public at the Warners' Theatre were not aware of any of that. The première, appropriately enough, was held just a couple of hours after the end of Yom Kippur, the sacred Day of Atonement which played such an important part in the film's story.

Once the film was over, Jolson himself went on stage. "Folks," he said, "I was so happy that I couldn't stop the tears."

The *New York Times* was equally moved. Mordaunt Hall wrote: 'The success of this production is due to a large degree to Mr. Jolson's Vitaphoned renditions.' He went on: 'The Vitaphoned songs and some dialogue have been introduced most adroitly. This in itself is an ambitious move, for in the expression of song, the Vitaphone vitalises the production enormously... It was also a happy idea to persuade Mr. Jolson to play the leading role, for few men could have approached the task of singing and acting so well as he does in this photoplay. His "voice with a tear" compelled silence and possibly all that disappointed the people in the packed theatre was the fact that they could not call upon him or his image at least for an encore. They had to content themselves with clapping and whistling after Mr Jolson's shadow finished a realistic song.'

Something that had singularly failed to do more than just amuse in a one-reel had become charismic in a feature.

Rival film producers in the audience were seen to shake physically in their seats. The next day the wires between New York and California were burning with instructions from movie moguls to wire their studios for sound.

A week or so later, Jolson was making a fortune for himself in the cinema – or rather in one particular Los Angeles cinema, the Metropolitan.

As an experiment, he was for one week earning himself $17,000 for his engagement at the theatre, doing a one-man vaudeville act after the main feature – a now forgotten movie called *Out All Night*. The theatre itself could have been out all night pushing people away from the queues that began forming outside the Metropolitan as soon as it was announced he would be appearing there.

At the end of the engagement, the management presented him with a silver engraved golf club and asked him if he would do another week. Al took his money, and left for Lake Arrowhead – saving he thought it was unfair to compete with the cinema on the other side of the road from the Metropolitan. That was showing *The Jazz Singer*.

Nevertheless, everyone involved seemed well satisfied. *Variety* said: 'Jolson simply took the town by storm.'

As for Al himself, he told the paper: 'For the past eighteen years, I've been appearing in legitimate productions doing eight performances a week. When the opportunity presented itself for me to go to picture houses, I looked at it from the angle of a following I never had before – people who were dyed-in-the-wool picture addicts and who never paid the $4.40 top which I was getting with my own shows' (the highest ticket for the cinema was 60 cents).

'My drawing power in the musical comedy field has been limited. In the picture business, it is not.'

Meanwhile, *The Jazz Singer* was proving how right he was. Within two weeks of its New York opening, *Variety* was reporting it was 'breaking all records between Chicago and the Pacific slope'.

Careers were smashed as studios realised that faces which had previously sent millions of women into swoons belonged to voices which would now transport them into hysterical laughter.

For Al Jolson it was the greatest moment in his stupendously successful life. He loved to see the crowds gather nightly outside the Warners'. Every evening for weeks, he and Lee Shubert would go into the theatre just before the film's end in time to hear Jolson singing Kol Nidre in the synagogue as his father lies dying.

Hal Wallis, later to become head of production at First National and then at Warner Brothers itself, was at the time in charge of publicity. 'I've never known a performer who took to working on a film like Al Jolson,' he told me. 'He took an interest in everything. When I wanted him to meet the press and talk about what we were doing, he did so – and brilliantly.'

The talking picture took its toll of show business much quicker than anyone could have guessed. It not only killed the silent picture, it assassinated vaudeville.

The Keith-Orpheum circuit, who controlled and ruled a vaudeville empire that stretched from one end of the United States to the other, wound up their theatre interests and joined with the Radio Corporation to form a new film studio – RKO.

That sort of effect of *The Jazz Singer* was not the main concern of Jolson and Warner Brothers. They knew they had a hit on their hands and that was the way they liked it.

The story differed from the one in the Jessel stage play.

Instead of the erring boy returning to become a cantor for the rest of his life, there was a happy ending of a different kind. Jack Robin sang Kol Nidre to make his father happy on his death bed but he went on to see his mother cheering proudly from her seat as he sang 'Mammy' on the stage of the Winter Garden.

And, of course, it had to be like that. No audience could really be expected to see Al Jolson give up show business – even in a film. It might have caused a revolution as big as the one Jolson had wrought on Hollywood.

The people who shouted 'Al . . . Jolson . . . Jolson . . . Al' for what seemed an eternity inside the Warner Theatre were merely acting out the prologue to the story of what instantly became known as the Talkies. The film quickly went round the world and if there were European cities without sound equipment in their cinemas, it did not matter. *The Jazz Singer* was shown from the Danube to the Dnieper as a silent picture.

The film was to make $3,500,000 net profit and before long Jolson's own stock in Warner Brothers was to be worth $4,000,000. As to his stock as a film property, it was priceless.

Publicly the other studios and the other stars were to dismiss 'this novelty – talking pictures.' Chaplin – of whom Jolson had written glowingly in a full page *Variety* advertisement the year before, praising *The Circus* as 'the greatest thing I've seen. Dem's my sentiments' – continued to stick the tiny moustache to his upper lip and to carry his little cane as he had always done. He vowed in the Press never to make a talkie.

Privately, everyone who counted in Hollywood was having nightmares. The local electricians had never had so much work in their lives. Studios changed overnight. Half finished silent films were scrapped completely or had sound sequences added.

And, of course, Warner Brothers wanted Jolson for another picture.

Harry and Jack had plenty to occupy themselves with, in the new Jolson career. They were also convinced that for their hot new property they had an equally hot new story.

They felt that *The Jazz Singer* had made Jolson above all a sentimental actor. It was a mistake Al himself was to regret – but not for a few years yet. The new film script had him in the role of the father to a dying child. All the emotions he had used as a son escaping from the fringes of his father's prayer shawl he was now displaying again, running after his little boy's pram. The picture was to be called *The Singing Fool.*

Again, it was a silent film but with the addition of snatches of dialogue and with a few songs which Jolson sang both with and without his blackface makeup. Looking back on the film now, it is easy to see where he was happier. He was stilted singing to an empty camera lens. He needed live voices to shout back at him when he sang, and there was nothing like the sound of applause to set the adrenalin running through his body, but even without audience participation he could escape from reality easier in burnt cork. The mask helped him as it had on Broadway, although only a fraction of his magnetism showed through. At the time, for those people who had never seen Jolson live, it was enough.

The Singing Fool was a picture racked with problems. For one thing there had to be a little boy to appear with Al as his son. For weeks mothers managed to break the Warner Brothers' security net and get on to the lot just in time for Al's entrance or just as Director Lloyd Bacon moved in. Cleaners mysteriously produced little boys from underneath their aprons. Waitresses managed to find them hiding on their coffee trolleys.

In the end, the part went to a youngster called Davy Lee – who years later said his principal recollection of the film was 'Uncle Al's bony knees'.

Finding a suitable new song for the film was another problem. One by one, songwriters submitted melodies and lyrics, and one by one Jolson threw them in the wastepaper basket.

In the end, he tracked down his old sparring partners, DeSylva, Brown and Henderson, who between them had supplied so many of the old Jolson hits – including one that was to be included in *The Singing Fool* already, 'It All Depends On You', and 'I'm Sitting On Top Of The World' and 'Keep Smiling At Trouble' for which DeSylva shared the credits with other writers – and were usually eager enough to write for him.

The song writers were at a party in Atlantic City when the long distance operator announced that Al Jolson was on the line from California.

'Listen fellers, I've gotta have a song, yah hear?' he told them. 'It's a song to a little boy – a little guy who's dyin' and his dad's near heartbroken about it. Do Jolie a favour and yer won't regret it.'

The idea of King Jolson, the man who had taken the Winter Garden by storm, who had thundered through the Metropolitan Opera House singing 'Swanee', wanting a silly song like that made the trio dissolve into hysterics.

'We've got to do it as a gag,' said Buddy DeSylva. 'Who could take a thing like that seriously?'

So between them they threw in every ounce of schmaltz they could sliver from one song. As the lyrics called for tears, DeSylva, Brown and Henderson laughed. By the time the song was finished, they felt so ashamed of what they had done that they got a bellboy to mail it to Jolson for them. None of them could bring himself actually to deposit the number in the box.

Jolson laughed, too. As people put it forty years later, he laughed all the way to the bank.

The new song was called 'Sonny Boy'. When audiences heard Jolson weep over the grey skies in the picture, they wept. When Jolson smiled before the song reached its climax, they smiled. When he broke down over the boy's death, the people out front discarded their soaking handkerchiefs under their seats.

For years afterwards, intrepid explorers were reported hearing Arctic Eskimos and African tribesman winding up ancient phonographs to listen to scratched discs of Jolson's 'Sonny Boy'. The recording became the world's first ever disc to sell a million copies. It went on to sell two million and then three million.

As for *The Singing Fool* itself, Warner Brothers had had the brilliant idea of staging its opening on Jolson's own stamping ground – the Winter Garden. Once more, he was the king of his own theatre and behaved like one. When he wanted to go out, the latest Rolls Royce import was provided for him. When he wanted to go to a ballgame, De Pinna's – New York's smartest men's wear store – provided him only a vicuna coat – which he promptly returned after the game. 'I only took it on approval,' he insisted.

For ten years, *The Singing Fool* remained the most successful movie of all time. Only in 1939 did *Gone with the Wind* overtake it.

The picture was to make $5,500,000. By the end of 1929 Warner Brothers – near broke when they made *The Jazz Singer* – had made a net profit of $7,271,805. Someone calculated it was a 745 per cent increase in their takings.

The once tiny studio was now the giant of Hollywood and their prize asset was Al Jolson.

Eleven months later a new Jolson picture opened at Broadway's Warner Theatre – *Say it with Songs*. Songs that Al Jolson again sang to Davy Lee. And that was not the only similarity.

DeSylva, Brown and Henderson were again brought in to repeat their 'Sonny Boy' success. This time, they didn't laugh and, predictably, this time not as many people cried. But 'Little Pal' was a reasonable enough follow-up to 'Sonny Boy' and Jolson and Warner Brothers' interpretation of him as a film star continued to mean money at the box office.

It had not yet dawned on the Warner moguls that they were hardly doing justice to their hottest property. Nor did Jolson yet realise what was slowly happening to his career.

He was making huge sums of money, $500,000 a film. It was phenomenal for that time, and the audiences were flooding into the cinemas to see him. Or were they? There were already rumours that each Jolson picture was turning out to be just a carbon copy of the one before.

Not enough people in high places, however, had realised it and the process continued. No one began to ponder the thought that as the novelty of the invention wore off, the public might be more demanding.

When films were being advertised as 'All talking – All singing – All dancing', Jolson's was not among them. The monster he had created had begun to bite.

Even before *The Singing Fool* had been released, Al was saying unpleasant things about the films he was making.

'It ain't so bad,' he said about one picture. 'But *The Jazz Singer* – a monkey could have played it, and did.'

Jolson was made to measure for the big Hollywood spectacular musical. But he didn't get one. Perhaps the studio bosses realised he would have ordered all the other singers and dancers off the set and taken the cameras over for himself.

One fact is certain – given the right director, Jolson the actor might have come to the fore as Jolson the dynamic personality had on Broadway. But it didn't happen.

He didn't get the directors he needed – probably because the best were frightened of him – and his talents did not get the chances they justified.

The Jolson on the screen in those days was in more ways than one just a moving shadow of the real Jolson.

But other things were happening to him. The Shuberts had managed to wean him away from Hollywood for four weeks to play in the Chicago production of *A Night in Spain*. He got $10,000 a week for the stint and so broke all records for show business fees. Eddie Cantor reputedly had earned $5,000 a week from Ziegfeld, and Marilyn Miller, the darling of the age, who had won the hearts of Broadway audiences washing up while she sang 'Look For A Silver Lining' and was Al's friend Jack Warner's current mistress had taken a weekly cheque for $6,000.

Lee Shubert had won Jolson's agreement to the Chicago deal only after a helter-skelter fee-chasing battle between them. Shubert said Jolson could have $5,000 for the show. Al said 'No.' '$6,000?' Shubert rejoined. Again Jolson shook his head, lit a cigar and walked to the door.

'All right – $10,000,' Lee agreed. 'You realise this makes you the highest paid actor in the world?' he said with obvious pain. 'Sure.' said Jolson. 'But you're the richest producer, ain't you?'

'I won't be,' said Shubert, 'if I have to pay actors like you.'

The conversation might have had some poignancy ten years before. But Jolson was used to the sort of superlatives Shubert put to him. Being the most *anything* in the world were now just words to Jolson. He always had been the greatest – and as far as he was concerned he always would be.

As he told *Motion Picture Classic* magazine in an article they headed 'Oh, Mammy', 'Not that I don't have a lot of fun in life, understand me. I'm always kidding. If I break a leg I enjoy that experience. If I make a million I enjoy that one. I like all sorts of things, too. I like to eat in a hash house with a bunch of galoots and I like to doll up in an open-face suit and have the head waiter in a swell hotel call me by name. . .'

He also enjoyed going to Texas Guinan's night spot in Manhattan. Tex, as the showbiz giants knew her, had, like Jolson, been a Shubert star. And like Jolson she frequently appeared on stage with a horse. But at her own nightclub, Tex was queen just as much as Al had been king of the Winter Garden. She would announce her own acts, introduce the girls of the chorus and welcome out loud her celebrated guests.

One night Al was at Tex Guinan's place and it was profoundly to affect his life. He walked into the club in full evening dress, as always, looking immaculate and acknowledging the welcome the assembled company were giving him.

He sat down with Eppy and Harry Akst, trying to keep his mind on the show in front of him. Just sitting in an audience was always a hard job at first. But then a girl in a chorus caught his eye.

'What's the name of that cute little dark one?' he asked Tex.

'Her name's Ruby,' the club owner replied. 'Ruby Keeler. But keep away. She's Johnny's girl.'

'Johnny?'

'Yeh – Johnny Irish.'

Al was plainly shocked at the news. Johnny Irish Costello was taking over the New York crime rackets in much the

[136]

same way that Capone had taken Chicago. And one did not cross razors with Costello or his gang too lightly.

For Al it was a ticklish predicament. He was plainly attracted to the girl. As she danced, she became more and more fascinating to him. There was a cute smile on her face that he found endearing.

He certainly did not want trouble from Johnny Irish nor did he want to admit defeat to Tex. And in situations like that, Jolson, always a gambler, had to be brave.

He went up to Ruby after the show and liked the smile she gave him even more than he had when she flashed it across the footlights. They talked and liked each other.

But at that stage neither was taking the other very seriously. To Al she was just a pretty face and had what certainly appeared to be a nice trim body to go with it. To Ruby, it seemed just another case of the big star using his charm to approach a chorus girl. Her mother had warned her about such things before she left home and there wasn't much a chorus girl didn't know. She was prepared for any likely advance.

The said good night to each other and that was the end of it – or so it seemed.

Months later, Al was at a Los Angeles railway station to meet Fanny Brice on one of those show business welcomes that delighted the publicity agents. She got off the train accompanied by two young girls. Fanny introduced them to Al, 'Mary Lucas. . .' Al smiled like a gentleman. 'And Ruby Keeler.' There was a blush on the young brunette's face as she was introduced to Jolson. Of course, she remembered him. How could she possibly do otherwise? But did he know who she was?

Because this was a showbiz gathering, the agents were there in force, too. Including Al's own man, William Morris.

As tough as Al was with most of his contemporaries, his heart melted like butter when faced with a pretty show girl. Looking at Ruby through the corner of his eye, he told Morris, 'Get that girl a job dancing for $350 a week. Say Jolie says she's the best little hoofer he's ever seen.'

Morris, whose New York office was already managing Ruby, thought it a wonderful idea. Whether he thought Ruby was worth $350 a week or not was relevant – he was on ten per cent.

The next day Morris personally made the calls. 'Jolson says she's great,' he said on the phone to the owner of one of Hollywood's smartest clubs. 'I'll think about it,' replied the man – and then did what both Jolson and Morris knew he would do.

He rang Al at his apartment. 'This kid Ruby Keeler?' he asked. 'Is she really that swell?'

'Really is,' said Al.

Ruby opened the next week at the club – for $350 a week. Every night after the show there was a bouquet waiting for her from Al.

When she returned to New York, Johnny Irish sent for her. Irish was as soft as far as women were concerned as was Jolson – but he was inclined to take that softness to greater extremes than the singer ever did.

When he saw that Ruby was quite clearly more interested in Jolson than she was in him, he had the word passed through the gang grapevine that it might be a good idea for Jolson to come to see him. Al did just that – like a prospective bridegroom calling on his father-in-law.

'Ruby loves yer,' said Johnny Irish without any formalities. 'So you'd better marry her – or there won't be a certain singer on Broadway no more. Get me?'

Jolson got the idea. 'See, I got this picture opening next week,' he said, adopting the vernacular of his would-be executioner. 'As soon as it opens, I'll marry her. I love the dame, I tell yer.'

Al and Ruby were married at Port Chester, New York on 21 September 1928. He was (at least) forty-three. She was nineteen.

Ruby's parents objected to the marriage right up to the time the ceremony was performed by a justice of the peace. Cantor Yoelson and Hessi shrugged their shoulders at a new *shiksah* daughter-in-law. They had become resigned to the

[138]

fact that their Asa was following the traditional show business pattern of marriage-divorce, remarriage-divorce-marriage again. They did not like it, but they accepted it because there was no alternative. They would have been pleased if this time there had been a nice Jewish girl to get to know. But it was not to be and there was nothing they or anyone could do about it.

The papers, meanwhile, splashed the story of *Abie's Irish Rose come true*. *Abie* the big Broadway stage success was now being made into a film and Jewish Al and Catholic Ruby seemed to epitomise the tale.

The gossip columnists loved every detail of the story. Wherever Al and Ruby went, the newspaper men and women went, too.

When word leaked out that the pair were going to Europe for their honeymoon, every pier in New York was blocked with Press photographers and reporters trying to seek them out.

'This is for keeps,' Al told them on the deck of the *S.S. Olympic,* and gave Ruby a fond squeeze. 'How about you, Honey?'

'For keeps,' she said.

In London and in Paris, they were fêted as the top people they were. They made a surprise visit to London's Piccadilly Theatre where *The Jazz Singer* had just opened to a mesmerised audience. When Ruby saw the crowds gathering around her new husband, for one brief moment she wondered what she had done. Had she married a man or a cult?

As for the audiences, it was easy to see why they went so crazy.

On 14 October 1928 the London *Daily Sketch* reported, 'Al Jolson, America's highly paid revue star – he gets $3,000 a week – has at last overcome his fear of appearing before a British audience.

'Until last week, Jolson was so nervous that English audiences might not like his work that he refused offers to appear here for fifteen years.

'Now he has made a personal appearance at a London theatre. He made an instantaneous hit.

'Jolson came on the stage of the Piccadilly Theatre on Friday night following the showing of his talking picture *The Jazz Singer*.

'He came on the stage to say a few commonplace words of appreciation at being in London. He stayed twenty minutes, keeping audiences in roars of laughter with funny stories. Even then they would hardly let him go.

'Jolson was thrilled with the reception. "It's better than New York" he said again and again.

'He said, "After this I simply must appear on the London stage. I would like to appear in revue. Anyway, I promise I'll be here sometime soon."'

As for his picture, the paper noted, 'It was made obvious that we are on the eve of a revolution in cinematography and that the talking picture will introduce an entirely new type of entertainment that will sound the death knell of the sort of thing to which we are at present accustomed.'

And there was this statement to end, 'One day Al Jolson is going to sweep London theatregoers off their feet. Film fans meanwhile can look forward to *The Singing Fool*.'

In America, they were looking forward to Jolson's fourth picture *Mammy*.

Jolson never did play live in a London theatre, but his pictures were eventually to be even better received there than they were at home. In Hollywood, even the studio heads were beginning to worry about Jolson's screen image, but he was still universally known – and mimicked. Theatre owners organised Jolson contests, one of which Al entered himself under a false name. He came third.

By the time *Say it with Songs* came out – in this film Al was sent to jail on trumped-up charges, to be deprived of his baby girl – more than one critic noticed the sameness of the offering.

Al, however, was happy to collect his half-million-dollar salary cheque – no one had ever earned anything like that before – and Warners were more than happy to add their signature to the paper. They talked about the future but didn't worry about it. While Jolson drew the crowds, it seemed that the same sort of meat was just what they were wanting, and that was what they were going to get. And if it wouldn't last – well, what did?

'Jolson,' said Jack Warner. 'Jolson lasts.' Others shook their heads. But Warner ordered plans for another picture with Al – and the same sort of formula – to go ahead. No one told Jolson that perhaps the customers would be more demanding in future.

Even Al, himself, though, thought it wise to tell one newspaperman, 'As for "Mammies" and "Sonny Boys", of course they aren't real. In real life Sonny boy would generally rather sock you on the jaw than climb upon your knee. Most of the Mammies instead of having hands all toilworn and that sort of thing, are stepping out with their boyfriends and having a good time. But that's the very reason why the public loves 'em.'

To Al, the public was still everything.

When he and Ruby returned on the *Olympic* from their European honeymoon, a new home was awaiting them at Encino, a few stones' throw from Hollywood. Al carried Ruby over the threshold for the cameramen. The couple had a meal together and just as the bride was settling in, Al decided to go for a short walk – 'to help the food go down, honey,' he explained.

He was away for the rest of the evening and a few hours into the morning besides. 'The guys at the fire station saw me as I passed by,' he explained to Ruby, 'and I gave them a song or two.'

Ruby didn't argue. After all, she wasn't married to a man. She had teamed up with a legend and she knew she would have to share him.

And Hollywood was treating Jolson in a way that even this movie capital had never matched before. When Jolson films had their premières in those days, it wasn't just a matter of searchlights, screaming sirens and all the microphones that could be gathered into one place. When there were Jolson films, there had to be special Jolson tickets, too – in real silver foil on which a black and white Jolson silhouette had been superimposed.

In early 1929, while Al was still in California, Ruby took the long train journey to Pittsburg. Flo Ziegfeld had signed her for a tap-dancing role in the new Eddie Cantor show *Whoopee!*

Al regarded it as a mere bagatelle, a whim that the little woman ought to have satisfied. And he knew that Ziegfeld was only trying to capitalise on her marriage.

Al joined her in Pittsburg, soon after the show opened – and saw red. She was billed as Ruby Keeler Jolson – below the name of Eddie Cantor. 'How can you have a Jolson below Cantor?' he asked Ruby with a pleading look on his face.

The idea of Cantor having top billing riled him so much that he took her out of the cast the next day.

A couple of months later, Jolson and Ziegfeld met on a train. The big producer gave Jolson another proposition. 'I'm got just the part for Ruby in my new Broadway show. Give her a chance.'

Al signed the contract for her soon after they arrived in New York. Jolson had a new role – his wife's business manager.

She came to New York and signed herself for what was the biggest opportunity in her young life. One that she was determined to grab with everything she had.

She was to dance in *Show Girl,* the big new Gershwin show at the Ziegfeld theatre that also featured Jimmy Durante and his partners, Eddie Jackson and Lou Clayton.

Jolson was a paragon of magnanimity all the way. He liked his wife's role and he liked the money he had forced out of Ziegfeld for her to play it – at not less than $1,000 a week. And he didn't want to turn the taps on his wife. After all, she was another Jolson and wherever she went, his name went, too.

Show Girl opened for a pre-Broadway run in Boston with Ruby biting her nails alone in her dressing room thinking about the responsibility her husband had put into her dancing shoes more than 3,000 miles away in California.

But unknown to Ruby, Al had followed her to Boston, stayed

in another hotel and, as the orchestra struck up the overture, was waiting in the foyer of the Colonial Theatre.

When the lights went down and the curtain went up, Jolson walked down the centre aisle with Ziegfeld at his elbow.

For him it was an unbearable experience. Ruby now had a big role and he was merely sitting in the audience – waiting. Seeing his wife perform to a full house while he sat in the dark was pure torture; as George Burns put it, 'It gave Jolie a pain in the ass.'

So he decided to get in on the big number himself.

By the time the orchestra had struck up for Ruby's entrance and the chorus had begun the opening bars of the song, Jolson could contain himself no longer.

He stood up in his seat, raced down the aisles to the foot of the stage and joined in the chorus . . . 'Liza . . . Liza . . . skies are grey. . . When you belong to me . . . all the clouds will roll away.'

Worries rolled away too. The audience went crazy. They cheered Jolson as they'd never cheered anyone else – certainly no one else in that theatre. The great 'Ziegy', who knew a show stopper when he saw one, beamed at the response. 'Do that every night, Al, and you can have half the show,' he told him.

Al's face shone, too. But he wasn't committing himself. When *Show Girl* moved to Broadway and the Ziegfeld Theatre, Jolson moved, too. And when the orchestra struck up 'Liza', Jolson came in on cue.

Ruby seemed pleased enough to hear him . . . at first. But she didn't know her husband well enough to realise that the reaction of the crazed audience was like a bell to a boxer.

She tried to tell Al that she didn't want him to upstage her, but didn't get very far. And the next morning's papers made her task that much harder. For the one thing that seemed to interest the news hounds about *Show Girl* was Jolson's performance in the stalls. That was all he wanted to hear.

He phoned Jack Warner in Hollywood and told him to hold up work on his new film. 'I'm stayin' on in New York for a couple of days – to keep Ruby company.'

[143]

Keep *her* company he did – and the audience, too. For the whole week, Jolson was at every *Show Girl* performance, and when Ruby went into her 'Liza' number, Jolson did too.

And as the performances went by, there was no one who seemed more tickled with the continuous Jolson contribution than Flo Ziegfeld himself. *Show Girl* was roundly condemned by the critics as the weakest 'Ziggi' show for years. Now it was in the fantastic situation of Al Jolson working for nothing to save his arch rival's show – much to Ruby's chagrin. Years later, she would claim she hated him for it.

No one bothered much about Clayton, Jackson and Durante. The audience had probably heard better music from Gershwin and, although Ruby herself had a certain curiosity value, it was plain that all the audience really wanted to see and hear was Jolson. And that meant that Al was in his element as only he could be. And as he could never feel on a film sound-stage.

But he couldn't stay in Manhattan for long. There was the small matter of his $500,000 new film for Warners at Burbank. Soon after his return West, he had the Bell Telephone men at work – setting up a direct line between his Encino home and Ruby's New York apartment.

One of the first calls he got, however, was not from Ruby but from Ziegfeld. His tap-dancing star had fallen from the top of the spiral staircase she used in her 'Liza' number and had been rushed to hospital with a broken ankle.

For Ziegfeld the accident was almost fortuitous. Jolson was in California and who wanted to see *Show Girl* without him? The show was closed and Ruby followed her husband West – with her ankle in a plaster cast.

To most outsiders they seemed a happy couple. She went with him to the races – more than once adding her two-cents' worth of advice and picking up enough winners to make Al shake with joy. She followed him to the prizefights which more and more were becoming a Jolson 'thing' – on one occasion he had even sparred with Jack Dempsey. The really big public occasions for Al and Ruby were the Hollywood premières.

Al enjoyed these occasions a lot more than he did other people's Broadway first nights. For the one thing about a film opening was that people went to see who was going to the cinema, not just who was actually up there on the screen. And going into a theatre was something Jolson did better than anyone else.

He only had to smile as he got out of his car, hitch his silk hat to a jaunty angle, or to whirl his silver-topped cane to feel as if he were at the Winter Garden again. And the people in the crowds only had to see him to be his audience.

And Al enjoyed being seen. He bought Ruby fabulous presents – diamonds, fur coats and cars. In one year, Al bought three of the latest Mercedes models imported specially for him from Germany. He gave one of the cars to Ruby – the cheapest one, the *New York Times* was pleased to note.

But soon after their marriage, there were buzzes of the couple's scrapping. The rumours didn't persist at this stage, and those that might otherwise have stuck were dismissed as the usual Hollywood gossip. But there was no getting away from the fact that the couple were from completely different environments.

She may have been *Abie's Irish Rose*, but for all his fabulous success he was still Abie, with the Jewish mannerisms, the almost insatiable desire for gefilte fish, and the frequent use of Yiddish phrases which to his ears said things that could never be expressed quite as adequately in English.

Ruby was small town Irish – with an aunt in Montreal who was a nun. Was there a conflict over backgrounds? No one said so at the time – but not long after the wedding, Jolson went to Chicago for a cosmetic operation to his Jewish nose. Some acquaintances noticed that Al really did seem to change.

He may have been the big star on stage and on screen, but at home it was plain that Ruby was beginning to twist him around her little finger.

The gamblers on both Broadway and Sunset Boulevard

were taking odds on the marriage surviving six months. Soon after their first anniversary, Jolson gave a Press conference in which he pointed to Ruby's finger. 'Look,' he said. 'No matter what she's doing, that ring never comes off.'

When *Show Girl*'s run was over and Ruby's leg had healed, the Hollywood columnists were talking about Mrs Jolson following in her husband's footsteps. Al plainly didn't like the idea – until Warners made it abundantly clear that a little tap dancer couldn't be much competition to a singer and personality like the Great Jolson.

'Right then – but only if I'm her manager,' Al insisted once again.

When Jack Warner phoned him to offer Ruby a part in his new picture *42nd Street*, Jolson put on the hardest business front he knew – which was hard by anyone's stardards after nearly twenty years at the top of the show business tree and a generation with the Shuberts.

He and Darryl Zanuck discussed it all in their ringside seats at the Hollywood Bowl during a boxing match.

'I want $10,000 for her first picture just like I made in *The Jazz Singer* during its first weeks,' he said.

Ruby plainly could not believe what her ears told her.

'You really ought not to ask so much,' she whispered tugging at his sleeve. 'I'd do it for $250 a week. That's still a lot of money.'

'Look,' Jolson chided her in Zanuck's hearing. 'Am I your manager or not?'

She didn't have to answer. Zanuck had a contract made out for $10,000 just as Al had known he would. There was only one further stipulation. 'Don't expect me to see yer work,' Al said. 'I don't want to watch other guys kissin 'yer.'

For Jolson that would be as bad as hearing people applaud her. But the ink on the contract had cast the die. Ruby Keeler was in films and on the threshold of what seemed like a never-ending partnership with Dick Powell.

Every time Jolson saw the two together, he squirmed – but more because of the success they were making in show business than the possibility that they could be having an affair. In fact, that was the one thing Jolson never alleged.

But he told one reporter, 'I couldn't bear to see some other fellow kissing her. I know it's always done, but it would drive me crazy to see it. How would you like to see a strange man kissing your wife, even though you knew it was just for a picture?'

He was persuaded to like what was going on by the money. And Jolson, like everyone else in 1929 was money crazy – although he rushed into nothing, bought stocks and made investments only after the strongest professional advice and then frequently advised his advisers. Some say he knew the money market as well as he knew show business. The gambler in him made him hedge all his bets.

When he and Ruby were married, the newspapers printed stories that he had settled $1 million on his bride. Jolson denied the stories – but not the fact that he could have done so had he chosen to. He was, without much doubt, the richest man his side of the footlights.

When everyone was putting money into the stock market, Jolson was, too. He speculated widely while others merely dabbled. But when in October 1929, Wall Street crashed, Jolson was not one of those queuing to jump out of skyscraper windows.

He was listed as having lost $4 million that day. But it wasn't the end of his world, by any means. He had securities and investments worth at least another $2 million to fall back upon and money invested in overseas bonds that were almost unaffected by the Wall Street crash. He also owned a lot of real-estate. What is more, when everyone else was selling at rock-bottom prices, Jolson was carefully buying this débris, knowing it was likely to recover.

Harry had not been making things easy for him – spreading more and more stories about the way Al was chiselling him out of his own career. Some of the stories were more true than others. But the crash did show Al's generous side – although there were cynics suggesting he merely wanted to show how big a man he could be in time of trouble. The facts, however, speak for themselves.

When the dust had finally settled in Wall Street, Al's stockbrokers and accountants began a systematic call on his friends in show business. Eddie Cantor had one of these messages.

'Al said to offer you anything you want – $50,000 or $100,000. Whatever,' said the voice. And it was a true gesture. Why didn't Al make the calls himself? No one knows. On the one hand, it might have made the offer seem even more generous and genuine had he done so. On the other, it could well have been that he felt too embarrassed.

Some people thought Jolson never did anything without a motive. It is difficult to see how he would have gained materially by this sort of life-saving gesture. Admittedly, another incident involving the two entertainers does seem rather more in character.

Al and Ruby were in Mexico with Eddie Cantor and his wife Ida. Cantor spent a few more dollars than he wanted to on some perfume for Ida. He saw the look on his wife's face when she heard how much he had paid for the scent.

'Don't worry, Ida,' he said rolling his banjo eyes – an involuntary action on which he capitalised in the theatre; he didn't invent it especially for his act – 'I'll win it back for you.'

He tried to recover the money in a crap game that night – and ended up losing $11,000. At the sight of this huge loss, Jolson collapsed in a fit of hysterical laughter. 'Meet my friend – the businessman,' he said pointing to Cantor. But then he always did like using Eddie as the foil for jokes.

On one occasion, he had phoned the Cantor residence saying he was from Beverely Hills Water Company and advised that since the supply was going to be cut off for forty-eight hours the family ought to stock up. That evening he walked into Eddie's house to find it lined wall to wall with pots, pans, cups, plates and bottles filled with water. 'Can I have a glass of water, please?' he asked – and then admitted the joke.

When Al started work on his fourth picture, *Mammy*, he began to wonder himself whether Hollywood itself was such a good joke.

But even so, another Jolson was concerning himself with Hollywood.

Harry moved to the West Coast with Lillian in 1929 and took a page advertisement in *Variety* – announcing he had signed a contract with the Universal Picture Corporation to make four films. The contract he had – the pictures he didn't.

One day he and Lillian were called to Universal to hear that the studio were not taking up his option. Al had had nothing to do with it. What seemed to be yet another tough blow to the elder brother was simply proof of a hard, unpalatable fact – Harry just didn't have the talent.

Universal liked the idea of having a Jolson of their own. At the time of the contract the name would have sold tickets had it belonged to a performing kangaroo. But by late 1929, it was no longer enough. It wasn't enough for Al and it certainly wasn't enough for Harry. He'd recently had a thumping row with his brother over a magazine's request for him to write Al's life. Harry said 'Yes.' Al said 'No.' And no it stayed.

Mammy had Al as the leading member of a minstrel troupe. He sang Irving Berlin's famous number that was to epitomise the Jolson career and to be his epitaph. 'Let Me Sing And I'm Happy'. That was not quite all he wanted. Much more his demand was – let me hear applause and I'm happy. And now he was quite clearly not hearing enough people clapping till the milk trains clattered home.

Eight

Almost Like Being in Love

THE 1930S WERE TO prove to be something of a watershed in the Jolson career. Ruby and public tastes were both having their effect on the way he saw life and if the Jolson leopard wasn't going to change his spots himself, there were plenty of influences being brought to bear to try to change them for him.

But a lot of the old glory was still there and he entered the decade making the same sort of money that he had ten years before, and confident that nothing could knock him from his pedestal. Indeed, he was still being treated like a king. When in 1930, he made his one and only appearance at that Broadway temple of vaudeville, the Palace, he was left in no doubt that this was the way show business still thought of him.

Many years later, Judy Garland – the one artist constantly compared with Jolson – was to sing, 'Until You've Played The Palace, You Haven't Lived'.

Well, Jolson had lived, all right, and just to satisfy himself, he did play the Palace – for just one evening's benefit performance. He was sitting in the stalls when the MC called him on to the stage. He sang only one song, but for more than an hour he held the audience spellbound like old times just listening to him ad-lib. He had finally done the one thing he had wanted to do most. 'I'll play the Palace when Eddie Cantor, Groucho Marx and Jack Benny are on the bill together,' he used to say. 'I'm gonna buy up all the seats and shout "Sing slaves for the king".'

Right: Sinbad was the role. Al Jolson, the sensation of Broadway.

Below: 'Watch me,' he said, 'I'm a wow!' In 1911, newly arrived at the Winter Garden, he certainly was.

JOLSON'S 59th STREET THEATRE
7th AVENUE and 59th STREET
Now Playing
Matinees WEDNESDAYS and SATURDAYS
The Messrs Lee and J.
Present
The Worlds Greatest Ente
AL
JOLSON
IN THE
New Musical Extravagan
"BOMBO"
In Two Acts
and Twenty Sce
Book and Lyrics by
Harold Atteridge
Music by
Sigmund Romberg
Staged by
J.C. Huffman
Dances Arranged
by Allan K. Foster
Produced Under the
Personal Direction
of Mr. J.J. Shubert

Left: By now he was what today would be called a megastar. Not just his own show—but his own theatre, too.

Right: Fooling around at home *c* 1912 with Louis Rosenberg, Jolson is on the right.

Above: Jolson in 1913. The fur coat meant he had really arrived.

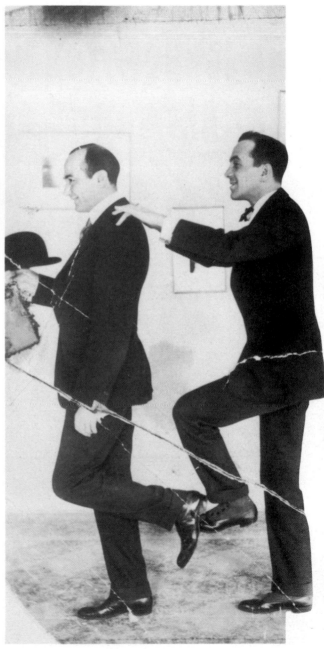

Left: Leaflets like this were distributed all over New York. In 1916 Jolson's name was the biggest at the Winter Garden — and the biggest on Broadway.

Right: His tunes became the popular songs of the day. (Francis, Day & Hunter)

TOOT, TOOT, TOOTSIE
(Goo' Bye)
Al. Jolson's
"BOMBO"
and
FEIST
NEW YORK

Above right: Al on honeymoon in 1928 with Ruby Keeler. *(The National Film Archive)*

Below right: Jolson the politician. At Marion, Ohio, with President Warren G. Harding *(left front row)*.

Left: Reliving memories of his own childhood in the synagogue and of the film that made history. Singing 'Kol Nidre' on the Day of Atonement, from *Hollywood Cavalcade*—a 1939 re-enactment of the famous scene in *The Jazz Singer*. *(Twentieth Century Fox)*

Above: Two 'greats' together— Jolson with Charles Chaplin.

Left: He even had a sparring match with Jack Dempsey.

Previous page: Al with Harry Langdon.

Above left: He always had the winner — except when it came to Ruby. He, however, tried harder to look happier than she did.

Left: Inside, he wasn't nearly so glad. Bing Crosby was grabbing at the Jolson throne — and Al knew it. It's just possible that on this occasion, his winnings were higher than Bing's.

Far left: Down Mexico way — in *Go Into Your Dance.*

Right: With Peggy Lee.

Above: The two Jolsons: Al 'Larry Parks' Jolson and Al 'Asa Yeolson' Jolson. *(Columbia Pictures)*

Below left: The 'Jolson' that the post World War II generation got to know—Larry Parks made up for the title role in *The Jolson Story*. *(Columbia Pictures)*

Right: 'That's my boy.' With Asa Junior, 1949. *(The National Film Archive)*

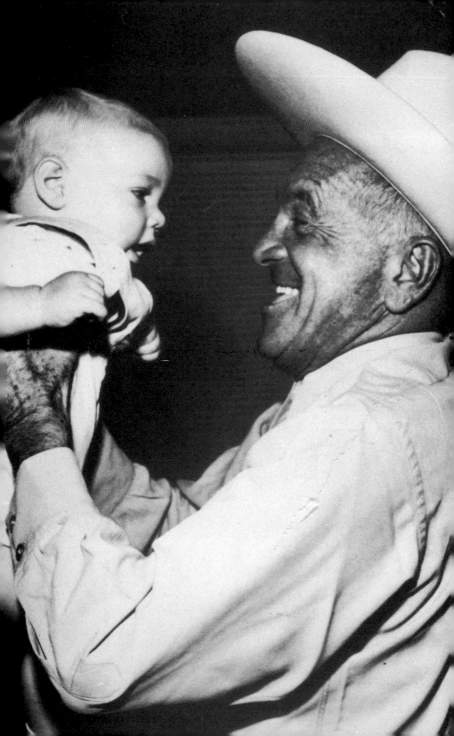

Left: Painting the town. With Erle soon after their marriage.

Below: The last month. Jolson in Korea, 1950. The GIs loved him . . . and so did the United Nations.

Above right: Al calling the tune again just like in the old days. The executive looking on had reason to be glad that he did.

Below right: Jolson the racegoer. Next to audiences, he loved the thrill of the racetrack best.

'This is how you do it.' In 1949, Al once more showed Larry Parks precisely how every movement in every song had to be done. The result was *Jolson Sings Again*.

For a time it seemed as though vaudeville was biting into Jolson. The man who had been no less than the God of the legitimate musical stage had succumbed to the embraces of the illegitimate sister – but at a price. New York's Capital Theatre booked him for just a week – for $15,000, and with a contract stipulation that he would get half of everything over a gross of $100,000.

The bets were on that Jolson would clean up another fortune. Broadway expected it of their king. But for the first time in his meteoric career, in a stage life that wouldn't know the meaning of the word failure, things were going ever so slightly wrong.

The week's takings showed that Jolson – with just Harry Akst at the piano – had made well under that $100,000. The writing did seem to be there up on the wall. And it was painful for Al Jolson, of all people, to see.

But by anyone's reckoning, he was still a top entertainer – although being merely top was never really good enough for Al. He had to be supreme. And when he heard whispers which told him that perhaps he wasn't that any more, he wondered in his heart whether they were true.

He made two films in 1930. *Mammy*, he told journalists proudly, was his best yet. Some reported it as such – both as their own view and as a faithful repetition of what the entertainer had told them.

One noted, 'It's possibly too sentimental a title for a film that was billed "Sing with Al. Laugh with Al".'

The film was novel in many ways. For one thing it featured a new score by Irving Berlin – always an event. Also, its final reel was in Technicolor, another Jolson almost-first. But the story was so trite it was embarrassing. Here, he was the man in a minstrel troupe who was being blamed for shooting his interlocutor, supposedly his rival in love.

On the run, he hides in his mother's house – in a scene too reminiscent of the reunion sequence in *The Jazz Singer*, although nothing like as poignant or effective.

There were a few new songs for him to sing, it is true – but again the limitations of the movie camera were making themselves as obvious as his own discomfort. Only when Al was singing in blackface in the minstrel line did a glimmer of the old Jolson come through. Perhaps for anyone else the scene might have been a shining moment. For Jolson it was just a glimmer.

The theme song for the picture was 'Let Me Sing And I'm Happy'. But he plainly was not being allowed to sing enough to be happy enough. He was trying to do the impossible and – paraphrasing something George Jessel was to say about him – attempting to trap the Pacific Ocean into a bottle. And neither Warner Brothers nor anyone else could do that.

In London, the great showman C.B. Cochran remarked wryly, 'The Jolson I saw on the screen is not the Jolson I knew in the flesh. It was a Jolson without a soul.'

Jolson was now astute enough to know what was happening – and what he was doing to his career for a mixture of money and the everpressing desire to entertain.

He confessed to *Screenland* magazine, 'I made two good pictures. I made *The Jazz Singer* and *The Singing Fool*. I showed 'em what I could do.

'Then they start tellin' me they can't find enough good pictures. All right – I'm reasonable. Can you find me two good pictures a year? "No." Can you find me one? It seems they can't. So I take what they give me and live in hope. And I find that the pole is only greased one way – down.'

And he added, even more sadly, 'I make good in two pictures – that's not claiming too much is it? All right, they tell you a movie star's life is just so long – then he goes out. Well, Lord – I didn't have any life – I didn't have my first five years even. I died a premature death. After all, it's not such a long time since *The Jazz Singer,* is it? I haven't turned senile since then, and my hair's still black.'

Jolson still had plenty of pep, the writer noted. He spoke striding up and down, with his 'mouth out thrust'. But he added 'mood follows mood'.

Jolson's moods told him what was happening – and there was little he could do about it.

Paramount Pictures tried to get into the Jolson act by

offering him $6,500 a week for a tour of their theatres in the South West States. Jolson turned it down.

Later in 1930, Al made *Big Boy*. It was a filmed version of the Winter Garden success, complete with horse.

In Hollywood, he continued to have his own stable, and now more than one observer was heard to say that his real horses seemed to be making more for him than the ones up on the screen and proving to be more enjoyable.

For years *Big Boy* had the distinction of being the only Jolson film never to have been shown on American television – because, it was suggested, the South regarded it as glorifying blacks and the North as ridiculing them.

It was a hotpotch of a picture in which Al, as Gus, tries to remember some of the things his grandfather (Al again) used to say and sing. At the end of the movie a theatre audience is heard to 'dare' Al to sing 'Sonny Boy'. It was a joke but no producer ever let him forget that his name was Al Jolson and that he was to sing Jolson songs.

Actually, *Big Boy* – though conceivably offensive to some, and undoubtedly never seen that way at all by Jolson himself – was the first inkling that Al could be better on screen than anyone ever imagined.

Because he was in blackface throughout most of the movie and because it seemed to him like being in a Broadway show, most of the Hollywood inhibitions were gone and he reacted accordingly. Seeing *Big Boy* is the nearest a modern audience could come to experiencing Jolson at his greatest.

For three years, Jolson was to make no more films, and it was to be five years before he was back at work on the lot for Warner Brothers. The hot property had now cooled down under the Hollywood sun.

'Sure I miss the stage,' Jolson had written in a signed headline for *Theatre* magazine in July 1929, and so had shown his usual insight into the way his business ticks.

He told the magazine that he loved to be able to shout back at an applauding audience. 'Keep it up, I love it,' – which he never could do from the screen. 'I meant it. I still love it. I still love an audience. And if the making of talking pictures

[153]

meant that there would be no more audience or offer no substitute, I would chuck them tomorrow – this very night.

'Sure I miss the stage,' he repeated. 'At first I missed it more, while making that first picture of mine *The Jazz Singer*. And I miss it a little less each time I come back to Hollywood to make another. Little by little a new sort of fascination and satisfaction that picture making brings is atoning for the lure of the footlights and the thrill of the first-night audience.'

And in typical Jolson form, the one principal example of this atonement was for him to be able to pass a queue lining up outside a cinema and hear children buzzing, 'That's Al Jolson.' As he said, 'Comparatively few of them would ever have known me had it not been for my pictures.'

What Jolson wrote was true. But it only went part of the way. He also said that sometimes he felt 'like one of those dolls whose strings are pulled to the right for a smile and to the left for a sad expression. I couldn't wait until evening came, when friends would be gathered around who would ask me to sing. . . I hungered for the live sound of actual people.'

The truest part of all was that those kids who now knew Al Jolson's face from his pictures didn't know how great he could be in the flesh or just how that doll became a ball of fire as soon as the strings of the theatre curtain were pulled.

Abe Lastfogel of the William Morris Agency in Los Angeles put it in a nutshell, to me when he recalled, 'Jolson was a little man – until he got out on to a stage. Then . . . he became a giant. When he left the stage at the end of the performance, he shrank to a little man again.'

Al's desire to hear a real audience applaud again was to be satisfied. In 1931, Jolson was back on Broadway. On 17 March he opened at the Nora Bayes Theatre in *The Wonder Bar* – his first Broadway opening since *Big Boy* at the Winter Garden in January 1925.

It is not remembered as Jolson's greatest show – for one thing the book of this show proved more difficult for Jolson to discard in his usual way. But at times he tried – and when he tried, he generally succeeded.

To demonstrate that his power over an audience was still

intact he told them four jokes, one after the other without stopping – and jumbled the punch lines from one gag to the next. The audience roared their heads off. What Jolson had said was totally unimportant. It was the way he said it – and, indeed, the fact that he had told the stories at all.

The Wonder Bar was supposed to be the name of a restaurant-cum-nightclub in Paris run by Monsieur Al – Jolson, himself. The music was by Irving Caesar and Rowland Leigh and the highspot of it all was a caberet performance featuring Al. In this he excelled – in a way that even Jolson had never done before.

He sang, for instance, his own favourite song from *Der Heim* – the Yiddish term for the ghetto from which his music had really all sprung – the one about the cantor's audition for the tailor, the shoemaker and the coachdriver.

And he sang Irving Caesar's 'Oh Donna Clara' in English, German and Russian – for which Caesar laboriously coached him.

His Russian version of the song was so impressive that the great bass Fyodor Chaliapin got to hear about it and came along to see how this ghetto Jew from his own country had made out.

He was singularly impressed. So much so, that the two Russian-born singers became close friends. Chaliapin would frequently ring Jolson during the day and say 'Arll, we both have no matinée today. Why not come around to my hotel and we have some wine and we have some caviare and perhaps a couple of girls. . .?

It was an invitation 'Arll' was happy to accept. Girls were always an attraction – much to Ruby's regret. But Mrs Jolson was in Hollywood following her own career and did not always hear what was going on on the East Coast.

But the friendship between Jolson and Chaliapin blossomed. It was a meeting between equals. Each admired the other's singing and since Chaliapin was in no way a rival of Jolson's, the entertainer was flattered that such a great name from opera should be interested in him.

Once, he had the bright idea of working with Chaliapin

and got Eppy to think about it too. 'I'm gonna do *The Jazz Singer* in grand opera,' he told his startled manager. 'Chaliapin is gonna play my father – the cantor.'

It never happened. And no one thought it would – except Jolson who saw this as just the challenge his career needed.

But for as long as *The Wonder Bar* was playing at the Bayes Theatre it seemed as though no challenge was necessary.

'The old Winter Garden's fair-haired boy has come home,' noted the *New York Times* – confirming again, for anyone who needed confirmation, that there was no substitute for a live audience to this man who would gladly have given away the fees he was receiving in Hollywood for the sound of a theatre's floorboards vibrating with his applause.

It became obvious during rehearsals that it was the same old Jolson.

He bounded back and forward, with brown bowler cocked on his head; to the back of the stage one moment, right in the lap of the audience the next.

The Wonder Bar was a revolutionary show. It had no curtain and the café staff moved backwards and forward on stage throughout the performance to add the touch of realism that no Jolson show had needed to have before.

The Wonder Bar had its uses. It also cemented another friendship – although it was one that, in a couple of years, was to be sorely tried.

Walter Winchell, Broadway's legendary columnist, had Jolson to thank for being allowed back into the Shubert empire. The Shubert brothers, in one of their imperious bans on people they thought had crossed them – all the New York writers were doing that, they believed, and so they started their own newspaper – refused to allow Winchell into any of their theatres. Since the Shuberts owned more than half of Broadway's real-estate, this was a considerable penance for anyone who regarded the theatre district as his beat.

More than an hour after the advertised opening time the first performance of *The Wonder Bar* still hadn't started that first night at the Bayes Theatre, Jolson got to hear of the ban on Winchell and refused to go on until the columnist had been admitted. As soon as he was shown through the front door, Jolson gave the word for the orchestra conducted by Lou Silvers to play the overture and start the show.

Although it was difficult to ignore the book, he managed to get away with some of his old tricks – and the sort that only Jolson would dare perpetrate.

When he first arrived in New York, he bumped into George Jessel. 'Come along to the theatre tonight and I'll introduce you from the stage,' he said.

Sure enough, just before the curtain went up, Jessel was at the Bayes Theatre. And sure enough, just as he had been promised, Jolson was out front waiting to greet him.

'You know there's a number later on with a lotta bales of straw lying around in the background. Hide behind one of those bales and I'll bring you out so that the folks can clap you! You'll have a swell time.'

'Great,' said Jessel.

When it came to the straw number, Jessel was in the wings waiting. 'You want me to go out now?' he asked his host.

'Sure – just wait behind that bale over there. Get down real low so that no one'll see you.'

Jessel got down, just as he had been told, and crouched uncomfortably as Jolson marched on to the stage for what was anticipated would be the big introduction for his guest.

Instead, someone in the audience shouted for a song. It was more than Jolson could resist – at any time. He sang the number – and the audience begged for more. And more they got. An hour and a half later and to the sound of the creaking of Jessel's joints, the guest straightened himself out, walked towards the singing Jolson and told the audience, 'This . . . said he was going to introduce me to you tonight,' and walked off.

Jolson got the laugh. Jessel took a cab home.

But he still fell for the same gag at a benefit show. Jolson had persuaded his arch-rival to join him on the stage 'while I sing one or two songs'.

The 'one or two' songs became five or six, then nine or ten and Jessel was still standing next to him. Finally when Al

[157]

shouted, completely oblivious to his guest, 'Folks you ain't heard nothin' yet,' Jessel pushed in front, dropped his trousers and shouted, 'And now you ain't seen nothin' yet' and hobbled into the wings with his trousers around his ankles.

But despite their rivalry, Jessel from time to time played Al's confidant. Whenever he felt uneasy about Ruby – whether she still loved him, whether she didn't think he was too old for her, or whether she was getting too involved with other men – he would ask George's advice.

On one occasion, Al showed Jessel a new ring he had bought for his wife. It had cost a small fortune, but, he figured, represented an insurance policy on Ruby's love.

'Yes Al, I'm sure she'll like it,' he told him time and again before Jolson finally plucked up enough courage to give it to her.

Al was constantly defending Ruby against what he considered to be assaults on her honour. On one occasion, a drunk insulted her at the Coconut Grove. Al gave him a punch to the jaw and as the drunk fell, the man's friend joined in the attack on Jolson. But comedian Joe E. Lewis was there – and got to the second man before he could do any damage. Ben Lyon was with them too – and he held up the arms of Jolson and Lewis. 'The winners,' he proclaimed.

The Wonder Bar ran for seventy-six performances. When Jolson returned to Hollywood, there was a new hit for him to sing whenever he had the opportunity. 'Brother Can You Spare a Dime?' said all that needed to be said about the Depression.

But that was a word that Jolson didn't like. And early in 1933, he mounted a political soapbox to say so.

He was still a name that drew crowds. And when people wanted a name either to raise money or to put forward a new political philosophy Jolson's was more than good enough.

In San Francisco, Jolson told a luncheon rally, 'I've travelled all over, but here I haven't heard the word that I've heard in every other city . . . I see smiles on your faces because you think I'm going to say something funny . . . well

[158]

I'm not . . . I ask you today to cut out that word and stop using it because it's hurting us more than anything else. Cut out that word "Depression". Will you do that from now on? Cut out that word "Depression" and substitute "panic". You'll be nearer to it.' And the luncheon guests applauded wildly.

He said he had invested like everyone else. 'I bought stocks that were supposed to be blue chip. We were told "Invest in the backbone of the nation." Well, I bought the gizzard.'

The guests now laughed, patted Jolson on the back and he went outside singing 'Brother Can You Spare A Dime?' to the men waiting in the soup kitchen queues.

And he sang it on the radio, too. Jolson had been slow to realise that radio was the really big medium, after all it cost nothing to turn a dial. But, finally admitting to himself that pictures failed to show the true depth of his personality, he was reluctant to take on something that would rob him of yet another dimension.

He eventually succumbed when Chevrolet offered him his own show on the NBC network, for $7,500 a performance. The half-hour shows went out weekly on Friday evenings with Al singing some of his old songs, some new ones and some that others had made famous. He also introduced a galaxy of other performers.

It was a frustrating mixture and the guests were the most frustrating part of the whole deal. He couldn't turn on the taps now to drown the applause the other people received. And even when the studio audiences were applauding *him*, he realised that they were clapping the cue cards rather than the real Jolson.

'I've just got a load of bum jokes here,' he told his producers, who smiled indulgently and steered Al on to another topic.

When he could get a word in edgeways, neither the network nor the sponsor would agree. Jolson wanted to vary the routine. Instead of the usual mixed bag of what was really radio vaudeville, he wanted to be able to put his own version of the Winter Garden on the air.

He wanted to be able to star in his own dramatised versions of famous plays and films.

'Al, we know what's right,' the men from NBC and General Motors told him – and, although no one apparently said that what was good enough for General Motors was good enough for Jolson, it was doubtless thought. It was also pointed out that $7,500 a programme wasn't peanuts. Kate Smith, the sensation of the airways at this time, was getting a mere $50 for her regular fifteen-minute shows.

Al sang 'Toot-Toot Tootsie', 'Dark Eyes', 'The Cantor', 'Avalon', 'Sonny Boy', 'Little Pal', and fifty or more other songs during the series. But he only completed fifteen of the twenty-six shows he was contracted to produce.

He wasn't happy with radio in 1932. He couldn't understand why everyone went crazy in the operations booth when he would throw away the script to ad-lib his way through. Nor did they like the way he moved about. It brought back memories of his early recording experiences – although instead of a strait-jacket, he was now given two microphones. The trouble, too, was that Jolson was singing to the studio audience rather than the people at home – and it showed.

When Jolson went back to Hollywood soundstages, he was again experimenting – but this time very much the victim of the experiment.

Some idea of the way things were moving had already come early in 1930 when Jolson was making *Mammy*. He told *Screenland* magazine that he loved the movies, but there were doubts. 'No more blackface for me, though,' he announced, 'I'm through with that. When I saw myself in *The Singing Fool* and how good I look – like Barrymore or somebody – I decided I wasn't going to sing "Mammy" again.'

The words in themselves didn't mean a thing. *Mammy* was just about as blackface a role as one could imagine. *Big Boy* was even more so. And he was to go on singing 'Mammy' for as long as he lived. But something was in the wind.

Hallelujah I'm a Bum was the Big Experiment. Looking at

it today, it is quite clearly the most adventurous Jolson film of them all and artistically one of the best. But the Big Experiment became the Big Flop.

Lewis Milestone was the director – undoubtedly the most imaginative Jolson had ever had. He was fresh from *All Quiet on the Western Front* and had a reputation that he was jealous to preserve. Rodgers and Hart provided the music and lyrics for the new film and they could never be bad. Their title song summed up a lot of people's feelings about money in those Depression days. And Depression, despite Al's strictures, was on everyone's minds.

'You Are Too Beautiful' the love ballad of the picture, was one of the smoothest Jolson ever sang.

But he didn't put on blackface once and his acting had to cope with dialogue written entirely in rhyming couplets – and cope he did. This was a new Jolson, a Jolson whose acting had made great strides since the embarrassing days of *Mammy*. But it was a Jolson no one seemed to like.

This story – about a gang of tramps in New York's Central Park who escape the cares of the economy by becoming the dropouts of their day – was panned by all the critics and the public stayed away.

The film cost more than $1,250,000 – a colossal sum in those days. And United Artists lost nearly every cent of it. Not that it was a lavish production. It certainly was not. But it was hit by the sort of gremlins Jolson would never have allowed to interfere with him on Broadway.

Just before the picture was completed, for instance, Roland Young, who had the key role of the Mayor of New York, fell ill and as the Mayor was in most of the scenes nearly all the film had to be reshot. Frank Morgan took over the Mayor's role.

Then it was discovered that most of the vital slang words would be incomprehensible to people outside the United States. So those scenes containing this dialogue had to be shot again, too.

There was also title trouble. Bum, someone realised, had a completely different meaning in England – and a most impolite one at that. So the title was changed for British distribution to *Hallelujah I'm a Tramp* – and so was the title song which had to be completely re-recorded.

In its life, the film had more titles than most pictures have reviews. In turn it became *New York, Happy Go Luck, The Heart of New York*, and even *The Optimist* – which anyone working on the film just had to be. When it was re-released twenty years later, it was called *Lazy Bones*.

The picture had been made by United Artists on the basis of a contract Jolson had signed with its studio head Joseph Schenck the year before – a contract that has since gone down in history.

Al had agreed to do three pictures for United Artists for $25,000 a week for forty weeks – a sum no one had even dared contemplate before Jolson came on the scene. It was drafted and signed when both Jolson and Schenck were on holiday in Palm Springs. The only paper they had with them at the time the deal was first brought up was a paper bag, and they clinched it all in a few minutes.

It became known as the banana-bag contract.

The next picture Al was due to make was going to be *Sons o' Guns*, a Great War story based on the Broadway show that had starred Jack Donohue. But Jolson decided it was not for him, and the role went to Joe E. Brown

Al told the studio which had been founded by Mary Pickford, Douglas Fairbanks and Charlie Chaplin that if they wanted him to work he'd do it for nothing. No one asked. And for the first time in twenty years, the hint was taken that Jolson needn't bother to work. The other two pictures stipulated in the banana-bag contract were never made.

It was an excruciating time for Al. For just as his star seemed to be falling, Ruby's was rising – and rising like a rocket. Warners loved her in *42nd Street* and signed her for more pictures – like *Gold Diggers of 1933, Dames*, and *Flirtation Walk*. They were all hits.

Al quipped, 'I'll be known as Mr Ruby Keeler yet.' Certainly, she was no longer being billed as Ruby Keeler Jolson.

Ruby, meanwhile, told reporters 'I'm still puzzled by the life of a movie star. My singing voice is not powerful enough to fill a theatre.' And she was right. Her talents were strictly limited.

Jolson told the world that Ruby was his, and that, he said, was all he really cared about.

'This one really *is* the perfect marriage,' he told people time and again – but he seemed to tell it principally to convince himself.

The gossips in Hollywood had been hard on Al and Ruby – although probably no harder than they were on any other star. Since both were stars in their own right, they could perhaps be forgiven for being doubly hard on this team. But they really ought to have realised to whom they were sizing up.

When Walter Winchell wrote a few stinging words about Jolson in his column, the singer took the law into his own hands and the feathers really began to fly. It was at the Hollywood Bowl just as the crowd were thirsting for blood at a boxing match. They got their glimpse of blood – but it came from the ringside, not from the fight on the bill.

Winchell was on one side of the ring and Al and Ruby were on the other. When Jolson saw the columnist, he charged over from his seat to where Winchell was sitting.

'Hello Al,' the writer said standing up and offering his hand. But he sat down again very quickly – as quickly, in fact, as Jolson could push him down with one fell punch. He got up again, rubbing his jaw from side to side, but Al punched him again.

'That'll teach you,' Jolson shouted. 'Write things about my wife, will you?'

Al smiled at seeing his victim lying semi-prostrate in his seat. But not for long. The next moment, there was a blow on his own head – from Mrs Winchell's shoe.

There were several stories about the cause of the fight. One was that Al had been made angry when Winchell wrote a new film scenario for Twentieth Century Productions about a show girl's relationship with New York gang leader

Larry Foy. Since Hollywood had never forgotten the stories told about Ruby and Johnny Irish and since other gangster names were continually being bandied about whenever Ruby's name cropped up – without any evidence whatever – Al immediately assumed that Winchell was referring to her.

Al said he really grew angry when Ruby began to cry on seeing Winchell walk into the stadium.

'And you know what that does to a fellow,' he told reporters on the way out.

'Ruby said to me, "I'll bet you're sorry that happened." And I told her "No, I'm not sorry." Now all we want is to be left alone.'

After the fight, the newspapers dubbed Jolson – 'The Hollywood Carnera'.

And Al took it all in good part. For one thing, it was keeping his name very much to the fore and in July 1933, he needed every notice he could get.

'Funny,' Al remarked. 'You can sing *Mammy* songs for 100 years, wear out your poor old kneecaps on splintery stages and talk on the radio till you're hoarse as a bullfrog – but you have to sock a columnist before you really become famous.'

The people who had up till now come to hear Al sing and to watch the way he performed on stage were now interested mainly in his biceps. 'He's as fit as a marathon dancer and as brown as a beach lifeguard,' said one writer after seeing the exhibit.

Tempers were frayed for days after the incident. 'Winchell sent word he was going to get me like I got him,' Jolson said with a note of triumph in his voice.

'Well, I'll meet him in a room or in an alley in the daytime or in the night. I'll show him again how an old guy of sixty-two can lick a young guy of thirty-six.'

It was the same old Al, never allowing the facts to interfere with a good story. *Who's Who in the Theatre* that year gave Jolson's age as forty-seven. He was more likely to have been forty-eight. But Al wasn't going to allow any protests on that score. He had a story to tell and a case to present.

'The fellow is an ego maniac,' he said joining the fight

against Winchell again. 'He can't take it.'

The fight with Winchell was in anger and Al was left with a permanently crooked little finger – and rumours of a $500,000 suit for damages brought by the columnist. But the two men made it up again soon afterwards.

As a gesture of his renewed friendship, he sent Winchell a jar of 'the famous Jolson salve'. And indeed it was famous. Al collected recipes for old wives' cures as avidly as he had formerly collected good notices. He had cures for diseases no one had ever heard of, least of all contracted.

But this was just part of the Jolson make-up. The biggest entertainer of all time couldn't do anything small. When he talked about his illnesses, they had to be of epidemic grandeur. The World's Greatest Entertainer was still also the World's Greatest Hypochondriac. He read the Medicine section of *Time* magazine before the one on show business. When there was a new miracle drug on the market, he ordered it by the jarful, long before the neighbourhood pharmacy had their supplies.

But he could put this hypochondria to good use. The biggest fear Jolson ever had was that one day he would develop a worse case of tuberculosis than he had experienced as a boy. At the first sign of coughing, he'd make his way to at least half a dozen doctors before he could rest assured that his lungs were not going to be seriously affected. And when he felt ill or was likely to develop TB, he'd ring the William Morris agency and ask them to book him into the Saranac Lake sanatorium – not for a treatment, but for a show.

As Abe Lastfogel told me, he earned the sanatorium hundreds of thousands of dollars by the frequent benefit concerts he ran on site.

For some time, benefits were the only work Al was doing. When he got up on the platform, he was the old Jolson again, king of his own world. And when he was the king, the other entertainers around him were once more his willing subjects.

On one occasion in the early 'thirties, Jolson joined George Burns and some of the cream of the Hollywood party circuit at a benefit in San Francisco – a Friars Frolic, organised by the Friars Club. Jolson was last on the bill – his constant position even when he didn't have a picture contract. It was after the people had heard all the songs and laughed at all the jokes they thought they could possibly stomach in one evening.

'You ain't heard nothin' yet' said Jolson as usual – and produced his own orchestra of a dozen violinists to augment the very adequate backing which had already done yeoman service for everyone else on the bill.

So for Al, the orchestra had to tune up again. 'We knew that we were going to have another Jolson performance,' Burns now recalls 'and we were not disappointed.'

Jolson was always available to raise money for show people and also for Jewish refugees whose plight in Germany was getting slowly but surely known. He was no longer a religious Jew but accusations against his lack of religious feeling – even though he was almost never seen in a synagogue or a temple – or about other Jews were likely to hit a raw nerve.

Some people said that the big fight with Winchell was not so much what he had written about a girl like Ruby but that he had mentioned in his column that Al had had to work on the Day of Atonement, the sacred Yom Kippur fast. And that he took as a personal affront as he would any hint that he was not a practising Jew.

A couple of years later, Al was to have a celebrated row with Joe E. Lewis over the comedian's decision to back Max Schmelling in his fight with Joe Louis, the American Brown Bomber.

Lewis had become annoyed about the number of times his name was confused with the fighter's, and so announced that every time Joe Louis was fighting, he'd back the other man in the ring.

Jolson – who had helped raise money for the comedian after his throat had been slashed by Chicago gangsters – was incensed that his friend could consider putting money on a man who had been lauded by Hitler and the Nazis.

'How can you bet on that Kraut?' Jolson asked Lewis, who was at least as Jewish as he was himself. Lewis put his money on the German and lost. Jolson was delighted – so delighted in fact that he patched up the quarrel.

But he wasn't delighted with his own career.

Screen Book magazine noticed the way things were going and had the temerity to ask, 'Is Al Jolson through?' They reported how Al looked the night that *Hallelujah I'm a Bum* was premièred in New York.

Jolson had flown into the city from California especially for the occasion. He told startled reporters that his mind was finally made up. He was going to retire from the screen. That retirement was to last exactly twenty-four hours.

Jack Warner, who was in charge of production at the Brothers' studios, got him on the telephone the moment he read of the news and Al's agreement to do three more pictures at his old home.

But there was a bitter venom in his voice as Jolson spoke of the things that had happened on the set of *Hallelujah I'm a Bum*.

'No directors should expect a star to leap off a bridge into the water at sundown,' Jolson declared. 'I decided, picture or no picture, I wasn't going to do it and get double pneumonia.'

Instead, he now revealed, he had dreamed up the idea of wearing a rubber suit under his linen clothes. 'It looked like a swell idea until I jumped in the water. Then I found that the suit kept me afloat.

'I bounced on the water like a rubber ball. So I had to come out. No more pictures like that for me! On the film, Lewis Milestone would stay up all night before a day's shooting and emerge with three pages of script!'

So, *Screen Book* reckoned, there were grounds for dis-illusionment on Jolson's part.

'Jolson appeared on the stage [at the *Hallelujah* première] deeply tanned by the sun. There was the same outward confidence and poise as of yore. But to the observing there was something lacking. Cold-hearted Broadway thought it detected a note of apology in the Jolson voice, a tone of a valedictory in his manner.

'Maybe Jolson, as does Broadway, feels that he has had his brief day of success on the screen.'

But he did go back to Warner Brothers and made a film version of *Wonder Bar* (this time without the definite article). Was he finished on the screen? Again, the critics wondered. And with good grounds – there had never been so little Jolson in a Jolson Picture before.

Here was a whole galaxy of talent – Dolores Del Rio, Dick Powell, Kay Francis and Ricardo Cortez – and Al Jolson as Monsieur Al. But, although frequently swamped, not to say almost forgotten in parts, there had never been a better Al on the screen.

He seemed more polished in every way. In one delightful tongue-twisting scene with a supposedly Russian aristocrat, a great deal of that old magic returned. And in the final production number, 'Goin' To Heavn On A Mule', there was Jolson as only Jolson could be. Far from being lost in the crowd, as some critics suggested, here he was finally mastering the camera. But it was all too brief a glimpse. The monster had not only bitten its creator but it was slowly chewing him, too.

Yet as far as Al was concerned, he was happy – in a rather sad way. He had begun kidding about leaving the screen while still working on the *Wonder Bar* film.

Between scenes, he'd burst into unscripted song. That was never a novelty, but now he asked the people around him to take note of the lyrics, 'Headin' for my last closeup,' he'd warble. 'Git along, little Jolson, git along.'

And he'd add: 'Jolie doesn't work here any more . . . I'm sure that I've told you this before.'

The trouble was, he said, Warner Brothers didn't understand.

'They all think I'm kidding,' he told Jack Grant in *Movie Classic*. 'I told one of you newspaper boys once before that I would never make another picture after this one . . . I tell you I'm through with movies. I'm quitting. I'm getting out. And I know a lot of other synonyms to express the same idea, in case they still don't get it.'

He said he had no quarrels with the studio. 'It's all of them put together and called Hollywood, the town where your personal-social-life, I mean – is based on your success at the box office.

'If your most recent picture slips, so do your friends.'

In the 1980s, such a statement would earn the rejoinder 'Man, you just spoke a book.'

The truth was, Al noted angrily, people were removing the word 'Hallelujah' from the title of *Hallelujah I'm a Bum* when they wrote captions for his pictures.

'The only reason I've filmed *Wonder Bar* is to make 'em change their minds. Word got around that it is going to be pretty good – pardon, colossal – and right away the same guys who a few months ago wouldn't speak to me are calling me 'old pal'. It just isn't on the cards for me to be as I have been in these last few weeks.'

Jolson was plainly worried about the way his career was turning. He was the third richest man in Hollywood, the experts guessed – after Charlie Chaplin and Harold Lloyd – but he was unhappy about his status in the world.

He said that when he appeared at a benefit performance even his father – now eighty-six years old by his own reckoning – didn't bother to go to see him.

Most of all, though, he was worried about Ruby. She was doing better and better and the more gushing her notices were, the harder Al took it.

Warner Brothers, as a publicity gimmick, put out a story that she was receiving the biggest fan mail in the studio. Al reacted by calling his wife 'big shot'. It was the one phrase he had to employ to be sure of a row between them.

He'd make things difficult for her in company by emphasising how hard he worked to get her first contract with Zanuck. He'd proudly tell friends how he pushed up the studio from its $250 a week offer to $1,250 for every full week before the cameras. 'I don't know why Zanuck didn't hear her gasp,' he'd repeat to Ruby's constant embarrassment.

Jolson now told everyone that as far as he was concerned, he was saying good-bye to Hollywood. 'And I mean good-bye,' he added.

Meanwhile, he brought Ruby's mother, her brothers and sisters and her dog out to California from New York – he got on well with his in-laws. 'Ruby's Ma regards me as the head of the family,' Al said with a smile. That was the sort of response he wanted from a mother-in-law.

Before Al announced he was giving up films, he gave up records – without announcing it.

The man who had at one time cut more discs than any of his contemporaries had done nothing since recording a selection of the Irving Berlin tunes from *Mammy* early in 1930. In 1932, he waxed another selection for Brunswick of the songs from *Hallelujah I'm a Tramp*. When they did about as well as the picture, he gave up recording. Indeed, he was to make no others for thirteen years.

But, nevertheless, he decided to give radio another chance. On 26 June 1933, he launched the new NBC series *Kraft Music Hall* – a name he was to be connected with on and off until his last year. At first, he was to be just the programme's guest star, but on 3 August he became the permanent host for the show which had the joint aim of projecting Jolson and selling Kraft cheese. And he had grandiose plans for the series.

Instead of just singing, he was going to star in the radio play he had wanted to do when he first started broadcasting. But it began with the usual dull vaudeville routine – and with almost consistently disastrous results. Early on in the series, one writer had headlined his piece, 'Al Jolson – don't make us cry again.' Another wrote, 'His show is getting too humid for comfort.'

But every writer noted that when Al sang 'Brother Can You Spare A Dime?' on the air, he brought the house down.

It was a number which, of course, always had. As George Burns recalled for me, 'When Al sang that song and turned his coat collar up and the brim of his hat down, you believed him so much that you wanted to empty your pockets to give him a dime for a cup of coffee. Yet everyone knew Jolson was worth $20 million.'

It was not beyond Jolson's ingenuity to turn his coat collar up and the brim of his hat down even on the radio. When he sang 'Sonny Boy', he had to find a child to come and sit on his knee as he sang. But there was one very real advantage that radio had over the movies. It allowed him to hear applause as he sang – even if there were a glass wall separating him from his audience. 'But they always applaud on cue,' a critic noted appreciatively.

Comedy was always the sticky part of radio for him.

'It becomes tiresome always being a song and gag man,' he said.

'After half-a-dozen broadcasts, I knew the comedy would have to go. There are just so many jokes in this world and radio is a Frankenstein in the way it devours material.

'Although you might think I'm immune from criticism, I've never been able to grow a thick skin. It's far better for you to leave your audience than for them to leave you – and remember, it only takes a twist of a dial.'

Radio was more exacting than the screen – 'and ten times more exacting than the stage. In the broadcasting studios, you work with a stop watch. The laughs are timed to the split second, and the pace is more rapid.

'In the theatre, you have the chance to ad-lib if the pace is slow. You have the chance to put your audience in a receptive mood by a few funny asides or an impromptu joke. But at the microphone, you stand or fall on your script – and so much of your personality as you're able to project over the ether. It's really pretty terrific.'

Jolson got his way and started work on radio plays. It paid off. There was an adaptation of *The Jazz Singer*, *The Singing Fool*, and *Green Pastures*. He also starred in a radio version of *Porgy* – the Du Bose Heyward play that had been the sensation of the Broadway season.

Jerome Kern got to hear about the radio success and offered Al the lead in a new operatta he was planning on the *Porgy* story. 'It's just what the doctor ordered, Jerry,' Al told him. 'Get to work. But why not make it an opera – an American grand opera?'

Kern thought about it and said he would truly get to work. But by the time he had assembled thoughts on the idea for the Theatre Guild, George Gershwin had beaten him to it. He decided he wanted a real Negro for the part – not Jolson in blackface.

The rest is theatre history, what became *Porgy and Bess* was a Gershwin triumph – if a belated one, because it was not until long after his death that its full worth was to be appreciated. While Gershwin was still alive, no one had been able to decide whether it was a good musical comedy or a mediocre opera.

As far as Jolson was concerned, it was just another idea that didn't come off. Another plan which was doomed was his entry into really big business.

In November 1934, Jolson and a man called Albert J. Karch brought an action against an investment concern whom they charged had lost millions through their neglect.

Al told the Supreme Court that he had 2,200 shares in the company. Karch had 400. The matter was settled without either man getting any money from the firm. Jolson didn't seem to worry. He was more concerned that he should not lose Ruby the way he had lost his money or the role in *Porgy*.

To cement their marriage he bought a new ten-acre estate at Encino as their little love-nest. The gossip writers enthused over its principal attraction – electrically operated gates.

When Ruby complained of all the tourists filling the pews of the little Catholic church in their neighbourhood, Al provided the money to buy a new one – so that the Indians who were being pushed out of the old building by the rubbernecks could get a look in. Also he hoped that it would make Ruby happy.

Nine

What'll I Do

IN 1934, OBSERVING LIFE with the Jolsons was like watching a marathon ping-pong game. Neither had any intention of damaging their marriage, but for both there was a sub-conscious sense of trying to score.

If Al called Ruby a big shot, she wanted to show him just how big she really was – and in her own right.

Al, for his part, was constantly trying to prove that the great Jolson was anything but a has-been. He didn't like radio, but he worked hard as it because it was the big medium of the day. And there, of course, we have the whole Jolson enigma in a nutshell. It was all relative. Al had a regular radio spot at peak times whenever he wanted it. He had offers of pictures and he could have had a Broadway show any time he gave the word. Few people in show business would have asked for more, but Jolson was not like anyone else in show business – or any other business, for that matter.

He wanted more than just to be in the public eye. He positively needed to *shine* in their eyes. He wanted to be a living memorial to himself, constantly receiving the adulation of his public. But in 1934, he had slipped a couple of places down on his pedestal and he didn't like it.

His radio reviews gave him constant heartache. On 6 April, 1935, he opened a new series on the NBC network for Shell Oil – under the title of *Shell Château.*

The first programme with Al singing, introducing guests and taking part in the playlets for which he wanted to gain a new reputation as a serious actor, was received warmly and he felt more encouraged than he had been at any time since first seeing a microphone.

But the *New York World Telegram* heard the second show and shook its head. 'Dull to embarrassing' was the way its critic summed up *Shell Château* Number Two. And rubbing it in, went on, 'If our glossy reports of last week led you to listen to the second broadcast, we're sorry.'

Al was sorry, too. But the show continued to get good ratings and was to be one of Jolson's most successful forays into radio. Where he did not score on the air was in the jokes he told. He didn't write them and sometimes he couldn't read them – they were so bad that only the joke writers themselves probably knew what the punchlines were meant to convey. This was something entirely new to Jolson – to tell a joke and hear it received in absolute silence. When he quite obviously hadn't scored, he'd give an embarrassed cough in an attempt to bridge through to the next item.

The writers gave Jolson , a man who would effervesce at the sight of a promising gag, stories that made him bubble in indignation – but no one took any notice. His contract specified he had to tell them. There were always painful puns to be inserted wherever possible – like the time that he said he had supervised a prison outing to an Army fort. The prisoners and the soldiers played football and the men from the jail won. 'It just goes to prove,' Al told his audience, 'that the pen is mightier than the sword!' It was one of his better jokes and received a tittle of laughter for the offering. But the audience reaction would not have been strong enough for him to bother to turn on the taps, had it been for anyone else.

When he greeted Bing Crosby's wife Dixie Lee as his guest star he remarked, 'It just goes to prove that love is around the crooner.'

But was there enough love for Jolson? Jack Warner, for whom Al could still do no wrong offered him a chance to prove to himself that there was. Instead of competing with each other, he suggested that Al and Ruby should work together – in a film.

When Al said yes, the big publicity machine went to work in

[174]

a way it had never had an opportunity to do before. It was in Warners' interest to stress just how happy the Jolson marriage was. The film was to be called *Go into your Dance* and the publicity pictures made the whole of life a dance for them.

Al Jolson was still the World's Greatest Entertainer, they said, and theirs was the world's greatest show business marriage. The old poses of Al in semi-profile, winking, were there to give the old message, 'You ain't heard nothin' yet.' Except that this time, there was always Ruby at his side. It wasn't going to be just a Jolson picture – at least not just an Al Jolson picture. He and Ruby were getting equal billing and Al tried to accept it the way the studio ordered.

'It seems *Wonder Bar* was a hit,' he told the *New York Sun*, beating his breast in the old Jolson fashion. 'All of a sudden people wanted to see me again. It was like an attack of renewed youth.' What it really was, was an attack of renewed Jolson and it did Al's constitution a world of good.

And he told the man from the *Sun* something he wouldn't have dared mention a few years before. 'They are actually paying money to see me!' It was all taken for granted once – now it was news. But Jolson was bubbling again and it was quite clearly good to see.

The studio publicity department prepared new question-naires about the Jolson career – they, too, would have been unnecessary just a little while before. They listed his favourite pastimes – racing, his favourite food – gefilte fish, and his favourite film to date – *Wonder Bar*, of course. They put down, too, his own least favourite film – *Hallelujah I'm a Bum*, of course. It had been made for United Artists, and now he was back with Warner Brothers.

Go into you Dance came just at a time that Al's radio work hit a setback. Like all artists he was caught up in the midst of the row over music royalties by ASCAP, the American Society of Composers, Authors and Publishers.

In 1936, the Music Publishers Holding Corporation, the licensee of all Warner Brothers songs, withdrew from ASCAP. They had had an arrangement whereby they had twenty per cent of the ASCAP stake and now they wanted more. When ASCAP refused, MPH withdrew its songs and banned all Warner Brothers movie songs from the air.

When Al said he wanted to do 'I Love To sing' from his new picture on the air, he was told, 'It'll cost Warner Brothers $50,000 to get one of its songs played on NBC.' So he couldn't sing his own songs on his own programme.

But he could plug his new film by talking about it. And he could say nice things about Ruby till it came out of the drapes of their home, the kitchen sink and the floorboards. Whenever he saw a newspaper man, he was full of the sort of praise for his wife he felt he was expected to offer.

'Maybe I'm prejudiced,' he said. 'Go ahead – sue me. But I'm honestly of the opinion that Ruby Keeler is the ten best women in pictures all rolled into one! Ruby has the faculty of bringing to the screen the sure sweet qualities she has in real life – charm, sweet sincerity and winsomeness.

'I'm Ruby's most severe critic and her most devoted admirer.'

The whole of Hollywood was buzzing with the news of the picture and the married couple who were starring in it.

A great deal was made of the theme song in the picture 'About A Quarter To Nine' and the *New York Sun* announced well in advance that the première of the movie was going to be staged at a quarter to nine.

The same paper reported the Jolson-Keeler marriage as 'still a very genuine mutual admiration club and never a word of trouble'.

And the *Sun* drew a very interesting parallel between Al and Ruby working on *Go into your Dance* and Douglas Fairbanks and Mary Pickford breaking up after working on *The Taming of the Shrew*. 'But the Jolson household is still serene,' it said, assuredly.

Nevertheless, there were occasional glimpses of the pain on Al's face when he saw Ruby getting the sort of closeup that he deemed his own right and his alone. Occasionally, too, he seemed to take over from the director Archie Mayo.

'Sweetie,' Al called as Ruby moved from one scene to another 'why not do it that way?' He was as sweet as the names he was calling his wife but there was no mistaking the fact that he wanted to be in charge. 'Honey! I think I'd do it like that if I were you,' he'd add for good measure.

Not that Al was faultless himself. In fact, many a scene had to be reshot after Al had called his wife 'Ruby' on the set when he should have referred to her as Dorothy.

Go into your Dance was a big success. But it was Jolson as part of a team that the public wanted to see. The public cried for more Jolson-Keeler pictures, and it seemed the logical thing to happen. The big number in *Go into your Dance* had the couple walking arm in arm, with Al – in top hat, white tie and tails – singing 'About A Quarter To Nine' to Ruby in her flowing evening gown.

It was the big hit of the film and because it was, provided Al with more cause for worry. 'They don't want to see me any more. They want *us*.' So there were to be no more films with Al and Ruby doing a double act.

'I'm going back to radio,' said Al. 'At least there *I'm* the star.'

And an expensive star too. In one of his early broadcasts for *Shell Château* he welcomed golf professional Sam Parks Junior, who had just become the national champion.

'What's the name of the place where you're instructor?' Al kidded, throwing the script aside in the old Winter Garden manner. 'The Summit', said the pro with a note of pride in his voice. 'But that's a rotten hotel,' Al rejoined – as the men behind the glass observation panel put hands to their foreheads in sheer disbelief. They knew what to expect.

The next day it arrived – a writ from the Summit Hotel Company demanding $100,000 in damages.

The matter wasn't settled for four years – by which time Jolson himself had been dropped as co-defendant. NBC was ordered to pay $15,000. Al had meanwhile parted company with his network and joined CBS.

He was always slightly intemperate on the air and it was hardly surprising that a man who relied so much on his own personality on the stage should find it so difficult to behave differently in front of a radio microphone. But that was Jolson.

On one of his very first radio interviews he sent shivers

down the spines of refined old ladies who had tuned into the star's return home from Europe. It was at the time that he fled from D. W. Griffith.

'How's the beer in England, Al?' a radio reporter asked him. 'Beer? They drink it warm in England. Personally, I think they should have put it back into the horse.'

A little later on, he was personally responsible for NBC introducing censorship on all broadcast scripts. He had got embroiled in a discussion about Clara Bow. 'Oh, she's sleeping catercomed in bed,' he quipped. The protest flooded in from offended listeners.

Early in the thirties he had predicted great things for a newer medium – television. The Bell Company had asked Jolson, the man who was generally first in anything new, to try his hand at what they forecast was going to be the biggest thing in the history of entertainment.

They ran a pilot programme from the Astor Hotel – with Al starring. He liked it. 'It's like radio, movies and the stage all put together,' he said. 'This really is going to be great.'

But Bell decided they still had plenty of work to put into television before anyone could be asked to pay for air time or buy sets. And the man who was first to appear on the small screen in America never made another live TV appearance.

Early in 1935, however, he had another career to think of. Al was a father. As suddenly as that. Or rather Al thought himself as a father. He and Ruby were in Illinois with George Jessel when they passed the Cradle Orphanage at Evanston. Jessel knew the priest who ran the orphanage and introduced the Jolsons to him.

'Why don't we take one of these kids?' Al asked Ruby –without really having to wait for her answer. He knew it all too well. It was something they had been talking about for most of the years of their marriage.

Ruby realised that Al was not going to be able to give her a child of her own, just as he had failed to father one for Henrietta or Ethel. She had been dropping hints along these lines whenever the opportunity arose. They had planned to adopt twins – a girl for him and a boy for her, just as in the song.

But they settled for one. They chose a seven-week-old boy. On 7 May 1935, in Chicago, they formally adopted him, under the name of Al Jolson Junior.

There was however one stipulation – the Jolsons had to bring him up as a Catholic. It was a detail about which Al didn't bother to tell Moses Yoelson in Washington, when he made his next trip to the capital. He knew it would hurt the old man and there was little point in doing that.

Instead, Al set about becoming a father in every way he knew. He bought the biggest pedal cars, the biggest teddy bears and the best baby clothes for 'my son'. When he and Ruby had a row over the boy, he'd call out to her, 'He's my flesh and blood.'

Two weeks after the baby was first carried into the nursery at the Jolsons' Encino home, he became seriously ill. The child was rushed to hospital and for two nights Ruby kept vigil by the cot, just like my other mother.

The crisis passed and the baby went back home. Al was like a dog with two tails. 'Dat's my boy,' he'd say when the youngster spoke his first words. For this seemed to be the best Jolson role yet. He wasn't worried any more about being a superstar. Here was an opportunity to give all the warmth he had previously given so lavishly to his audiences to this one little boy, the boy he was convinced was going to follow in his footsteps to become the World's Second Greatest Entertainer.

'Why not?' he'd say to friends who appeared a little sceptical at the idea. 'He's my son, ain't he?'

He'd wheel the baby between the orange and the grapefruit trees in the garden of the big house in Encino. He'd stop to talk to the gardener and ask him for some flowers to give the child to hold. 'Don't you think he looks like me?' he'd ask him. The incredible thing was that Jolson really believed that he did.

For a time, Al was obviously very happy in his new life of retirement.

The local community took full advantage of his presence among them and his absence from the studios. The Chamber of Commerce at Encino elected him their President. On 28 December 1935, Al Jolson became the town's Mayor.

He really was happy now. He was a big shot in his town, in his family – and with a son of his own, he felt a big shot to himself. And that was the most important thing of all.

And he was taking interest in other things. He bought the rights of the best-selling novel *Penny Arcade* – and sold them to Warner Brothers on condition that they starred James Cagney in the lead. (The film was made – with Cagney in the lead as Jolson requested – under the title *Sinners' Holiday*.)

And in June 1936 he joined hands with one of Hollywood's ace showmen – Sid Grauman, the man behind the famous Chinese Theatre on Hollywood Boulevard. He wasn't going into the theatre business, nor was he going to make a film with Grauman's money. Instead, he became Vice-president in a company that the theatre owner had formed to dig for minerals in the Black Hills of South Dakota.

Jolson put in some money, but drew out no minerals. Yet he didn't seem unhappy. He had his Sonny Boy to take out, to play with and to talk about on the radio.

At one time, so many people wrote to hear more about Al Junior that he tried to persuade Ruby to allow him to bring the baby into the radio studio. She said 'No' and Al Junior stayed in the nursery. All this wasn't doing Al's public image any harm either.

Early in 1936, he started work on another film, *The Singing Kid*. But that didn't go smoothly for either Jolson or Warner Brothers. It was one of the most ambitious Jolson films to date – with a number of exterior shots that never failed to give problems. For Jolson was once more behaving like the big star he had been six years before, and the people in the studio, who would have been delighted to execute his slightest whim back in 1930, were a lot more choosy in 1936.

So, when Al insisted on getting his own way and started showing the small print in his contract to prove his point, the rows were inevitable.

Jolson was required in one scene to sing in the street – with traffic all round him and people walking up and down the pavement. Jolson sang his heart out. But the studio men knew what to expect. The big Jolson voice was drowned every time someone walked by and when a car appeared in the distance.

'Al, we'll have to dub your song in the studio,' Director William Keighley told him.

'No dubbing,' said Al. 'I either sing it as it happens or I don't sing at all.'

So to satisfy Al's demands for realism, the street had to be completely recreated on the studio lot.

It was all symptomatic of the way Al was feeling while making *The Singing Kid*. The film was about a top-line entertainer who loses his voice. It began with a medley of Jolson singing some of his best-known numbers, 'Mammy', 'Swanee', 'Rockabye', 'California Here I Come', 'April Showers', 'A Quarter To Nine' and 'Sonny Boy' – all but the last in blackface.

But what seemed from the start to be a pure Jolson vehicle turned out to be yet another occasion for him to be swamped by other people. His co-star Beverly Roberts had just as big a role as Ruby had in *Go into your Dance,* and this alone didn't exactly please him. To make things worse, in the musical numbers 'I Love To Sing-A' and 'Save Me Sister', Cab Calloway and the Four Yacht Club Boys seemed to be around more than he was.

Jolson was unhappy all the time he was on the set – and for the first time members of the crew could be heard talking about the 'cruel Jolson'. There was none of the idolatry he had experienced from the wings of the Winter Garden. No more indulgent shrugs from fans who hoped somehow one day to get Jolson genes swimming in their bloodstream. 'He was the cruellest man I've ever known,' said one top Hollywood figure who had his break working on that picture.

Beverley Roberts sparred with Jolson almost from the moment they first met. She was introduced to him on the set just as she was about to be tested for the female lead. 'I was rushed through by the makeup department so quickly that I went on to the set with my hair dripping wet,' she recalled years afterwards on a television programme.

'Jolson roared with laughter when he saw me and the director said 'What are we wearing for hair this year – mouse's nests?' I was indignant – just like a firecracker. And I think that's how I got the part. Al admired how I reacted to the way I was being treated.'

Jolson hated *The Singing Kid.* 'That's it,' he said when it was all over. 'You can't treat Jolson like that, no more crummy pictures for me. I'll decide in the future what I'll play.'

The film prompted yet another bust-up with his brother Harry. Early in the thirties after Harry had come to Hollywood for a movie career which ended before it began, there had also been an equally disastrous business venture for the elder Jolson brother. He and Lillian had put all their savings into a restaurant they called 'Harry Jolson's Rendezvous'. But not enough people chose it as their rendezvous and when they did, too many of them escaped the formality of paying the bill.

Al came to the rescue and appointed Harry his personal agent. He sent him a telegram with the message. 'WITH THE SALARY I GET, IF I WORK ONE WEEK, YOU'LL LIVE A YEAR.' And Al arranged for Ruby to be one of Harry's clients, too.

With Ruby, it was merely handing her the contracts Warner Brothers and First National were rushing for her to sign. For Al, the contracts were few, far between and not all to his liking. Even the radio producers were mentioning names like Bing Crosby and Rudy Vallee to Jolson, and suggested that he start crooning their way if the air waves were to keep on lapping.

It was more than the ego of Al Jolson – the man who had shown everyone else the way – could stand.

In 1936, *Variety* printed an announcement from the William Morris agency, 'We are proud to announce that Al Jolson has exclusively authorised us to represent him for the negotiation of radio and theatre engagements. Any other person or persons purporting to represent Al Jolson in the connection do so without his authority.'

The writing was on the wall for those other persons – all of whom seemed to be Harry Jolson. A letter was sent from Harry's attorneys demanding $75,000 damages. It never went for trial. When Al next met Harry in the street he gave him a new car as compensation. 'With my career in the shape it's in right now,' Al told his elder brother, 'I need an organisation like William Morris to represent me.'

The agency got Al a new CBS series for Lifebuoy Soap. It was called *Café Trocadero* and was to run for four years, although the title was dropped after the first two shows.

There was a consistent pattern of Al singing 'April Showers', introducing guest stars – including Ruby – and fooling around with his regular sidekicks, Martha Raye and a very successful Greek-dialect comedian, calling himself Parkyakarkus (real name Harry Einstein).

The Shell programme meanwhile had been used for the radio début of a bright child singer called Judy Garland.

Radio was now becoming undemanding for Jolson, although when he wanted to do so, he could sparkle as soon as the green light indicated he was on the air. On those occasions, he treated the microphone as one of his old live audiences, and made love to it just as he had in the days when he was king. To listen to one of those Jolson performances was to be admitted to an enchanted land. But you had to turn the knob to take your choice and sometimes there was no enchantment – merely the sound of a man bored with himself.

And when he was bored Jolson had to find new diversions. He bought more horses and told bigger stories about his successes. He bought a piece of prizefighter Harry Armstrong, sharing the ownership deeds with George Raft.

He also had the first really serious row with Ruby, flaring up at suggestions that his career was through, calling her names and storming out of the house.

But every now and again, a columnist would do a piece on Jolson and every now and again he felt the better for reading it. *Metronome* magazine in the mid-thirties was still describing him as 'The first salesman of songs' and adding, 'He may have a song that isn't so good. The Jolson pipes have been chipped by time of a bit of their platinum, but you'll get the song and it will either thrill you or you will subconsciously feel that he is driving the song home. If you happen to have the latter reaction, class yourself in the minority. For Mr and Mrs Public like the way Jolson sings a song. One of the greatest proofs that they do, lies in the fact that they've supported so many of his imitators.' For the magazine noted Jolson didn't bother about breathing from the diaphragm when he sang – he merely breathed when he needed to do so. What did matter was that his songs came from his heart.

'And that is where Jolson sings 'em from. That is the priceless ingredient in selling a song. Diction is important, phrasing is another, accompaniment a third – but the story and the heart appeal must be there ... he still remains champ.'

It did him good to read things like that – even when he hardly believed it himself. But when he had a sympathetic audience to listen to him, he was as much champ as he had ever been.

And never more so than when he appeared on the Hollywood party circuit. He needed no agents to book him into celebrities' homes and he needed no persuasion to sing at the piano which formed an obligatory part of all these show business shindigs.

Everyone at the party would sing or tell jokes, but if Jolson were there, he'd expect to be asked to go on last. There was one party to which he and Ruby went, however, when the expected did not happen.

George Burns and Gracie Allen were giving a party at their Beverly Hills home for Damon Runyan and the Burns and Allen parties were always different affairs. George Burns liked telling stories that made him the life and soul of his own party. He also liked to sing. 'Why shouldn't I? – I'm payin' for the piano player!' was how he put it to me.

Burns was just getting into the swing of things by the time

his ninth or tenth number had ended, and his guests were either talking in corners of the main room with glasses in their hands or listening appreciatively. All except Jolson. 'He was getting a pain in the ass,' Burns recalls with a distinct twinkle in his eyes.

After about the eleventh Burns solo, Jolson did the unheard of thing. He went up to his host and *asked* if he could sing.

'Sure, Jolie,' said Burns pointing the way to the piano with his cigar, 'go ahead.'

Al gave the pianist instructions to play the accompaniment to 'Rockabye Your Baby With A Dixie Melody' and had just got into the refrain when Burns sidled up to him from behind and joined in.

Jolson looked at Burns – and bristled. He stopped singing, grabbed Ruby's arm and her fur coat and marched out to their car, parked outside. As they went, Burns followed – still singing '. . .and when you croon, croon a tune – from the heart of Dixie.'

It was the sort of trick the Hollywood set loved to play on their big names, but Jolson didn't like it. A year or so passed before he and Burns teamed up again.

In 1937 Jolson and Sid Grauman were in business once more, too. This time, it was the traditional means of showing a film star's recognition by one of his peers.

Grauman invited Jolson to preserve his hands and feet in the wet cement of the Chinese Theatre. Al, naturally, went two better. He held his fingers outstretched in his favourite 'Mammy' pose – and preserved his left knee at the same time with an arrow pointing to it to explain its significance.

Meanwhile his radio show went on . . . and on. The *World Telegram* wrote in 1937, 'His air show is flimsy but his magnetism and vitality make it appealing.' And that at a time when people were saying he was completely washed up. By Jolson standards, he was, but that only goes to prove just how high those standards had been.

And he was still the centre of attraction wherever he went – although there were times when he appreciated this less than at others. He was at Los Angeles' Olympic Auditorium with Chico Marx one day in 1937 when a man who thought Jolson's talents somewhat lacking decided to prove his point – by throwing a bottle at him. 'Come on down you coward and fight,' challenged Jolson – who had been slightly cut by the flying glass. Chico was slightly hurt, too – but neither saw their assailant.

By 1939 Jolson was feeling restless. He was about fifty-four now and regarded as the elder statesman of show business. But it was not a role he relished. He was still recognised wherever he went, but there was none of the old crazed adoration he had experienced and demanded in the past.

Young girls queued up to see him enter the CBS studios, but he had a sneaking feeling that they would have done so for any celebrity who was on the air every week.

And he had his share of spongers, too – people who knew he was good for a dollar or two, and too big to turn them down.

There was the time he was in Miami and walked into the bar of the hotel where he was staying. At his entrance, the juke box played 'Sonny Boy'.

'I can't get enough of that song,' said a woman at the bar, 'lend me a couple of nickels.'

Jolson pushed a coin to the woman and said excitedly, 'The next five are on me.'

When the woman recognised him, she stammered, 'You're Al Jolson.'

'Sure and you knew it when I walked in,' Jolson answered. 'What's the idea of that corny routine?'

He knew what to expect. The woman was on hard times. Her husband had put a thousand dollars on a horse and had lost. What's more, it wasn't his money – it was Al's. It turned out that the husband was the desk clerk at the hotel and had taken the money from the safe soon after Jolson checked in. Al had left his cash there for security, and had not yet missed it.

'I don't soft soap that easy,' Jolson told her – and ordered her to get her husband. He took them both away in his car –

not to the police station as they had feared but to the local greyhound stadium. There, he gave the man $500 – and instructed him to put it on a dog he believed to be a sure fire thing. The dog produced a $3,000 dollar win.

Al took his $1,500 from the winnings and allowed the desk clerk to have the other $1,500. 'Let this be a lesson to you,' he warned. 'Never bet the horses – if you've got to bet, bet the dogs.'

Legend has it that the couple's son saw Jolson just before he died. 'Sure I remember your mother,' the star told the youngster. 'And you mother still owes me some money.'

'How much?' asked the boy sheepishly.

'A quarter. I gave it to her for the juke box and she never returned it.'

But the fact that he could afford the time to play games with people like that worried Jolson as much as the stolen $1,000 had worried the desk clerk and his wife.

He asked William Morris to get him back into films. Easier said than done. It was plain that Warner Brothers did not want the man who had given them life and it was equally plain that no one else did, either.

Eventually, Twentieth Century Fox took the bait. What they were offering was not the star part, or even the second supporting role – but the third billing under the names of their top box office draws, Alice Faye and Tyrone Power.

But it turned into an exciting choice – although just how exciting took a few years to register.

The film was to be called *Rose of Washington Square* – all about a singer who falls for a good-for-nothing professional gambler. The rough plot outline was so much like the story of Fanny Brice – the title song had been introduced by Fanny in a Ziegfeld show in 1920 – that the star threw libel suits at Twentieth Century Fox and collected.

Jolson was in it just to be Jolson. He played a character on the same vaudeville bill as Alice Faye, who became her friend and who was to warn her just what a low-life her husband (Tyrone Power) was turning out to be.

But he also sang – in blackface – the old Jolson songs like

'Rockabye Your Baby', 'Toot-Toot-Tootsie', 'California Here I Come' and even 'Mammy'.

He had plainly never acted and certainly never sung like it before on the screen. It was not so much a new Jolson as the old, recapturing . . . himself.

The film set no records at the time. But people who saw it took notice. In the *New York Herald Tribune*, John K. Hutchens said it all, 'It takes a motion picture – the one called *Rose of Washington Square* – to remind you of it and even then you didn't know whether it was pleasant or sad to reflect upon. But there it is, anyhow, a whole chapter of theatre flickering past you in the little while a film requires, and there in the middle of it was one who had been peerless in his field some twenty years and more ago.

'The other stars were in it, impersonating (after a pattern) characters suggested by real people of the same era, one a famous singing comedienne, the other a shoddy crook to whom she was fiercely and incredibly loyal. But the other, Al Jolson, was pretty clearly playing Al Jolson.

'In the picture, his name was something else, but no one would be taken in by that. Who but he had ever donned burnt cork, sunk to one knee and inquired lyrically after his celebrated Mammy in the Deep South? Indeed, his Mammy must have been copyrighted.

'Your haven't seen him on a Broadway stage either in years – neither has anyone else – and even then, he was a figure out of the show business past. The show was a foreign novelty freely adapted in the Jolson uses and entitled *The Wonder Bar*, and it marked his return to the stage after five years in which he had been a great man in Hollywood.

'It wasn't a generally good show, but that didn't matter. It never had mattered. A lot of the Jolson shows hadn't been masterpieces of musical comedy writing. They hadn't needed to be. All they had needed was the tumultuous Jolson vigour and the smashing Jolson style, unique and incomparable in the theatre of his prime and never equalled since by any popular singing star.

'He was already a legend of the occasion of that return and

this picture set you thinking of it. . .

'As far as the theatre is concerned, you think of all this as in the past, because you don't expect ever to see him there again. As long ago as *The Wonder Bar,* he didn't seem entirely happy about being back on the stage, which is an exhausting place – and now he is fifty-three. Perhaps it is just as well that he doesn't come back.

'Perhaps his style wouldn't do today, however painful such a notion may be to anyone who can remember even a few years into the past.

'At the performance of *Rose of Washington Square* attended by this department, the younger generation was somewhat less than tolerant even of his trademark, the immortal 'Mammy'. You would never have thought it could happen.

'But since it did, you are glad that there are at least this and other film records of him, though they are the merest suggestion of what he once was. You will be very surprised if you ever see anyone else who was as good in the same way.'

No other Jolson film since *The Singing Fool* had generated that sort of comment – although it was not nearly prophetic enough. But for 1939 it did the Jolson fame as much good as a dozen blood transfusions – although this was really the only sort of blood Al had ever needed.

Later that year Twentieth Century Fox featured him in another supporting role – in a Technicolor opus called *Hollywood Cavalcade,* which also featured Alice Faye, but this time with Don Ameche in the main male lead.

Al's part was so small that he was billed right at the end – 'With special thanks to Al Jolson'. It was a fictional love story set around the story of the cinema. There were the Keystone Cops, custard pies and Rin Tin Tin. Al just sang one song – *Kol Nidre*, in a remake of the synagogue scene from *The Jazz Singer*, right at the very end of an extremely indifferent movie. 'Kol Nidre' was chosen because all the other *Jazz Singer* numbers were in their original form, Warner Brothers' copyrights.

He did it while working in the studio on another picture

starring Don Ameche. It was a smaller role than the one he had had in *Rose of Washington Square* – but somehow it was a more important one.

The picture was *Swanee River* – supposedly the life story of Stephen Foster. Jolson pretended to be E. P. Christie, the great minstrel who sang many of the Foster ballads for the first time.

But once again he was simply playing Jolson, although this was an effervescent Jolson quite obviously delighted to be back at work again. He sang 'The Old Folks At Home' in one of the most memorable performances of his screen life. People who had seen Al on the Winter Garden stage now felt that at last the studios were getting near the real Jolson, and were featuring him in just the sort of part he should have had ten years before. Of course, the cinema had progressed technically a bit since those days and that showed, too.

But Al's marriage to Ruby had plainly not progressed at all. There were inklings of what was going on in Ruby's mind every time she and Al were seen together. They both looked morose. He was heard to shout at her in public. And it was affecting their home in the sense that most breaking marriages do. The biggest sufferer was Al Junior.

To what extent, came home to Al the day when the child met him at the airport. He had been away for a weekend with George Jessel and was excited at being met by the joyous youngster. Al, with a strong suntan, raced down the steps of the aircraft, grabbed the child in his arms, lifted him up and cried 'Who am I, sonny boy?'

'You're the Jew,' said the child callously. Even under his suntain, Al Jolson blanched.

'It was the only time I ever saw him humiliated,' Jessel recalled for me.

[190]

Ten

All Alone

THE HARDEST PART OF being married to Ruby Keeler was for
Jolson to be able to convince her just how big a star he had
once been. And never did it come any harder than when he
was working – doing the same kind of work that his
contemporaries in the business were doing very happily, but
without causing the sort of sensations he had once come to
regard as his right.

In 1939 he did a radio broadcast from a new hotel run by
the Paley Brothers, controllers of the CBS network for whom
Jolson was then working. Mickey Rooney was on the bill
with him for the show, which went no further than the area
covered by the local radio station. It wasn't even heard by the
guests in the hotel. The MC was Rudy Vallee.

Ruby had a table at the back of the restaurant and couldn't
hear the show presented on the stage at the other end of the
room. Vallee paid a fulsome tribute to Jolson as he
introduced him. 'He's one of the greatest talents of all time,'
he said. 'He's the man with the thrilling voice.'

When the show was over, Jolson went over to Vallee's
table. He asked him to tell Ruby, 'what you had said about
me on the air.'

But even if he had convinced her about the throne he had
once occupied on Broadway – and his scrapbook would have
done that adequately enough – it was not sufficient for him to
remain her idol.

One evening, when Jolson was playing bridge at the home
of his friend, George Levy, Ruby phoned. He didn't want to

interrupt his game, but the butler insisted that it seemed important. He left the card table with a 'spade bust'. All the bidding had just stopped as Al called 'three spades'. It was going to be another Jolson killing.

He came back to the game from the phone, looking ashen. But he took his seat and said nothing. Then slowly reached over to his partner George Burns. 'What's the bid?' he asked. Burns replied, 'Three spades.' And Jolson answered: 'I double.'

In the space of minutes, Burns told me, he had forgotten that he had made the bid himself. He was looking at eight spades, but he wasn't aware of it. The partners looked at each other and knew what the phone call had been about days before it was in the papers.

When Jolson returned home the day *Swanee River* was completed he found that Ruby had kept the promise she had made him on the telephone. She was gone . . . out of his life. She had packed her things in the Mercedes and driven with Al Junior to her parents' home.

Al was in tears and had to be comforted by the servants. Eppy came over to try to soothe things for him. Finally, he rang through to Ruby's mother, but she wouldn't allow them to talk.

He wrote to Ruby, made more telephone calls and begged her to come back to him. And he tried to keep a stiff upper lip when talking to the Press. But the man who had made a profession out of crying on the stage and screen found it almost impossible to convince outsiders he was happy when he really wasn't.

On 26 October 1939 the *New York Herald Tribune* reported that the pair were parting.

'Jolson appeared broken hearted,' the paper noted. It said they had decided to part after he had shouted at her at a boxing match. 'I hope everything will work out all right,' he told the *Herald Tribune,* but without much confidence that it would.

He had just learned that she had already consulted lawyers. But he insisted, 'These are family troubles – not important enough for divorce.'

Later he said he had decided that the only thing to do was to face the fact that they were apart and be generous. He offered her $400 a week for life – and $50,000 in a lump sum if she married again, with a $100,000 trust fund for Al Junior.

Ruby's lawyers told him to forget it – until it came to court.

Meanwhile, Al stayed alone at their Encino home and Ruby and Al Junior stayed on with her parents.

Al's misery increased every time he thought about Ruby. In his own way, he loved her deeply. The trouble was that he had been given the sort of challenges that were too bitter to accept. At first it was a matter of being reconciled to the life of a soberly married man far from the spotlight that he needed so badly. And when that wasn't possible, facing the even harder prospect of having a wife with a career more dazzling than his own.

For years, there had been rumours of Ruby and Al sparring verbally with each other all night long. When she had gone, Al seemed to miss that as much as the more loving moments.

He asked Harry Akst, his pianist, to spend the night with him so that they could just talk the hours away. Akst slept in the same room – in Ruby's old single bed – night after night. In the afternoons, he'd go to the racetrack with him. In the evenings, to the prizefights. In between, he recalled years later, there were fights with his own wife – apologising for having to eat dinner with Al instead of with her.

'I didn't know then how close I was myself to Reno in those weeks,' Akst said shortly before his own death.

At the track Akst regarded it as his duty to bet with Al and lose with him. At least, he assumed Al was losing with him. But Jolson never actually admitted it to him any more than he had to Jessel.

'You didn't have the winner, did you Al?' he asked incredulously. 'Ha! Ha! I didn't have his sister,' Jolson replied. In those painful times, he needed his moment of triumph – even if he had to create it for himself.

In time, Ruby was to become much happier about her separation than she was when she first appeared before the court, four days before the end of 1939. Then, she had filed for divorce on grounds of extreme cruelty and physical suffering.

The judge heard tales of Jolson 'publicly humiliating me. He would shout and call me names,' she told him.

'He called me stupid and kept me up all night calling me names. He would sit at the table and refuse to talk, and just leave me to keep up the conversation. Then he would go upstairs to bed and leave me to entertain our friends. . . Whenever I expressed an opinion, he would say "That's wonderful. Do you know about that, too? You are too smart."'

The judge asked: 'Did he say that in front of friends?'

'Oh, yes,' she replied. 'He criticised the friends I brought into the house and at a restaurant we had bitter quarrels. He would never agree with me about anything, and when I suggested things he would fly into a rage. He never takes me anywhere.'

Even after Ruby's statements to the judge, Al hoped for a reconciliation. She had been given an interlocutory decree, but he hoped their marriage could be salvaged from the wreckage. 'Who knows?' he told reporters.

'It takes a year for a divorce to become final. And Ruby's a wonderful girl.'

If there were a chance for a reconciliation, it was through Al Junior. Ruby had been given custody of the boy. For weeks Al would see the youngster on Saturdays or Sundays and take him for long drives or on outings to the nearest ball game. But these afternoons were always painful.

Al confided to friends, 'The kid's growing away from me.' After a while, it became all too painful.

Al agreed not to see the boy again. Instead, he was concentrating on his career. He had big plans – and remarkably enough, Ruby was still playing a part in them.

Earlier in 1939, Al had done a deal with a stockbroker friend called George Hale. He had come to Jolson with the script of a show he had been offered and asked Al to look it over for him. It was all about a radio singer's dream of the Wild West.

Originally, the show was to be called *On the Line* – with a

[194]

score by Rodgers and Hart. But by the time Jolson and Hale came to an agreement, Burton Lane and E. Y. ('Yip') Harburg had come up with a new score and the show was retitled *Hold on to your Hats.* Ruby was to be the lead dancer.

And for the first time in nine years – since *The Wonder Bar* in 1931 – Jolson was coming back to his old Broadway as the star in his own show. Actor-manager Jolson revelled in the chance of recreating his old greatness.

Ruby was contracted to appear with him and this he saw as the possible chance of recapturing her, too. It was arranged that she would open at the Shubert Theatre in September 1940 after a six-week trial run in Chicago.

He sent her roses every day of the first week and paid for her to stay at an expensive hotel. She sent back the flowers and also the items of jewellery that he plied her with later on.

On the stage, he acted as both star and producer – but not husband. When he found fault with Ruby's dancing, he'd tell her so. He'd shout and he'd rave and Ruby would walk out. In the evening, there would be more roses and more gifts – all of which were returned to him.

Finally during the Chicago run, Ruby walked out on him for the last time. She was replaced on the stage by Eunice Healey. And once again, he tried to replace her in his mind with horses.

Every spare moment, he'd drive to Arlington, Chicago's main track, to take his mind off his lost marriage. When the show hit a sticky patch in rehearsals, he could be heard muttering, 'What's going on at Arlington? I gotta get there.'

He was notably nervous – walking up and down on the stage, seeking the nearest water cooler for a drink. Just as he had in the old days, he'd regularly poke his head into the box office and see how many tickets were being bought.

A reporter told him he was looking good. For the first time in weeks, he smiled. 'Hollywood took it off,' he said, rubbing his midriff. 'But no more Hollywood for me. And no more marriage either. You can put *that* in caps. This is the life. Sure I'm tired. Never tireder. These rehearsals are costing me $100 a minute. A hundred. Hear that – a hundred. I'm going to the doctors,' he told the Pressmen who were gathered round to hear every word the way he wanted them to, and the way they had not done for a long time. But he didn't see a doctor. He found his way to the track at Arlington.

That night, with Eunice dancing in Ruby's place, he seemed a different man. The *New York Times* noted that he stood in the spotlight 'while the old timers out front sent a wave of applause that washed down from his shoulders all the loneliness for the stage that Hollywood put there. He bounded around the stage and was all movement, and remained so for the next three hours.'

On 11 September, 1940, the curtains parted at the Shubert Theatre on Broadway. The prodigal son was made to feel as though he had really come home.

Brooks Atkinson, the 'Butcher of Broadway', was cheering with the rest of them. In his *New York Times* piece he wrote, 'It's all right folks. *Hold on to your Hats* has arrived at the Shubert where it opened last evening, and the musical comedy season has begun with enormous gusto.

'For this is the show that is bringing Al Jolson back to Broadway after an absence of nine years.'

And then, coming right to the point, he went on, 'If you think you have lost some of the old fondness for him during the interim, prepare for a pleasant surprise. He is a little older now, his hair is a little thinner. But none of the warmth has gone out of his singing and none of the gleam has departed from his story telling.

'By great good fortune, he is also appearing in one of the funniest musical plays that have stumbled on to Broadway for years. Hold your sides as tightly as the title directs you to hold your hat.'

He was pleased to welcome Martha Raye to the show with Jolson. A young lady called Joanne Dru, who a few years later was to do well in Hollywood, escaped his attention. Jolson and Raye, who were already working on the radio together, were, he said, a combination that 'is just about perfect'.

Jolson was 'the magnetic minstrel who has a way with a song and the power to capture an audience instantly'.

And the *New York Post* joined in the rhapsodies.

'It took Al Jolson in person to remind us what an extraordinary entertainer he really is. His throaty hymns to Mammy may in memory have become easily resisted. But Mr Jolson in person and in action is quite a different proposition. The people who can match his personality in our theatre are rare.

'He is at once host and performer, minstrel and crooner, hero and autobiographer.

'From the moment of his first entrance when he settles from a chair on the centre stage to talk directly to the audience he establishes his pre-eminence as he banishes formality. He is the perfect master of ceremonies, not only for the musical in which he is appearing but for himself.

'As a confidence man, Jolson spills his public secrets with a breezy surety belonging to a vanished race of vaudevillians.'

Yes, Al had come home. Once more he was going to be the king. And he once again held his head up high when he walked down Broadway – as often as not with the show's new junior female lead Jinx Falkenburg, a few years later to be one of show business's most exciting glamour figures.

There were rumours that they were about to marry and Al was quite clearly flattered to be seen in public with her and the posse of dogs she usually had around her.

Once more, he enjoyed the tricks he had always played on Broadway before. Once more, he threw away the book and once more he managed to infuriate other people.

He and Jessel crossed swords on the Shubert stage just as they had nine years before. This time it was not over Jessel himself but a girl he was taking out. Jessel was having an affair with a chorus girl and had arranged to meet her after a performance of *Hold on to your Hats.* He sat in the stalls and waited and waited and. . .

While the rest of the audience were thrilled beyond measure and while everyone in the company was obviously delighted to just sit down at the back of the stage and listen,

Jessel was going crazy. Finally, he marched on to the stage, took his girl by the hand and walked out with her.

'I had a dame and Jolson was holding her up,' he told me, 'What did he expect me to do?'

But Jolson seemed happy. On 28 December 1940, a Los Angeles judge gave Ruby her final decree and he didn't mind any more. It had taken a year and two days. Jolson promised to pay her $400 a week for herself and Al Junior.

Not long afterwards, the amount was changed to a lump sum payment of $50,000. Ruby had married a real-estate magnate called John Lowe. The cruel part of this marriage was that Al Junior's name was changed to John Lowe Junior.

Al felt he had been hurt so much by the lack of affection from the boy that he did not want to fight it. When he had asked the boy to come to see the show his mother had forbidden him to do so.

To console himself, he took Jinx wherever he went – to the races, to Lindy's, to nightclubs. Rumours of romance grew stronger and the talk was of a new Jolson marriage. But it never happened. *Hold on to your Hats* was all the romance he wanted and his loving audience appeared to be giving him what was needed.

He even managed to settle his own part of the suit with the Summit Hotel Company over the Shell broadcast, by offering four tickets for the show to Leo Heyne, the proprietor. As far as he was concerned the radio libel had been forgotten – with all the recent libels on his career.

But five months after the show's opening came a cruel blow. He caught a severe chill and was rushed to hospital with suspected pneumonia. The show that had delighted him and had thrilled the Broadway audience just as of old had to close.

Jolson went to Florida in a state of acute depression. He insisted that Eppy stay with him, and talked to him night after night about his wasted life – just as he had to Harry Akst a year before.

'Success is great,' said Al. 'But does anyone love me?'

It floored Eppy. But it was the truth. In recent months, Al

had felt the warmth of love from afar. But there was none for him by his own fireside.

In July 1941, the show revived in Atlantic City. The local critics and the public loved *Hold on to your Hats*. But Al thought his voice was leaving him. His old fear of the stage had returned. For the first time in his life, he installed microphones in the theatre in which he appeared.

He sang with all the old gusto – new songs like 'Don't Let It Get You Down' and 'She Came, She Saw, She Can-canned' and old ones like 'Hello, My Baby', 'Alexander's Ragtime Band' – and his own songs like 'Mammy', 'Sonny Boy', and 'California Here I Come'.

But if the will were there – and sometimes it wasn't – the ability was missing. Again he was taken ill and again the show was forced to close. This time for good.

Al was more unhappy than he had been for years. And to make things worse, Harry was suing him again. He claimed that back in 1934, Al had agreed to pay him $150 a week to keep him out of the theatre and away from the Jolson name. He had paid for three years but had stopped doing so in 1937.

Harry was down on his luck. He had been trying to sell insurance – with about as much success as he had had on the stage – and he needed the money. He claimed $25,000.

Supreme Court Justice Samuel H. Hofstafter thought otherwise and dismissed the claim summarily. He said it had been a verbal contract and was 'repugnant to the statute of frauds, and could not be enforced in the courts'.

But his victory did not make Al any happier. The battle in the court was won – the fight in his family continued.

Eleven

Don't Forget the Boys

THE WORLD'S GREATEST ENTERTAINER was fast becoming a subject for the nostalgia columns in America's newspapers and magazines.

He continued to go racing, continued to make outrageous bets and to score equally outrageous coups on the track. He was on the air regularly on his own show and as the guest attraction on other people's.

But there were no more offers from Hollywood and when he threw in suggestions to his friends in the big studios, no one took much notice. The only stage work offered to him was the occasional benefit concert – and these were getting fewer, too.

What Jolson missed in idolatry on the stage, he tried to make up with his own bravado. He took it upon himself to be a father figure for other entertainers – some of whom appreciated it and some who did not. He was once on a benefit bill with Caesar Romero when the Latin star's joke on stage fell completely flat.

Jolson went up to him, 'You didn't tell that story right, son,' he said. 'You should have had more feeling in it and told it like this. . .'

Ruby was never completely out of his mind, but he found solace in the pretty girls he would always have around him. He always sent them flowers, booked tables at the best restaurants and always wore an immaculately-pressed suit. The man who had been the toast of Broadway now looked like a thousand other successful businessmen.

He gained a reputation as a charming escort. When he took a girl out more than once, he would tell her what dress to wear on their next date.

Nor did he restrict his advice to day wear. One Hollywood beauty of the time says that when she visited the Jolson home she would be shown into the bedroom where a magnificently expensive night gown and negligée would be lying on the bed. 'It's yours,' Jolie told her 'if you. . .'

But out of the public gaze Jolson was miserable. At the Hillcrest Country Club, the mostly Jewish haunt of the California showbiz set, he would buttonhole the other members and engage them in conversation.

People he wasn't prepared to acknowledge a few years before, when he was at the top, were now invited to share the latest Jolson joke. But the club's regulars like Jack Benny noticed that he was frequently alone.

'You'd see him in the corner by himself, looking very dejected,' Jack Benny recalled to me.

The Hillcrest and everyone else in the entertainment business were writing him off as a backnumber.

Early in December 1941, Al was in New York. He had made some business plans, had gone to see his lawyer and had talked to the people at CBS.

On Sunday mornings he would go out for long walks down to Broadway, the scene of his old triumphs. He managed the thought that it was perhaps rather nice to be able to walk down Broadway on a peaceful morning, with few other people around and no one to bother him for an autograph.

He was just getting ready for one of these pilgrimages to the past, when he asked Eppy to make him some coffee. While he waited, he turned on the radio in his hotel suite. He was just in time to hear the announcer break in with a news flash. Like everyone else listening to the programme that morning on 7 December 1941, he froze. It had just been announced that the Japanese had attacked Pearl Harbour.

Al walked down the ghostly deserted streets and thought. He came back to the Sherry Netherlands Hotel and made the decision that was profoundly to affect his life. He picked up

[201]

the telephone in his suite and dialled the White House.

Al Jolson was enlisting. And he was going to the top to do it. The operator put him through to Mr Stephen T. Early, personal secretary to President Roosevelt.

'This is Al Jolson, Mr Early,' he said. 'Those boys fighting the Japanese and Germans are going to need some entertaining. Well . . . I entertain better than anyone else. Get me to them.'

Mr Early was not able to offer much more than the familiar cry from unimpressed impresarios, 'Don't call us – we'll call you.'

But Al made sure that his agent William Morris would have more luck than others. In New York Morris himself, and in Los Angeles, Abe Lastfogel were both given Mr Jolson's personal instructions to get him overseas.

When Al went back to Washington to see his father – now in his late eighties – his step mother and his half sister and brothers, they noticed how Al had changed. He was no longer the cocky all-conquering success, he was visibly worried. They were also surprised to note just how frequently he was coming to Washington now.

But there were no gilt-edged invitations to the White House and he appeared more concerned to lobby the Congressmen than to see the old folks at home.

On Capitol Hill he'd talk to every senator who would see him. He would call at all the Armed Services' headquarters. And always with the same message, 'My name's Jolson and I sing. Let me sing to the boys. I'll pay my own fare.'

Finally, the War Department gave him the green light. They had just formed a new group called the United Services Organisation – USO. It had been set up to send entertainers to the battle zones – and Al could be the first to go under their plan.

Al didn't merely say thank you to the civil servant who phoned him, he sang it. If they had been in the same room together, he would have got down on one knee – and kissed him.

One of the first places to which Jolson was shipped was

Alaska. He had been given about a dozen shots before they let him leave for the frozen North with his old friend and accompanist, Martin Fried.

The broad facts of the trip Jolson told to *Variety*: 'We arrived in Anchorage at 9 pm, Anchorage time, and stayed at the Westward Hotel. When they told me to observe the blackout regulations and put my lights out, I had to laugh, for in this part of Alaska at midnight it is so light you can thread a needle on Main Street.

'We gave two performances in Anchorage – each to an audience of 1,500 soldiers. Each show lasted an hour and I almost wore the knees out of my pants singing 'Mammy'. But 'Mammy' really got a workout the next day when Fried and I gave nine shows – each of an hour's duration.'

What was missing from Jolson's own story of that Alaskan trip was the drama of this fifty-six-year-old in a private's uniform getting over to 1,500 men at one sitting.

These troops were warned that a great star was coming to see them. Rumours swept the camp that it was going to be Lana Turner. Counter rumours spelled out the name Dorothy Lamour. When Al Jolson was introduced the disappointment could be measured in decibels. But he arrived on stage cheerfully enough. 'Hello boys – I'm Al Jolson,' he called. 'You'll see my name in the history books.'

Someone laughed and then the vibrations of the laughter carried from seat to seat, row to row, like a falling pack of cards. When he heard the troops laughing, Al laughed and proceeded to tell another joke – and then another. The jokes got dirtier, the laughter grew louder and then suddenly someone called for a song.

Al gave them what they asked for. He chatted about home, told them what he thought of Hitler and Hirohito and was swamped by their whistling applause.

For the first time in years Al Jolson had found an audience. And the audience had discovered Al Jolson.

It could be wrong to describe this as the Winter Garden reborn. Not even in *Sinbad* had Jolson had an audience quite like this. As he joked in Alaska, 'You either stay here and listen to me or get buried by a hundred feet of snow. You've got no place else to go.'

But it was instantly obvious that most of the men in that audience would willingly have forsaken a sundrenched beach for just one chance to hear a performance like this again.

When the War Department had heard how Jolson had got through to the men, the USO were asked for more shows like it and Al was asked to do as many of them as he could.

He had established a new relationship with his audiences and they liked it as he liked them. It was as if he appreciated for the first time what it had been to be unwanted. He now relished the way he was able to get through to this new generation of admirers.

He refused to wear any badges of rank – and he insisted that priority be given at all his shows to enlisted men. 'The officers can stand at the back – if there's room,' he'd call.

He travelled from base to base by Jeep. In Europe he would stop a couple of men in the street and say, 'Hello, I'm Al Jolson – from the USA. If you don't believe me – I'll sing for you.' And he did. For two men on a street corner, there was a private performance of anything up to half a dozen numbers.

General George Marshall heard about these performances and decided that Al Jolson deserved campaign medals.

It was while on the first Alaskan tour that Jolson set a precedent he was to follow for the rest of the war. One young soldier called out to him, 'Kiss my wife for me when you get back to New York, will yer Al?'

'I'll do better than that,' Al called after him. 'I'll take her out to dinner. What's her name?'

The name was shouted and Al wrote it down with her telephone number. 'Any more?' he called. And almost 1,500 names and phone numbers were called out in chorus.

'I'll write down those I can – and I'll call them when I get back.'

And he did. No sooner was he back in his New York hotel than he started his dialling operations, 'Hello, Mrs Schwartz?

Sammy sends his love.' 'Oh, Mrs Murphy? I was talking to your Michael yesterday. Yeh – in Alaska. My name . . . oh, Al Jolson.'

From Alaska he was sent to the steaming jungles of Trinidad – singing the same songs and telling the same jokes.

He always tried to get into the spirit of the performance he was giving. He'd wear the same uniform all the time – although he sometimes donned a tam-o-shanter lent him by a Scottish soldier and he seemed happier than he had been for a long time.

But something happened in one base that first sent him into a mood of deep depression. Harry Akst had joined him now as accompanist and it was clearly a happy arrangement. The two men had become fast friends in the pre-war jungle of show business that was trying to exclude Jolson, and they had developed what was almost a telepathic relationship.

Akst was at the piano when Al called for requests at the first show. 'Swanee' called a youngster with a Southern accent as dark brown as his skin.

'You heard him, professor,' said Al. 'Don't let's keep the man waitin'.'

The piano sounded the first chords and Al got into the rhythm of the tune. He reached the chorus. 'The folks up north . . . will . . . see me no more . . . when I get to that Swanee . . . shore.' But the word shore didn't sound right. Jolson did a second chorus just to convince himself – and the same thing happened. He just couldn't reach the high notes any more – the notes he had regarded as his own trademark.

Back at the hotel where they were staying that night Al decided it was all over. 'I can't sing, Harry. And if I can't even sing "Swanee" I'm finished.'

'What yer talking?' Akst answered. 'Sure you can sing – only the high notes are a bit difficult. So forget 'em. Who worries about high notes? Crosby doesn't – and he's doing all right. That sort of singing went out with vaudeville anyway. Nobody wants high notes any more.'

So at that moment Jolson decided to forget about high

notes – and concentrate on a voice that was sounding decidedly better the lower in register that it got.

The people out front did not mind, in fact they liked it. More than that, they appreciated this supposedly 'dated' style.

Jolson and Akst toured all the US bases in the Caribbean, getting hotter and stickier, but with Al enjoying every round of applause that came to him.

The USO flew him to England and Northern Ireland. Again the men were eating out of his hands. He told them what he had told their fathers about English beer – 'it should have been put back into the horse' – and again sang 'Avalon', 'April Showers', 'Mammy' and whatever they wanted.

But he made it a practice never to sing 'Sonny Boy' – unless he couldn't get away without it. 'I found too many guys crying for their own Sonny Boys,' he explained afterwards. 'And they've got enough to worry about.'

But England was not the happiest place for Jolson during the war. He was in a party of USO players which also included Merle Oberon and Patricia Morrison and before very long it was plain that they were not getting along too well together.

It was altogether a very unpleasant trip. Merle Oberon and the others constantly complained that Jolson wanted to be treated as the leader of the party – a role to which none of the group was willing to assign him. Al tried to get himself booked into Britain's own temple of variety, the London Palladium. There wasn't enough interest to guarantee the kind of house Al demanded even in those days from civilian audiences.

Al had always been insecure. That was why he needed to be treated like that Roman emperor. Now that he had lost his laurel-wreath crown, he could only think of the negative parts of his life – and, truthfully, it was all pretty negative. No non-military people wanted to hear him. No woman wanting to share his bed for his own sake – or for the sake of a ring.

Everything about this trip made him unhappy.

Also, London and the Savoy Hotel where they were staying

were a bit too civilised for the new Jolson. He was now used
to living in a tin hut with just a bunk for a bed. In a luxury
hotel he liked to be swamped by admirers – and no one in
England seemed to recognise him. His only happy moment
was when he bumped into Ralph Reader and was able briefly
to relive their days at the Winter Garden. 'They were great
days, English,' Al said with a tear in his eye. 'Great days.' He
feared he would never see their like again.

Every evening he could be seen pacing the floor of the
hotel entrance hall, just walking up and down, head bent
low, hands in his pockets.

He entertained groups of civilians in an air-raid shelter.
'You know why I'm in the shelter?' he joked. 'It's not that I'm
scared – but I'd look awful silly singing "Mammy" with just
one arm.'

The *New York Times* did a magazine piece about Jolson
entertaining in England. He was always surrounded by
cronies, the writer of the article, S.J. Woolf noted. 'It was as if
he were on Broadway.'

But 'the Broadway atmosphere which pervaded the rooms
did not dispel a feeling of nervous tension which surrounded
the showman in khaki. The Jazz Singer seemed more like a
doughboy waiting the zero hour than a Sonny Boy listening
for the curtain call.

'There were few jokes in his talk. The comedian was
playing a straight part. The lighter side of Army life
apparently had not made much of an impression upon him.
For, like many other comedians, at heart, Jolson is serious
and sentimental.'

Jolson told him why he had made the USO tours – now all
the time accompanied by Harry Akst, 'Some of the places
where those fellows are stationed are not ideal summer or
winter resorts. But the morale is great. As you go around you
can't help comparing this bunch with the bunch in 1918.

'These fellows have their feet firmly on the ground. They
aren't bluffing themselves. When I say this, I'm not handing
out propaganda. I have run up against fellows who kicked
because their food was not served on the finest china . . . I'd

be lying if I said they were all as happy as larks. But all of them want to know how things are going at home and they all feel that it's the things at home that they are fighting for.'

And he also told Mr Woolf, 'When the war started, I felt it was up to me to do something, and the only thing I know is show business.'

In Scotland, Al knew he still had something to offer. British troops as well as Americans sat spellbound listening to all the old numbers. Jolson's old line about the boys in front asking their grandmothers who he was became more relevant than ever. The British troops had never had a chance to hear him in the flesh.

One of them, a young RAF navigator named Harry Wayne, recalled: 'It was the most extraordinary experience. Here was a star we didn't hear every day on the radio, whom I barely knew of suddenly electrifying us all. Afterwards, I went round to see him. He gave me his autograph. I still remember it as one of my greatest moments.'

He went from England to Tunisia, from Tunisia to India. Always with Harry Akst. Always singing the same songs. And always making new friends.

He seemed to spend his life overseas eating nothing but Spam. When he was home he entertained Army, Navy, Marine and Army Air Corps bases all over the country. Again the staple diet was Spam.

But on one occasion the General decided that Jolson couldn't be treated like that. He invited Al to his home for a fried-chicken dinner.

Before he went he asked the General what his driver Micky Rosenberg could expect. The General said that the driver would get the same as all the other men. 'Spam?' Al asked. The General shuffled uncomfortably. 'I'm afraid, General,' said Jolson, 'Micky has to have what I have.' And he did.

In a base at Montgomery, Alabama, he had difficulty in proving to a young coloured private that he really was the man whom he claimed to be. 'OK son, I'll prove it to you.'

He gave the private a complete rendering of 'Mammy'. At the end, the youngster, wide-eyed, held out his hand to Al. 'I believe you *is* Mr Jolson,' he told him.

Later, there was a two-hour performance for the rest of the camp. The commanding general told him, 'You've done a wonderful thing for these men, tonight.'

In 1943 came the big blow. Jolson, the man who had been the first to go overseas and who had spent so much of the past couple of years trying to persuade other stars to follow him, was named by an Army newspaper as one of the performers who were shying away from the China-Burma-India theatre of war.

The paper – *CBI Roundup* – wrote that Jolson had avoided their area because 'the going is too tough'.

Jolson retorted, 'It's a dirty lie. These guys don't know what they're talkin' about. I've just never been booked into that area.' He certainly didn't have it easy.

In Dakar, he was faced with what he described as a 'hell hole'. And to make the point, he added for good measure, 'Dakar is the filthiest hole I have even seen. Every known insect is there breeding with every known other insect.'

Other places were easier – but not on the Jolson constitution. He and Harry Akst flew into South Africa and in Natal gave a series of concerts to military hospital patients. Of the first of these he said, 'I sang all the songs in my repertoire – and then Harry played numbers requested by the sick kids – and how they liked it!' This gives some idea of how long the concert lasted. After a short break, he repeated the performance for more patients.

He noted, 'Then dinner again with the men. Main dish – Spam! Oucha-ma-goucha! Awakened at 4 am. Raining cats and dogs. Ready to span the South Atlantic. But at the last minute the trip was cancelled due to motor trouble. So I gave another show at the hospital for the shut-ins who missed yesterday's shows.'

Jolson reported, nevertheless, 'Noticed a lot of the same faces.'

At dawn Al and Akst finally took off for Dakar. 'At 7 pm, we had dinner. You guessed it – Spam. And for dessert, a substitute for quinine called Atalrin – little yellow pills which Akst mistook for soda mints. They gave him a belly ache, which so far is the only belly-aching he has done. Just had lunch – broiled Spam! We're going to do three shows to-night – one for the officers, and one for the men as well as a radio show. Yes, the work is tough and the going sometimes rough. But compared with the tremendous job the boys are doing, who are we to complain?'

Jolson was a flag-waving patriot and there is no doubt he was genuinely moved by what he saw on those trips.

When he was not singing, Al was buying war bonds. In 1942, he bought the first ticket for the première of *Yankee Doodle Dandy* – the George M. Cohan story with James Cagney. The ticket was worth $25,000 to the cause. Later in the year he bought another – this time for $70,000.

In present-day terms he was a hawk. He regarded Hitler as the man who was personally exterminating not just the Jews – although he felt that deeply enough – but the whole of civilisation. The Allied troops, on the other hand, were the knights in armour who were going to save humanity.

There wasn't a man he met who didn't want to win that war and this impressed him with the same sort of infectious spirit that he himself had once used to infect his audiences. In his whole career there had never been a more reciprocal understanding with the people on the other side of the stage. What he gave out to the people on Broadway was only a fraction of what he delivered in Dakar.

It became all the more evident just how much Jolson was exchanging with his audiences when he made his return trips to the States between overseas tours.

In October 1942 Colgate Tooth Powder launched the *Al Jolson Show* on CBS. Jolson was decidedly unhappy about the new series. And the sponsors were unhappy about him – especially since he constantly referred to the product he was supposed to plug as 'toothpaste'. He was being paid to publicise tooth powder – someone else had the toothpaste account.

When he did name the cleansing agent correctly, he could sometimes be heard in off-mike – and certainly off-script references – to say other than the kindest things about it.

He had Monty Woolley to provide class to the series and there was Carol Bruce for the glamour and the female singing. She also provided Jolson with company outside the studio. He gave her the full treatment. There were flowers and always a note telling her what to wear. But it never blossomed into a long-standing romance. Sometimes he was a little too fresh for her liking. Nor could he get Ruby out of his mind.

Only overseas was he visibly happy again. He felt he had something in common with boys who had left their wives and sweethearts behind. In America he felt lonely and deprived.

The day before Al flew out to Miami – where his plane was to leave for Algiers – he received an urgent message to ring Mrs Mamie Eisenhower. She had heard that Jolson was going to meet her husband and wondered if he would be kind enough to deliver a note for him.

'Sure, honey,' he told her over the phone. 'What do you want me to say?'

And over the phone, Mamie dictated the note, 'Dear Ike: Al will give you this note and give you a sweet kiss from me – and also a swift kick, too, because you haven't written for so long.'

In Algiers, there were special orders for the singer to be taken to the General's headquarters. 'What do you know, Al?' asked Eisenhower. 'I've got a message for you, General,' he replied – and showed him the note. 'Well,' said Ike, 'when you get back home give Mrs Eisenhower back that kiss. As for the other. . .' he bent down, lifted up the flap of his jacket and instructed Jolson to carry out his wife's bidding.

On this trip life was harder than Jolson had ever known it in his life. In Sicily and Italy, he followed the advancing Allied troops through the 'hell and mud'. He made more tours of the other European bases. But he felt warmly rewarded.

In 1943, the *New Yorker* magazine reported in its diary, 'We've just heard from a soldier who was fortunate enough to be on hand at one of the entertainments presented before the troops in Ireland by Al Jolson and some of the other performers from the States.

'Jolson, our soldier reports, concluded the entertainment with what was obviously considered to be the best number in his repertoire.

'It was "Brother Can You Spare A Dime?" – and Jolson gave it, as the show people say, everything.

'No other happening in recent weeks has given us such a sense of this significant moment in history.'

On Jolson's fourth overseas trip – this time extended 42,000 miles as far as Karachi and back and entertaining 400,000 American troops on the way – he was giving sometimes four shows a day.

He was the talk of the entertainment industry – many of whom were content to keep him as far away from the home market as possible. The big money was in films and films were definitely not being made with the men at the front in mind. Some of the younger singers, who were anxious to keep their reputations intact, went out on one short USO trip and quickly came back – before the people at home had forgotten them.

When one famous Hollywood actor had to be commissioned as a captain before he would leave to entertain at military bases, George Jessel quipped, 'If that's the basis on which commissions are granted, then Al Jolson should be commissioned as a fort.'

In the South Pacific, Jolson sang, 'Is It True What They Say About Dixie?' and had boys from the Deep South begging for more. In New Guinea he sang 'Give My Regards To Broadway' and one of the soldiers out front wrote home, 'As he sang, I felt as though I were back in New York. Only a short time ago, New York seemed as if it were a million miles away. Then along comes Al Jolson and he drops the city right into my lap – Empire State Building and all – Boom!'

His audiences were adoring him more than ever now. When he had first gone to a military establishment he had been greeted with derision. Now the men in the forward positions knew what to expect. For them, he did not even

[212]

have to sing – although he did. Just being with him was enough.

While in North Africa the men out front thrust papers in his hand begging for autographs. He signed everything shown him – official passes and even the five-franc scrip notes that were common currency of the time.

The only thing one young soldier could find for Jolson to sign was an American $10 bill. Al took it and then gave it back to the youngster in khaki – unsigned. 'Son – my autograph isn't worth tying up this much dough. Invest it in War Bonds.' He then found a five-franc note from his own pocket, scribbled the name Al Jolson all over its face and thrust it into the gaping hands held out in front of him. 'Here, sergeant,' he called. 'This is on the house.'

Jolson, meanwhile, made speech after speech, begging the entertainers who had so far held back to come out and perform for the troops. 'Quit the Battle of the Brown Derby,' he implored, in an obvious reference to the Hollywood restaurant where the stars would meet to discuss the war and their jobs. There was a new respect for Jolson among everyone who knew of his work. When they joked about him, and particularly about his age, it was all in good heart. 'Al did a fine job in the war,' Joe E. Lewis quipped a few years later on, 'at least – until the Confederates captured him.'

On a brief spell back in the States between his Far East tours, the reality of his loneliness struck home. Because he and Harry Akst shared the same hotel suite they both gave up the privacy most men need from time to time.

Akst realised too late how much he needed this privacy. He was phoning his wife when he looked over into the corner of the room and caught Jolson – just sitting, looking out of the window with tears rolling down his cheeks.

'What's the matter, Jolie?' the pianist called, interrupting his conversation.

'Nothing,' he replied. 'It's just that I realise you've got someone to come home to,' Al answered. 'Who've I got? Who cares whether I live or die? Not a soul in the world.'

Occasions like that made Jolson realise the need to get

back to his audience as soon as possible. Another trip was being planned when, in October 1943, Al stood in an hotel lobby in New York reading a newspaper. Suddenly the type in front of him became blurred, the room turned over and over and everything went blank.

Several days later he woke up – in hospital, shielded from the rest of the room by the loose plastic covering of an oxygen tent.

He had picked up two bugs overseas. One was a recurrence of his old trouble – audience fever. The other was malaria. This time it was obvious that malaria had been the stronger of the two. Before long, it had turned into pneumonia, and for more than a fortnight Al was on the danger list.

After being discharged, he walked out of the hospital feeling so shaky that he wondered if he would ever get up before an audience again. Eppy was with him, so was Harry Akst, so was Martin Fried.

'Get me on the next plane to Europe,' he shouted at them. 'I've got to get back to my boys.' The friends gave Al a glass of lemonade and told him to relax.

There weren't going to be any more overseas tours, they insisted. And Al had better realise it. What they didn't realise was that they were dealing with Jolson. He had discovered again what it was like to be worshipped by an audience, and it was a religion he didn't want to see dying out too quickly.

It was quite clear that Al wanted to continue to work. It was equally clear that none of the old openings were available to him any more.

There was the occasional radio appearance – usually on a programme for war workers like his brother Harry, who was to spend four years on the assembly line at an aircraft factory.

But no one was offering Al the chance to sing before live audiences, or even before the cameras – especially, before the cameras. Hollywood just didn't want to know about him as a performer.

'Take it easy now,' the studio bosses told him truthfully. 'Enjoy yourself.' But that was something Al Jolson had never really learned how to do on his own in front of an audience.

[214]

He became more and more unhappy. He knew he was weak, but he knew, too, that he would become weaker still if he didn't have a new opportunity soon to recharge his batteries. And the fact that he had no social life only served to make him feel doubly inadequate.

At the Hillcrest Country Club he searched for new ways to make friends. And here the Jolson ingenuity succeeded where his jokes had failed. The talking point of the club was the fact that the war had struck from the menus their principal delight – sturgeon. Most of the club members like Benny, Burns and Jessel were sturgeon devotees. So was Jolson. But only Jolson knew how to break the embargo the State of California had imposed on this delicacy being brought across their lines.

Al had a friend in New York who could get hold of sturgeon and by various diverse means get it through to California. Every week, a parcel addressed to Mr Al Jolson would arrive at the Hillcrest brought by a refrigerated truck.

'Want a piece of sturgeon?' Al would call and his friends would come running.

'We know when Jolie was doing well again,' Burns joked to me. 'We didn't get any more sturgeon.'

Meanwhile, Al had at last found himself a job. An old admirer, Harry Cohn, boss of Columbia Pictures, invited him to become a producer. Columbia was the studio that was steadily making a fortune for itself with Rita Hayworth pictures.

Al was told he was to work on a picture called *Burlesque*. He was called producer and was advised that he was to supervise everything that went into the film. But before long he realised he wasn't doing very much.

They also hinted he was going to work on his own life story, but were not yet ready to commit themselves.

Sometimes he just sat in the studio – thinking. His depressions were frequently acute. At other times he was able to laugh at his new predicament. 'I had an office with couches and beds in it,' he told a group of his cronies at a lunch at the Hillcrest. 'For months, nobody called me. One day, the phone finally rang and I answered, all excited. A voice said – "Is that Shapiro, the plumber?"'

And with more than a touch of irony he told them about the big studio happening of the day. 'One of the other producers liked his men to laugh at all the jokes he told. And every one of those employees always did. Except today when one man didn't laugh. "Why aren't you laughing?" the producer asked this man. "Oh," he replied. "I'm leaving on Saturday."'

If Jolson could have told Harry Cohn he was leaving Columbia on the Saturday, he would have been equally delighted. The only thought was that he had nowhere else to go.

He rang the USO offices again and demanded that they find him more work. 'I want to go overseas and I want to go soon,' he thundered. But he had to agree he would never pass the rigorous medical inspections that were now compulsory before anyone was allowed to play at a base abroad.

'How about touring our hospitals?' he was finally asked. Once more Al could have kissed the receiver.

For a start, there would be a tour of the West and of the Deep South – and again Al was happy. He was doing the only work he ever wanted to do – and of course singing to an audience who really wanted to see and hear him.

He felt he was getting through to the sick boys even better than their doctors were. And he was finding new admirers in the nursing and medical staff, too. At the Eastman annexe of the Army Hospital at Hot Springs, Arkansas, he was mobbed by autograph hunters – when he finally decided to stop singing. There was nothing new in that. But on this occasion, one of his admirers made a deep impression.

Twelve

That Wonderful Girl of Mine

SHE WASN'T EXACTLY PETITE. Neither was she tall. Her hair was dark and it fell down to her shoulders. And as she flashed her white teeth in the crowd gathering around Jolson that night late in 1944, there was something about her that made Al smile, too.

She was wearing a white coat in a sea of white coats. And like the girls around her she giggled when the Jolson mock-Southern twang made a speedy quip about Arkansas hospitality.

'That was a cute little one,' Al mentioned to Harry Akst as they climbed into their khaki-coloured staff car outside the hospital.

'We'd better get some gas,' said Akst and directed the car towards the filling station just outside the hospital perimeter. As the car stopped, Al got out to stretch his legs and breathe the still warm air. They were on their way to Texas, but there was something about this last stop that made him want to linger a little longer in Arkansas.

The colonel in charge of the hospital was there, too, and Jolson took the opportunity of asking him to authorise a new batch of fuel coupons to cover the next stage of the journey.

As Jolson and the colonel talked, he noticed the brunette from the crowd a few minutes earlier shyly edge towards them. She had an autograph book in her hand.

'Would you write your name for me, Mistah Jolson?' she asked.

The way she posed the question was music to Al's ears. It was as though she had asked him to sing 'April Showers'.

'Sure, honey,' Jolson replied and gave her the sort of big wink he usually reserved for his audiences. In fact, as far as he was concerned, in this pretty little girl was a whole audience condensed specially for his use.

'What shall I write?' he asked her.

'Oh, just say to Erle.'

'How's that?'

'Erle-E-R-L-E,' she spelled.

Harry called from the driver's seat of their car, 'We're ready, Al.'

''Bye, honey,' Jolson said as he walked to his car.

'Nice kid,' said Harry as they drove off. 'Sure was,' Al mused. 'Erle. . .'

He talked about her incessantly all through the drive to Texas. When he checked into his hotel in the Lone Star State, her image was still before him.

He and Harry played cards but still he couldn't get her out of his mind. 'Funny thing,' he told his pianist friend, 'I haven't thought about Ruby all day.'

The two men went to bed at about 3 o'clock in the morning, but Jolson couldn't sleep. Finally, after about an hour of tossing and turning, he switched on his bedside light and dialled the long-distance operator.

'Get me the Eastman Hospital Annexe at Hot Springs, Arkansas,' he told her. 'Personal call to the base commander.'

The name Al Jolson was once again important enough to be passed to the colonel at any time even in the middle of the night.

'What is it, Mr Jolson?' the colonel asked trying not to sound too sleepy.

'Sorry to wake you, colonel,' Al replied. 'But you see it's like this. That pretty gal we were talkin' to last night. Think I might have a job for her in pictures. What was her name?'

The colonel said he didn't know. 'But I'll get it for you. Want to hang on?'

'Please,' said Jolson and waited.

The colonel woke up a captain who in turn got a clerk on to it. Within a short time the colonel had his answer.

'Mister Jolson? The girl's name is Erle Galbraith. She's an X-ray technician out here. A civilian.'

'Thanks, colonel,' Al said, jotting down her name on the pad beside his telephone. 'Yes – Erle.' And with that he was at last able to sleep. When he awoke, Al hurried through dressing and eating his breakfast and got to the writing desk in his hotel suite.

'Dear Erle,' he wrote, 'I think your face is a natural for the flickers.' And he offered her a stock contract at $100 a week. Just to put the record straight, he emphasised he was not in love with her. But that wasn't quite true.

He heard nothing for several days – although he still couldn't get Erle out of his mind. But then there was a call from a Los Angeles lawyer asking if he could come and see Jolson.

An appointment was made at the Beverly Hills Hotel and the lawyer turned up, shook hands and told him how much he had always admired Jolson at work. 'You haven't come here to tell me that, have you?' Al stressed. 'What do you want?'

The lawyer said he had some dear friends in Arkansas by the name of Galbraith. They had asked him to call on the singer to ask for more details about the offer he had made to their daughter. They didn't know he had become a movie producer but, even if they had, it wouldn't have been enough. Old men who made that sort of proposition usually had a different course of action in mind.

'Of course I'm serious,' Al told the lawyer.

'Well, Mr Jolson,' came the reply, 'it would be most unfortunate if you were throwing a curve.'

The language was more polite than Johnny Irish had used nearly twenty years before, but somehow the message seemed the same. But it didn't worry Al any more now than it had then.

His mind was made up. He wrote to Erle and told her to come straight out to the West Coast. In the letter he told her exactly which train to catch. The train arrived in Los Angeles eight hours late, but Al was there to meet her.

A bevy of Columbia executives were hovering in the background at the same time. For this girl, he told them, was going to be the new Rita Hayworth — 'and with a voice like an angel'.

When she demurely stepped down on to the station platform, Al was delighted at the sight before him. She was as beautiful as he had remembered her. The studio man next to him smiled, equally appreciatively, as Al nudged him in the ribs.

'Hello, honey,' Al said as he welcomed her and gave her a fond peck on the cheek. 'How have you been?'

'Mistah Jolson,' she replied, 'ah've been just fine.'

The man from Columbia looked at Al and Al looked at him. The truth of the matter was that Al hadn't remembered at all what this 'angel's' voice sounded like. But having heard it now, he knew pretty well what Harry Cohn would say when he heard it.

A screen test had been arranged for the following day and Cohn was waiting to see it. He respected Jolson's judgment and knew a man of his experience would be unlikely to sell him a pup. The test turned out the way Al expected — Erle had a face made for the movies, and a voice that quite obviously wasn't.

'I was quite floored by that Southern drawl,' Al said later. 'But I had only to take one look at that kisser, that little face and those big dark eyes . . . I knew with a dialect like that she would never stand a chance on the screen though. So I thought I'd better marry the poor kid.'

To make her feel better, Jolson used his influence to line up a couple of small non-speaking parts at Twentieth Century Fox. And with the euphoria of this new career before her, Al popped the question.

'Sure, I'm old enough to be your grandfather,' he told her. 'But I love yer.'

Erle was twenty-one. Al was sixty. As he expected, she turned him down. But she mentioned the proposal to her parents, who were prosperous, respected conservative people in Little Rock. Erle's uncle was General Claire

Chennault, the Flying Tigers hero of the China front, and the family were very proud of this connection. For their Erle to marry a singer who was older than they were themselves was quite out of the question.

While the Galbraiths – mom, pop and the elder brother, an Army sergeant – were discussing the audacity of the proposal, Al Jolson was being rushed to hospital. His malaria had struck again but this time the doctors noted a malignancy in the lung.

They decided there was only one way to save his life – although they were making no guarantees – and that was to cut a hefty slice off his left lung. To reach the lung, two ribs had to be chopped away too.

When Al recovered sensibility several days later, he pondered what the effect of the operation would have on a singer. 'I'll never sing again,' he told his nurse – and refused to see anyone. To Jolson the thought that he would never sing again was worse than a death sentence. His doctor said he would pull through. But to Al it seemed a promise of living death.

He just lay in the big white hospital bed and thought about the past, about the future and about what might have been. He decided not to think about Erle.

When he eventually condescended to allow them in, his visitors – Eppy, Harry Akst, his step brothers – came to offer good cheer but nothing any of them said could break him from the ever-mounting depression. But one visitor managed it.

Erle walked into the hospital room, sat by his bed and gradually got him to smile. She also managed to bring him back to thinking about a future that perhaps would not be as cloudy as he had feared. Before she left the room Al had proposed again – and this time she had accepted.

There was still a drainage tube in his back and he had to have injections to help him keep his mind on things. 'But I felt like a kid of sixteen,' he recalled afterwards. 'I knew I was head over heels in love.'

Al went to Palm Springs to convalesce. There, he wrote a

letter to Mr Galbraith asking for his daughter's hand in marriage. The father's letter came back by special delivery. 'You are old enough to be my daughter's father,' it said. The idea was preposterous.

Al told Erle what her father had written. 'I'll go home and see him,' she promised. 'I can twist Daddy around my finger.' This was exactly what she did and on 23 March 1945, just as the World War in which Jolson had fought as hard as any combat soldier was coming to an end, Al and Erle were married by a justice of the peace at Quartzite, Arizona. This time Moses Yoelson was not told of his son's marriage. In fact he hadn't even been told about his operation. The cantor was ninety years old and his own health was failing rapidly.

Together the Jolsons took a bigger suite at the Palm Springs hotel where Al had been convalescing, and moved in. But Erle wanted a real home. She had heard of a ranch-style house on the market that could have been built for them.

'It was,' said Al. The house which was being vacated by Don Ameche was the one Al had built after his marriage to Ruby. He had sold it by auction after the divorce. And as Erle said, it was ideal for them – although the memories were at first painful. But there was something about his new young wife that brought those memories into clearer perspective.

Ruby had wanted Al for herself but had the consolation of her own glittering career. Erle didn't want a career. She was only concerned with being with Al by the swimming pool during the day, or knitting socks for him as he gently sang to her in the evenings.

'Why don't you sing again in the movies?' she asked him with the naïvety of youth.

'But I can't sing any more – you know that.'

'You're singing now, aren't you?'

'Yeh – but this isn't the sort of singing I used to do on the stage. I need strength for that.'

She continued to knit and Al continued to hum. Could he have the strength to start singing professionally again? The suggestion pleased him.

Unknown to Erle, he had been doing some experiments with his voice. Somehow it wasn't the same voice he used to have – but it wasn't just that he couldn't hit the high notes. As he grew older he could accept that his voice had grown deeper. However after the operation, it had vanished. Now, though, it was coming back – at least four keys deeper than it had been before surgery and, although he wouldn't tell Erle this, he liked the sound of what he heard.

Milton Berle made Al the star guest on his weekly radio show and for the first time the new Jolson voice, singing the old songs, was heard in public.

'I'm not too strong now,' Al told his host, 'but they've promised me when I'm feeling a little better they'll let me go to Tokyo to sit in Emperor Hirohito's palace. And there I'll sing "Mammy".'

And he added, 'It's only now that I'm playing what you could call the Big Time. Of all the wonderful audiences I've played to in my whole life, the ones that gave me the biggest thrills were thousands of miles away from Broadway – in the jungles of the South Pacific and in the hell and mud of Italy.'

He meant it and the audiences knew he meant it. They quite plainly liked what they heard and the way Jolson sang his songs.

When he returned home he asked Eppy to try to arrange some work for him – a picture or two and perhaps his own radio series again. Yes, he thought, radio was just right. Not too strenuous – just the kind of work he could do.

Erle was right behind him. 'If you're well enough,' she said, 'do what you really like doin'.'

But Eppy came back empty-handed. Kraft cheese were looking for a new star for the Music Hall Jolson had introduced on its first programme all those years ago, but politely they said they didn't think Al was now the man for the job. He wasn't all that well and they didn't want to overtax him – besides, Crosby and Sinatra and young Perry Como were the voices bringing in the money now.

It was all true. On every radio station there were the cool, gentle crooning voices of these singers who had been hardly old enough to talk when Jolson was packing the crowds into the Winter Garden.

They were taking their singing nice and easily. No one, however, was giving the same chance to Jolson. He was turned down as every approach was made.

Eventually, however, Warner Brothers came to the rescue – but with something rather different from what Jolson was hoping for. They were planning a biographical picture based on the life of George Gershwin and wanted Al to play himself – singing 'Swanee'.

He was, however, happy to accept – and played the role with all the energy he could summon up, And, when it was all over, he refused to take a fee.

The film was called *Rhapsody in Blue.* But Jolson's part was merely a cameo – and although it gave him a certain satisfaction to be able to appear in blackface again, to stand before a camera once more and, indeed, to sing that song another time – it wasn't quite the same as being invited to take on a new challenge. He wanted to set the Mississippi on fire again and singing 'Swanee' in a biographical film about someone else wasn't really the way to do it.

The director, Irving Rapper was to tell me: 'We never thought he'd make it. Jolson was so ill most of the time, we were afraid Jack Warner would just call it off. But he did it – and how! For us making the picture, it was really the highlight of it all.'

Al knew just how much a highlight it was. In honour of the occasion, he gave Erle a new ring.

Decca Records made up for his disappointment by inviting Al to record 'Swanee' for them. And they plugged it in the film – without mentioning the non-Gershwin flipside, 'April Showers'. But although there was a lot of pep in the 'Swanee' recording – possibly a little too much because it bears a number of tell-tale signs of being deliberately speeded up by the engineers – the 'April Showers' version used a tired old arrangement that did neither Jolson nor the song very much good.

It was Al's first commercial recording for thirteen years and it seemed destined to flop, even though he had been promised five cents for every copy sold.

No one wanted Al Jolson as a star in his own right, and it plainly broke his heart. More than anything, it broke him up to realise that he wasn't showing Erle what he really could do.

'Tell her how great I was,' he'd implore visitors to their home – much as he had wanted Ruby to know of his previous triumphs. But, although Erle constantly reassured him that she did know just what a sensation he had been, he was convinced that she needed confirmation of the fact whenever it was possible.

He couldn't even find a spot on a benefit bill – the kind of show which producers would at one time have gone down on their hands and knees to ask him to appear in. By everyone's standards Al Jolson was now washed up. Erle asked him to allow her to help – by turning his despair into serenity. But the depressions came to the top all too often.

Then suddenly everything changed. The renaissance came unexpectedly – just when Jolson seemed resigned to his life of obscurity.

Thirteen

Me and My Shadow

IT WAS IN 1943 THAT the idea first hit Sidney Skolsky – soon after he himself had been hit by Al Jolson!

They were at a boxing match and Jolson saw the columnist sitting at the ringside. With one swoop the singer hit Skolsky's jaw and told him that was just the sort of treatment he could expect for printing such scandalous stories about him.

Skolsky was adamant that another columnist had written the item. It hadn't even appeared in any of the papers that were served by his column. Al was deeply apologetic. It was, he agreed, a case of mistaken identity.

The confrontation, far from souring the feeling between the two men, somehow only seemed to heighten Skolsky's long-standing idolatry of Jolson. And it planted the seeds of his big idea.

He had always been known as one of those writers on the Hollywood scene who played with vague notions and turned them into wild extravaganzas, who treated a thought like a baker treats a piece of dough. He didn't merely have an idea, he played with it, rolled it around and shaped it.

His idea was to adapt the story of Al Jolson to the screen and as a result there would be a film that would create interest and enthusiasm all over the free world. For it had everything a picture needed – colour, escapism and music. This, he felt, was his best idea yet. It had all the ingredients that people were now seeking as the effects of war were beginning to bite for the first time.

There were also none of the problems one frequently met when filming the life of a living person. The kids who bought cinema tickets knew no more about Jolson than they did about the private life of General Tojo – so all sorts of liberties could be taken with the script without anyone noticing.

Nor, he reasoned, could there be any problem about getting a younger actor to play the part. Jolson had not, after all, been seen on the screen for so many years.

So Skolsky – newspaper and magazine columnist and studio writer – started his determined effort to make his own idea a reality. Metro, Warners, Twentieth Century Fox, United Artists – all gave him the same answer, 'Save your breath and we'll save our dollars.'

The polites ones used a phrase Jolson himself had given to an eager Hollywood a generation before, 'You're daffy.' The less polite used altogether different language. Warner Brothers thought the suggestion was just about the most ridiculous idea that had yet been put on a desk in the executive suite.

Skolsky was not merely laughed off the Warner lot at Burbank, he was positively ridiculed. Big moguls chuckled over their champagne glasses at the stupidity of the idea and secretaries spilled coffee over the memos which rejected it.

Briefly, Skolsky had forsaken his column to work in the Warner studios as an assistant to veteran Broadway writer Mark Hellinger who had turned his hand to screenplays. He could, therefore, see the Warner reaction at first hand. Their attitude was that, since he had just made his guest appearance in their own *Rhapsody in Blue* film, they were now convinced that he was a has-been. An interesting has-been perhaps, but a has-been just the same. Even Jack Warner had had to admit it – reluctantly.

The old cliché of the boxing world was dragged out time and again – they don't come back.

Jolson went virtually unnoticed in *Rhapsody in Blue*. More than one theatre billed his name in the list of guest appearances as 'Al Johnson' and the record he had cut of

'Swanee' barely took enough at the music shops to cover the cost of waxing.

Only Columbia Pictures showed any initial interest at all in Skolsky's idea. And that was only when he was a producer for them. When Skolsky came back to them with the idea, Harry Cohn, Columbia's boss, did not laugh. He merely puffed at his huge cigar, muttered a few obscenities and showed Skolsky the door. But that was just what the writer had expected. Cohn was polite to no one. He was the man who had made Grace Moore an overnight hit with *One Night of Love*, and who had turned a seventeen-year-old dancer called Margarita Cansino into a star named Rita Hayworth.

Hollywood respected him because of his undoubted know-how. But everyone at Columbia seemed to fear him — most hated him. He had the reputation for being the hardest man in a city that fed studio chiefs on the broken down careers of lesser mortals. A one-time vaudeville singer who turned song plugger on the way to becoming a Hollywood producer, he was known to be able to reduce some of the toughest villains in town to tears. A smile from Cohn, said some, was worth more than a contract from anyone else.

What Skolsky did not realise was that Harry Cohn was also a Jolson devotee and that that was the soft spot beneath his walnut-hard exterior. In all his years in show business, there had been only one artist who could make Cohn sit back, smile and occasionally cry — and that was Al Jolson. While underlings bowed and scraped to Cohn, Jolson was his idol.

He had liked Skolsky's idea more than he had intended to let on when it was first brought to his notice. But there was one thing he had learned very quickly in business — never appear too eager.

Three months went by without word from Cohn. But then the phone rang on Skolsky's desk — and heralded the start of one of the most celebrated conversations in Hollywood folklore. It was the unmistakable gruff Cohn tone, 'Get your ass over here. You're working on the Jolson picture.'

The phone was put down, Skolsky smiled. The fight was on.

Two men, columnist and studio boss, who shared but one thing – an admiration for Al Jolson – were together in uneasy combat. And there was also Cohn's number-two Sidney Buchman to join in the verbal fisticuffs. He, too, was dedicated to Jolson about as much as he was to the business of making films. This man, who had been born in Duluth, Min., educated at Oxford and worked at the Old Vic in London, had seen Jolson entertain and been tremendously excited by what he saw and heard.

He had written some of the big Hollywood money-spinners like Frank Capra's *Mr Smith Goes to Washington*, which made James Stewart a top name, and had been largely responsible for the success of the Cornel Wilde film about Chopin – *A Song to Remember*. He was to play no small part in making Jolson's tunes songs to remember, too.

With the die cast, only one thing remained before the idea could really take root – to talk to Jolson himself. In all their long negotiations the man who was at the centre of it all had been left almost totally in the dark once the first idea for the film had been abandoned.

The occasional rumour had filtered through to his country retreat, but they were no more than rumours and as such just seemed to feed his constant depression. Jolson knew that Hollywood manufactured rumours as efficiently as it made films – only 1,000 times faster. And the movie capital's rumours were frequently 1,000 times more extravagant than the plot of any picture.

Confirmation that this was more than a rumour came to Jolson when he was in New York. He had a call from Jack Cohn, the producer's elder and generally estranged brother who handled all the organisation's business deals in the East.

To Jolson it was as though it were 1912 again with Jake Shubert asking him to play the lead in the Winter Garden's new show. Al was not just interested, he was already choosing the costumes he was going to wear and the songs he was going to sing. He would be in Hollywood, he said, just as soon as the reservations could be made.

Only once did he have real doubts – when the superstitious side of his nature began wondering if a living entertainer had ever had his life story filmed before. He remembered *Yankee Doodle Dandy* and breathed a sigh of relief. Yes, George M. Cohan had seen his film biography – and died a month later. Jolson swallowed and promptly tried to forget that mere detail. Here was that memorial he had been seeking for so long.

In the 1940s there was only one comfortable way to travel to California from New York and that was by train. Jolson had the best private compartment on the journey. The second best was booked by Jack Warner.

Now the man who had turned down flat any possibility of Warner Brothers handling the story of this has-been felt peeved at the idea of another studio beating him to it.

He now offered Jolson $200,000 for the story rights and specified that he would put the whole production in the hands of Michael Curtiz, who had done such a brilliant job with *Yankee Doodle Dandy*.

Jack also promised Al the Epstein twins, Julius and Philip, who – although their names weren't on the credits – had written *Yankee Doodle Dandy* and who had won an Oscar for the *Casablanca* screenplay.

Years later, Julius Epstein told me: 'I didn't know he made that offer. If he had, we'd have turned it down. We hated Jolson.'

That certainly wasn't the way Jack L. Warner saw him. He still believed that the sun rose and set to the sound of *Mammy* – and now that a competitor was showing interest in a Jolson biography, he was growing steadily more upset that the film could go to any other studio.

What he had not told Al was that he had been for some time planning a remake of *The Jazz Singer*, to mark the twentieth anniversary of talking pictures in 1947. He had already signed Dane Clark for the role and the studio's salesmen were at that very moment telling the nation's exhibitors about it. Now he was willing to drop his plans for the remake and substitute a Jolson biography in its place.

His idea was that, if for any reason – and he knew it would

be impossible – he couldn't star Jolson himself in the movie, he would have Clark in the part. Al was quite tickled with the idea. He liked the feisty young Jewish actor (whom he used to see at the Friday night boxing matches which were as much a religious routine for him as the ceremony welcoming in the Sabbath were to his father and his more Orthodox coreligionists).

Except that before talks could get any further, Warner had a violent row with the turbulent young star – who had already been voted the most promising newcomer in pictures. Clark had almost come to blows with his boss – and now Jack was suspending him from the studio. What was more, he was refusing to allow him to play in any other studio's pictures. He even told Columbia that it should have no ideas in that direction – and let Harry Cohn know that he wouldn't sanction any copies of either Jolson or Dane Clark films being made available to any other operation.

With Clark out of the way, Jack made further overtures to Jolson.

Sure Jolie could play the lead himself – after all, wasn't he a major stockholder in Warner Brothers? It was obviously the right thing to do. This was a company, he stressed, who had a doubly vested interest in wanting a successful film. And, Warner swore, there wasn't a grain of goddam truth that the project had once been offered to his studio and then turned down.

When Jolson booked in at the Beverly Hills Hotel, Skolsky was there waiting for him. Despite his recent association with it, there was only one word the singer had for Columbia – 'crappy'.

He was weakening now to the idea of repeating *The Jazz Singer* success all over again in the studio where both he and the film had made history.

Together Jolson and Skolsky discussed the idea of the new picture as they sat beside the hotel's swimming pool.

Al had taken a small room at the hotel when he first arrived at Beverly Hills. By the time he and Skolsky had finished their first discussions, he and Erle had moved into a bungalow in the grounds. The idea was worth seeing through in comfort.

Jolson admitted that he liked Skolsky's approach when he first contacted Cohn. 'Everybody's making biographical films,' he told Cohn, 'but no one's done one of the king.'

He and Skolsky chewed over and over again the important parts of his life and the ones which would make the best filmed story. Yet from day to day, Jolson varied the stories, contradicting himself with every utterance. Once more he was proving that, as far as he was concerned, there was nothing particularly sacred about the truth.

Skolsky stressed that Columbia were going to make this the big picture of the year. There would be no risk of its being submerged in the midst of a pile of celluloid and gathering dust as it probably would at a bigger studio like Warner Brothers. At Poverty Row, where Columbia was born and expanded into Sunset Boulevard, there was no such risk. For them, there was always one Big Picture, and the Jolson film was going to be that. Besides, Jolson could have half the film's profits.

It was that final clause which, undoubtedly, clinched things. 'Jolson a failure?' Impossible, he thought. If anyone had any doubt, Jolson – now with the ego of the past quickly returning – had none at all.

The Jazz Singer had made him a fortune in a deal that at the time seemed no more certain. What is more, here was the chance to make everyone sit up and take notice. It was the chance he had been waiting for. Not only would he have a good cheque at the end of it all, but he would also have the opportunity once more to do something that was still very much more important than eating – Jolson would be singing. A new public would be hearing the new Jolson voice.

He believed that that voice, with its individual sound, would go down better now that it had before. When Jolson first sang in a high tenor, that was how the audiences wanted it. Rudy Vallee, even Bing Crosby, sang that way when they first stood before the public. But now Jolson had his more robust, deeper style that seemed to be what the bobby-soxers were asking for. And he believed he had something that this new generation had never heard before.

He began to build a new picture of the future. Here was the chance, at last, to sign autographs again – which he never enjoyed but regarded as a necessary symbol of success – to be able to meet youngsters at ballparks or in theatre or cinema lobbies without being forced to say, 'Ask your parents if they remember me,' and wondering if, in fact, any of them really did.

Despite all these dreams, there was still more than a little of the old Jolson business sense left in him. He refused to sign his contract with Columbia until certain amendments had been made.

He wanted, in addition to half the film's profits, $25,000 for recording the songs in the picture. Cohn baulked, muttered more obscenities – and then imagined the scene in New York when his brother Jack heard about the price. Jack Cohn, he knew, would say 'No'. The thought of being able to pass one up on his brother and so prove that he had the better business sense, excited him.

Al, thinking of his last meeting with his own brother Harry, appreciated the beauty of this. The $25,000 clause was added and the picture was on.

Cohn and Jolson had dinner together to celebrate and to talk about old times – the days when the man now known as King Cohn could hardly afford the price of a seat in a theatre where Jolson was playing. The shape the picture would take, or any idea of who was going to play the role, had not yet been discussed.

But the Jolson rumours in Hollywood were mounting and the people who thought they counted on Sunset Boulevard were still laughing. And Jolson smiled as broadly as they laughed. Yet, as the doubts ran like a forest fire through the soundstages, they caught up with him – and he started doubting, too.

Over the previous months, the girl who had constantly picked him up when he was down, who dearly wanted to see him on top the way he had told her he had once been, now shuddered at the thought of a final let-down.

'This is it, baby,' he told Erle. 'I'm going to be great again.'

'Sure you are, Al,' she promised. If wishes came true just by working hard at them, the new Jolson career was born with that one sentence from the wife who had never seen audiences eating out of the palm of his hand.

She had realised soon after their wedding that feeding his ego was going to be as important as feeding his stomach. Now the honeymoon was over. She saw his moments of depression and wanted to see him on top of the world again. Perhaps, she hoped, the time might come when he would never have to beg friends to tell her how great he had been.

Nobody tells a story about Hollywood and its people better than songwriter Sammy Cahn. In his superb book of memories *I Should Care*[*], he recalls the time Al went to a party at Harry Cohn's house – to say one word and wait for the effects of what was really his audition.

Phil Silvers, always a magnificent mimic, played Cohn in a charade he devised for the mogul's pleasure. No one else would have had the effrontery to try it, but on this occasion the star guests were asked to imagine that Cohn was assembling *The Jolson Story* and trying to work out who could play the title role. Jule Styne said he had someone who might do, snapped his fingers, called out 'Boy! Boy!' and the real Al came in. 'This guy couldn't play Jolson's father,' said Silvers, but he agreed that he should be allowed to say one word.

The word was 'Mammy'. Jolson didn't sing it, but it was enough. As Cahn says: 'I've seen Al Jolson at the Winter Garden. I've seen him many, many places. But there was never ever any performance of 'Mammy' as there was that night. Never. Standing, backstage, all those talented people were awestruck. Except, for the benefit of assembled guests, Cohn, alias Silvers. He picked up the telephone, called Twentieth Century Fox and asked to speak to George Jessel. 'Hello, Jessel,' he said. 'You've got to dub this picture. . .'

The evening was notable for another reason, testifies

[*] *I Should Care*, London: W.H. Allen & Co. Ltd, 1975.

Cahn. He says Jolson sidled up to him carrying five pages of yellow legal paper, 'This Sinatra, is he a friend of yours?' Cahn told him he was. 'He'll never have anything like this,' he said – and then pointed to the list of stocks and shares the paper contained. Among them were 10,000 shares of AT and T.

Only a few days later, it looked as though everyone's doubts had turned out the way they either hoped or feared – depending on which side of Harry Cohn's payroll they were. Jolson's malaria returned – with a vengeance. He was rushed to the Cedars of Lebanon Hospital and once more placed in an oxygen tent.

The news was withheld from Cohn by the people who knew they kept their jobs only as long as he kept his temper. When he did eventually hear of Jolson's illness, the patient was already a little better.

Cohn and an aide rushed to the hospital – but not before Jolson had been warned that they were on their way. He persuaded his doctor to provide a pick-me-up. When the men from Columbia walked through the door, Jolson was sitting up with a broad grin on his face and threw his arms out wide to greet his guests as though he were going to sing 'Mammy'.

Cohn walked straight up to him like a consultant surgeon – except that he did not bother to remove his big cigar. He took out the Havana and dripping ash on the bedsheets, looked deep into the patient's eyes. 'You gonna die on me?' he asked. Even Jolson was speechless. 'Can you still sing?'

That was all Al needed. He jumped out of bed, pushed aside a medicine chest and warbled 'April Showers' as brashly and as tunefully as his one lung would allow. He had never tried so hard with a song in his life.

Cohn left him, muttering, 'The guy's gonna die, the guy's gonna die.' For the next three days Jolson was back in the oxygen tent. But the plans for the picture went ahead.

When he got back home again, Jolson felt he had only one mission – to show Harry Cohn and Sidney Buchman that he could still sing. Buchman, who had not taken over executive control of the picture, was the one who really counted.

Al felt there were spies everywhere. He wondered if the

postman were not really a Columbia scout sent to check up on his voice. The delivery boy, he feared, might be one of Cohn's crawling assistants anxious for the break that would make his own career with the same fell swoop that it would smash Jolson's.

If these were just hallucinations, they were the right kind of images at just the right time. He began to sing wherever he went – to prove the point to himself. He would chant all the old numbers in the kitchen just as he always had in the bath. Every guest who came round for an evening drink was treated like a Winter Garden audience.

There was a twinkle in his eyes that seemed to say, 'I'm not doing this just for you, you know. This is just a preview of how big I'm gonna be again. You see if I'm not.'

When Skolsky first suggested the film idea, Jolson had not seemed too concerned that this voice might come out of someone else's lips. As time went by, he grew more and more worried about the idea.

But Cohn, for whom a pretty girl or a handsome young man represented thousands and perhaps millions of dollars, was not prepared to entertain the idea of Jolson playing himself. Jolson had signed away his life – literally, and there was nothing he could do about it. The singer had begun to wish he had done the deal with Warner Brothers and told Cohn so.

It was then that Cohn amazed everyone around him. Jolson couldn't play the part himself – and that was final. However he could have a say in who did play it. There was to be no veto, he made that clear. But as adviser to the production team, they would hear what he had to say.

The newly-resurrected Jolson power was a new talking point in Hollywood. But an even greater one was the big question – who is going to play Jolson?

Day after day, actors came to be tested. And because they were to play Jolson, this could be no straightforward test. It had to be a test of endurance as well as of acting ability. The chosen actor had to be able to walk like Jolson, dance like Jolson and make love to an audience as Jolson had. He also had to look as though he were singing.

[236]

The first to be tested for the role was an actor of thirty-one who had been on the Columbia payroll since 1941. Jolson fidgeted in his seat before the lights in the projection room went down. When he saw the fellow in blackface trying to be him, he got up from his seat, and stormed out of the room.

'You tryin' to kill me or somethin'?' he shouted to Cohn. 'Fellers all over the world try to imitate Jolson. But are any of them like Jolson? Is that one a Jolson? He doesn't look right. He isn't right. Noboby can be right – but Jolson himself.'

Columbia were learning what a Jolson sulk was like. More advanced lessons in his technique came with every subsequent test he saw. Actors who were well-established and newcomers who had done practically nothing came and went. Jolson hated them all, and made sure that everyone knew it.

'You can't do it,' Harry Cohn was told. 'There's only one Jolson.' The megalomania of old had returned and with it the old Jolson habit of talking about himself in the third person.

But Cohn went on with the tests and more names were considered. There was Richard Conte, whose big moments playing hard-boiled gangsters were still before him. There was Jose Ferrer who at that time had no more thought of playing Toulouse Lautrec than he had of marrying Rosemary Clooney. And there was also Danny Thomas, a rising young performer who looked as though he could be more to Jolson's liking. However, he had one drawback.

Thomas – a Christian of Lebanese stock who looked more Jewish than Jolson – was advised to get his long nose shortened. 'This nose has been in my family for generations and I'm not going to change it now,' he thundered, and left – without the part.

Six years later, Danny Thomas played the lead role of the cantor's son in a Warner Brothers remake of *The Jazz Singer* – without changing his nose. But that is another story.

While the casting traumas went on, Jolson kept raising objections. 'He doesn't stand right,' he said of one promising performer. Or, 'He moves his arms too much.' Or – 'that one looks like a penguin.' And always there was the same comment, 'He doesn't look like Jolson.' Time and again he stormed out of the projection theatre.

Cohn at one time even suggested that he make a screen test himself. It would, he believed, prove the point that there wasn't a thing in the world that could make a man more than sixty look like a twenty-year-old. Even Columbia's makeup department – which prided itself at being the most expert in Hollywood – couldn't.

When Jolson realised that nothing could persuade Cohn to change his mind, he suggested a compromise, 'There's one guy who could do it,' he said. 'And that's Jimmy Cagney.'

Cagney had always been an actor Jolson admired. He had been particularly thrilled by his performance in *Yankie Doodle Dandy* and had secretly believed that Cagney had modelled his prancing technique in the film more on Jolson than on Cohan. He also had the same sort of build as Jolson.

Unfortunately, Cagney had had enough of being someone else's shadow and did not want to risk being typecast. He turned the offer down.

A youngster called Ross Hunter was tested – mainly because he was on the Columbia payroll. But he was rejected. Later Mr Hunter was to find it more profitable making his own pictures as a producer.

Finally, in absolute despair, Cohn called for a re-run of the first test he had seen. As he and Jolson watched a young man in blackface prance along the apron of the stage miming to a recording of 'Swanee' Cohn realised that the star of the picture had been there all along.

His name – Larry Parks.

Parks was perfect for the part for two reasons. Although he had made half a dozen 'B' pictures, while under contract to Columbia, with quite insignificant results, he was the sort of unknown who could carry conviction, without objecting to masquerading as someone else.

Also he was good looking enough to satisfy Cohn and he had shown a good enough indication that he was not going to be merely content with impersonating Jolson. He would give a performance that would be remembered.

The day after the second screening of the Parks test, he was signed. Jolson had to learn to accept the almost unacceptable. Someone else was going to play Jolson and he couldn't do a thing about it.

But he had his objections to Parks at their first meeting and he made sure Cohn knew about them. Parks was too tall, his hair was too bushy. Jolson still could not accept that anyone could play him. However, the men the columnists were soon to dub 'The two Jolsons' shook hands. Al, meanwhile, set about his side of the business – singing the songs.

There was one thing the man who had once been called the 'King of Broadway' and 'Emperor of Hollywood', was not going to allow anyone to forget. If this were to be his life, there was no tale to tell without the songs. The Jolson voice was going to knock them in the aisles once again. And the Jolson songs were the really vital part of the whole enterprise.

At this stage of the game, Morris Stoloff, Columbia's Musical Director was brought in. Together, he and Al spent hours going over the songs Jolson had sung through his long career, each one a milestone.

With Stoloff and arranger Saul Chaplin, Jolson went through his whole repertoire. It was agreed before they started that these had to be songs with which Jolson had been associated through the years, but they also had to be numbers that could appear credible to the more sophisticated post-war audiences of 1946.

So it was up to Stoloff to test whether they could make the journey in time. Old standards that Jolson had made great were abandoned simply because no one could really be expected to take them seriously now. New arrangements had to be found that would provide a synthesis of the old songs and their period and of the demands of the music-buying public of the present. He changed the old arrangements and orchestrations and made old songs new again.

If the film were to tell Jolson's story through the songs, Stoloff made sure that they would do so brilliantly. But the maestro admitted to me 'When I heard Jolson start to sing those songs I turned to jelly. That man still had a magic that defied description.'

The songs boiled down to those that were mostly Al's own favourites and, indeed, very few of the comic numbers with which he had begun his assault on Broadway – except 'The Spaniard That Blighted My Life' – and none of the old potboiling pops that he recorded in the early twenties were eventually included.

The film had to have the great songs, 'Mammy', 'April Showers', 'Swanee' and 'California Here I Come'.

There was also a 'new' song – and one that would become the hit number of 1946. It was called 'The Anniversary Song' – and came to be written at about six hours' notice for a scene in the picture that was next on the shooting schedules.

It was chosen completely by chance. Buchman pointed out that a suitable number was desperately required for a scene at the end of the picture where Jolson's parents – in the film his mother was still alive in the last scene – were celebrating their wedding anniversary at a party on the patio of the Jolsons' California home.

Nothing came to mind – until Al started to hum an old Viennese melody, long in the public domain. Saul Chaplin got to work on a lyric and new arrangements – and both he and Jolson had earned themselves a fortune. Both men have their name on the song's credits.

Saul Chaplin was to tell me: 'I was quite ashamed of that song at first. I gave Al and Sidney Buchman the lyrics in a great hurry and that was that. I really should have done better than "Oh, how we danced on the night we were wed. We vowed out true love though a word wasn't said." And then the way Jolson sang it. . . All the emphasis should have been on the word 'true'. He just ran over the word. Well, if he had done it my way, he could have improved it out of a hit and into a flop!'

The story of the picture was never as important as the songs. It would be a loose tale about the man who, even when he was down, appeared to have done more in twenty minutes than some people do in twenty months. Sidney

Buchman, who by now was the picture's godfather, is credited with working out the main story line.

It was he who decided to base the theme on the craving of this one man for the sound of people sitting in plush velvet seats, applauding until their hands were sore and their voices hoarse. When the 'other woman' in a man's life turns out to be an audience, a love story emerges to beat all others. It was too complicated to go into all Jolson's matrimonial troubles, so it seemed obvious to Buchman that the decline and fall of the marriage with Ruby said it all.

And in this Jolson was not nearly as difficult to please as he had been over the casting. He sat in on the story conferences and agreed right from the start that actual events and dates could be juggled around just as much as the studio wanted.

The picture's title? It was Harry Cohn who found the name. At first, *Minstrel Boy* was considered. Then came *April Showers*. The earliest publicity stills were captioned *The Story of Jolson*.

But Cohn made the final decision. 'There's only one name for this picture and you guys all ought to have thought of it,' he said. 'It's just gotta be *The Jolson Story*.' And the rest is history.

Long after the story line, the title and the songs had been assured, there was still one vital character uncast – Ruby Keeler. This proved almost as difficult as finding a Jolson. Again came the pilgrimages to and from the projection rooms and again the shaking of heads – Jolson's among them.

Cohn took some of the tests home and showed them to his wife Joan and their houseguests. One of these was a blonde girl who had been on Columbia's payroll for about as long as Larry Parks and who, up to that time, had made just about as much of an impression as he had.

She was Evelyn Keyes. 'Why can't I play the part?' she asked Cohn. At which point, Joan chimed in, 'Don't be silly, Evelyn. You can't play that role. You know you aren't pretty.'

Evelyn told me, 'At that point I was so determined to convince everyone that I was right that I yelled right back. All right – I know I'm not pretty. But I'm damned sure acting ability must have something to do with it.

'I worked harder at getting that role than anything else in my life. I sent Cohn telegrams every day. I phoned him twice a day, three times, sometimes half a dozen times a day.' And before long he gave in – she had the role.

Still another factor had to be considered. The story line was agreed – but it had to be written. A Hungarian writer called Bundy Salt was brought in first. Cohn asked him if he had ever heard of Jolson.

'I saw *The Jazz Singer* in Budapest,' he replied.

'Anything else?' asked the studio boss.

'I hear he's washed up.'

'Nothing else you know about him?'

'No.'

'Good,' said Cohn. 'You're going to write the screenplay.' But he didn't.

Laurence Hazard was mentioned and then rejected. Stephen Longstreet was finally brought in to do it. He is now a successful author and his other credits include the Broadway musical *High Button Shoes*. Alfred E. Green was appointed as director. He had been involved in Hollywood musicals almost since the time Jolson showed the world that there could be such things. Sidney Skolsky, whose idea it was in the first place, had the prestigious title of producer. All these names appeared on the film's opening titles. However, it was soon apparent that there should have been one other name there – Sidney Buchman.

He wrote snatches of dialogue, coached dancers, organised camera angles – and helped keep the peace between Jolson and Parks when it seemed that they were likely to have an argument. It was Buchman who decided with Jolson which characters were to be kept and which were best discarded. He also devised the ones which were to be invented.

When Ruby Keeler heard that she was going to be played on the screen by another actress she threatened legal action. So with wildly differing figures being speculated on around Hollywood, a financial settlement was agreed. Evelyn Keyes could play her part, and she could be seen starring in a musical called *Show Girl* and in films like *Gold Diggers, Flirtation Walk* and *42nd Street*. But her name wouldn't be Ruby Keeler. Instead, she would be Julie Benson, Mrs Al Jolson. It was an old Hollywood technique – and Al didn't mind.

There were other, more fundamental changes. His father was shown as an indulgent, kindly gentleman who was easily converted from his strict religious objections to show business to become an expert on the theatre. A man who, in early scenes, was never without his badge of religious orthodoxy – his skullcap – somehow lost it as the hair underneath became thin and as his beard turned white. He was also portrayed as having no objections to his son marrying out of his own faith.

And, as his mother survives throughout the picture, no attempt is made to complicate the issue with step brothers and sisters – or even his full brother Harry or his sisters Rose and Etta. They just didn't exist as far as Hollywood 1946 was concerned.

Neither was there a James Francis Dooley, an Eddie Leonard or an Eppy. In their place, a lovable character called Steve Martin – a complete figment of the imagination, although in many ways an amalgam of them all.

It was a sentimental story that could have been a success, on reflection, even without the music. Ludwig Donath was brilliant as Cantor Yoelson. His own miming to the singing voice of Cantor Saul Silverman was masterly and the home scenes with Mama Yoelson (Tamara Shayne) and their overstrong horseradish were full of the kind of shmaltzy hokum that brings tears and laughs from the most hardbitten of critics.

As Steve Martin there was one of Jolson's own favourite actors – William Demarest – who a generation before *The Jolson Story* had shared scenes with Al in *The Jazz Singer*.

Harry Cohn saw the way things were going early on in production – before Jolson had spent much time on the set and before he had done any singing. Within a fortnight of production beginning, he had lifted the budget ceiling of

$1,500,000 which he had imposed when the deal was first set up.

Now there could be more lavish sets, bigger orchestrations. And what would Jolson make of them? It was obvious from the moment he first moved on to the sound stage, and was shown into a soundproof glass booth where he was to record his songs, while the orchestra played in the studio below.

Since *The Jolson Story* was made, and has turned over the years into an international institution, it has become fashionable to think of Larry simply seeing the old movies, listening to Jolson's voice and then miming them on to film. It wasn't like that at all.

The director and the producer might have been satisfied with doing things that way. Larry might have been happy to use his imagination. Al certainly wasn't. For every number that Jolson sang, there was a shot on film – in Technicolor – of Jolson singing it. He mimed his own voice – not as well as Larry was to do it, it must be said – demonstrating for each one how he expected his 'shadow' to put over that particular number. It was almost like the technique Walt Disney adopted for his cartoons – acting out every scene so that his animators knew what sort of movements to put into their characters.

And, as Jolson recorded the songs, a mysterious thing happened. Only Morris Stoloff could hear the tunes through his own headphones, but the crowds gathered round for the performance just the same. They could see him move around just as he always had, and the old magnetism started working once more – even though they couldn't hear a note.

As Evelyn Keyes recalls, 'I remember just standing and staring, watching Jolson perform. It was uncanny. He was in the booth singing – but we could see him moving and the people were just overwhelmed.'

Jolson had been a backnumber up to that point – and Columbia a laughing stock, but it took just as long as the message took to travel for the people in the business to realise that he was coming back – and there was no point in laughing any more.

The rumours continued just the same. The principal one was that Jolson couldn't manage a tune any more and that the engineers had to piece together a melody here, a chorus there, before they could come up with anything that was technically acceptable. There were other days, so the stories went, when the Jolson voice wasn't usable at all.

But there was no more truth to that in this film than in any other. From his first test recording, Jolson proved not only that he could still sing, but that he had never sung better in his life.

Stoloff played round with the sound as it was recorded on the strips of film and joined the pieces together just as tape would be spliced today. But that was simply because he was looking for the perfection he eventually found.

If the commercial recordings he made in the years after *The Jolson Story* cannot be held out as proof – for by then the tapes could have been doctored as easily as the soundtracks – the numerous extemporary performances on radio or at benefit shows that followed did demonstrate that those rumours were a slander on the Jolson talent.

For weeks after the recordings were made it was impossible to walk on to a *Jolson Story* set without needing one's ears plugged with cotton wool. For there was Larry Parks miming to the old Jolson songs with the volume of his loudspeaker turned on as full as it would go.

He would stand in front of the mirror and rehearse the miming he would do on the screen. However, he was not going to be satisfied with merely mouthing someone else's words. For Larry Parks discovered very early on what was going to be the secret of his success in this role. He sang himself at full force the way Jolson had done. This gave him the action and put force behind the words, as Jolson did. However the recording always sang louder than Larry Parks ever could.

The result was that not only did Larry's lips move while Jolson outpoured the song, but the Adam's apple bobbed up and down as the vocal chords vibrated and – as one critic noted – even the fur on his moving tongue could be seen.

[245]

But there were still criticisms from Jolson. He came on to the set more and more often as production advanced. 'You don't move around enough, kid,' he told Parks — and proceeded to demonstrate exactly what he meant.

In Parks's dressing room, Jolson showed what his easy approach meant. First he moved a lamp, then a chair, finally a bookcase. And as he darted from one end of the room to the other, it appeared as though a tornado had hit the Columbia studio. 'See, kid,' he said. 'You gotta take it easy.'

Before the part was finally his, Parks embarked on what was probably the biggest character research programme ever conceived by an actor studying a role. He did more than read about Jolson, he found himself living Jolson's life.

His friends were given a special mission — to find all the old Jolson records they could get. They were delivered in boxes, by the truckload. Old pressings of 'Mammy', 'Sonny Boy', still older versions of 'The One I Love Belongs to Somebody Else' and 'I'll Climb The Highest Mountain' were treated once more with great respect.

Parks was then able to appreciate how Jolson's voice had changed. He didn't sound the same and he took deeper breaths. So he had to rehearse the breaths as well as the vocal arrangements. He could hear that, although the Jolson voice had changed, the way he altered his songs with the tremendous Jolson energy had not changed at all.

He raked up all the old Jolson movies, too. Warner Brothers were asked to supply prints of the early Jolson pictures. 'Hell, no,' said Jack Warner. But the films were found just the same and hour after hour Parks would watch Jolson at work in the Columbia projection rooms.

Scratched and faded copies of *Big Boy*, *Wonderbar*, *Go into your Dance*, *Swanee River* and — most useful of all — *Rose of Washington Square* were flashed once again on to the screen.

Rose was seven years old when Larry Parks first saw the picture in the Columbia theatre. It had never been a great film and, as we have seen Jolson very much played third fiddle to Alice Faye and Tyrone Power. However, it provided several good lessons in projecting the Jolson style – certainly the only pure Jolson film that did so. Now, all those years later, it is interesting to compare the way Jolson himself performed 'California Here I Come' in *Rose of Washington Square* with the manner in which Larry Parks imitated him in *The Jolson Story*.

Jolson was on the set almost every day, advising Parks. To help him get into the spirit of things, he took him to the racetrack – and to a synagogue. On the set as Al gave his advice to all the people hungry to hear him talk of the real old days, Erle would sit at his side – knitting.

There was a time during rehearsals when Jolson asked Parks to think twice about a certain gesture he had used in a song. 'Don't you remember how I used to do that bit?' he asked. The younger man admitted with embarrassment, 'I've never seen you work at all before a live audience, Al.'

'Wait a minute, wait a minute, son,' Jolson replied gleefully. 'You ain't heard nothin' yet.' The next moment, he was on stage and was giving what turned out to be a two-hour show – just for Parks.

In 107 days before the cameras Larry Parks lost eighteen pounds in weight – trying to show how Jolson used to woo the audiences. And generally Jolson was as happy as anyone with the way Parks was portraying him. He never admitted to forgiving the studio for giving the role to someone else and chided both Cohn and Parks when he thought the moment was appropriate. But deep down, he accepted what had to be accepted.

There was one scene, however, that he was not at all happy with. And everyone around knew it. The Jolson foot came down hard in a longshot scene when Parks was meant to dance down the runway at the Winter Garden, singing 'Swanee'.

Al was distraught. 'The kid just can't do it,' he said emphatically. 'And no one can do it – except me. Are you gonna have a film about me without 'Swanee'? Or are you gonna have a Jolson film without Jolson dancing – or without him whistling?' The answer to both those questions had to be, 'No'.

So in this one scene, Jolson himself played Jolson. People who prided themselves on knowing anything about the Jolson of old said that they recognised him. One woman writer said she recognised his overhanging paunch. But in 1969, when, one supposes, it did not matter any more and when the film was blown up into 70mm, this scene was enlarged to a close-up and there could be no further doubt. This certainly was not Larry Parks.

Probably the greatest problem that Larry or anyone else engaged in the musical side of *The Jolson Story* had to face was the undeniable fact that Jolson never sang the same song the same way twice.

When, for instance, he sang 'Ma Blushin' Rosie' the line ended in one take for the film '. . .don't be so captivating'. In another, it concluded, 'don't be so aggravating.' Parks was completely thrown. He already had enough trouble coping with the fact that Jolson never came in twice on the same beat.

This musical-chairs treatment of songs caused one of the famed rows on the *Jolson Story* set. Al was recording 'April Showers' for the soundtrack and, as usual, the ever-growing audience around him applauded with almost fanatical enthusiasm when it was all over. Everyone, that is, except Saul Chaplin.

'You left out something,' said Chaplin innocently and proceeded to show the way he remembered Al performing the tune on one of the now classic old pressings. Jolson was furious. Of course, he said, he couldn't give the song the old treatment. He didn't have the breath any more. And, he said, pulling out a bundle of banknotes, 'I made this in show business. What did you make?'

In the end Jolson took Chaplin's advice and changed 'April Showers' in the finale (its second appearance in the movie) to something resembling his earliest version – and it was clearly worth the effort.

Other recordings were made and then discarded – for a variety of reasons. There were two recordings of the old Jolson showstopper 'Rip Van Winkle' – one in German dialect, the other straight, but neither appeared in the film. A plan to interpolate 'Carolina In The Morning' was left on the cutting room floor – only to be resurrected three years later in *Jolson Sings Again.*

A scene where Larry Parks mimes to 'Sonny Boy' in a reconstruction of *The Singing Fool* scene was dropped after the film's first public performance – not because Parks's portrayal was inadequate but because it seemed to cut the story dead in its tracks.

Another number was thrown out because it appeared to have the same effect in the cinema as it had had when Jolson first sang it in a smoke-filled nightclub – the song about the synagogue cantor's audition. Jolson recorded it for a party scene and the picture's cast were so ecstatically excited by the way he put it over that White Anglo-Saxon Protestants found themselves learning the Yiddish words.

Larry Parks learned the words phonetically and even Jolson admitted he gave an incredible performance. But it had to be dropped. 'Sidney Buchman just decided that nothing, but nothing, could possibly follow that,' Evelyn Keyes recalled.

It was difficult to follow Jolson when he was on the set at any time. On some occasions, the only person allowed near him was Cohn. And Jolson was the only man in Columbia's history ever to be allowed access at anytime of the day or night to Cohn's own private office, an uncanny reprise of the situation at Warner Brothers after *The Jazz Singer.*

Any worry with regard to the business side of the operation had vanished for Cohn soon after Jolson first appeared on the set. Hollywood's best musicians had queued up to be allowed to join Stoloff's orchestra and he realised that his financial investment was secure – just as long as Jolson survived the shooting of the picture. What he wanted to be able to perpetuate was a feeling of mutual confidence between them – between producer and idol.

When a cameraman stopped the shooting of 'Swanee' because an arc lamp was flickering, Cohn flew into a fierce rage. 'No one stops a scene when Jolson is singing,' he shouted to the penitent cameraman and was about to fire him. But before any firing could be done, Cohn had cooled –

when he was reminded that Technicolor film cost something like fifty cents a second and they were wasting time.

Things went well between Jolson and Cohn. But this was not always the case between Jolson and Parks. Rumours grew of a succession of rows between the two stars. Parks at first denied it.

In June 1951 he told *Picturegoer* magazine, 'They were untrue. Jolson and I were enthusiastic co-workers with a sound regard for one another. There was never a disagreement between us. I confess that, at the outset, I had no desire to be Jolson, but that was certainly not through any lack of admiration. I simply felt I was not the one to do the role justice.'

Eighteen years later he spelled it out a little clearer, 'Al Jolson didn't want me to portray him. He wanted to do it himself. I got the part and when the picture started everybody called it "Cohn's Folly". They thought that Harry Cohn had taken leave of his senses. I met Jolson but never broke bread with him.

'The big problem was that Jolson sang every song as if he were going to drop dead at the end of it – at full volume all the way and my problem was to act out different emotions with Jolson singing at full pitch. It's very difficult to collapse in mid-song while the voice is at full throat.'

No one had any doubts though that however much Jolson accepted Parks and wanted him to do the best possible job, he still somehow resented him – whether he told him so in as many words or not. Yet to Evelyn Keyes he behaved totally differently.

'It's true, he was always performing,' she recalls. 'Wherever you went with him, he was on – you know, if you were sitting alone with him in a room he was giving you a performance. He had this extraordinary energy. He would perform all the time – and you found yourself being grateful. He was absolutely charming.'

He struck up this charming relationship with Evelyn after he himself had messed up one of her takes. This was for the scene where Julie Benson is impersonating Jolson. She is down on one knee, arms held out and singing 'California Here I Come'. In the film, Al Jolson, in the body of Larry Parks goes over to her, takes her hand and with a false look of anger on his face, says, 'Come here, my friend. I'll have to talk to you.' She, meanwhile, protests, 'Please, Mr Jolson, I'll never do that again.'

In fact, the real Al Jolson applauded her impersonation wildly – and so ruined the whole scene.

The Jolson Story took six months to shoot from beginning to end. Another six months was spent by Sidney Buchman in the cutting room, readying the picture for its first showing.

It was during those anxious moments wondering whether or not Columbia really had a hit that Al and Harry Jolson met again for the first time in years. Harry called his brother to say there was an urgent message from Washington – their father was dangerously ill.

They arrived at his small apartment near the synagogue where he had helped conduct services for so long, in time for the old man, now ninety-four, to pronounce a final blessing on his sons. He told them that, although their ways had not been his, he loved them still.

Harry had his wife Lillian to console him. Al had Erle. And at this moment he needed her warmth. At the time when he was feeling on top of the world again, as much on top as in the words of the song lyric in *The Jolson Story*, his past had caught up with him. The man against whom he had rebelled had died without seeing what could be his son's greatest moment.

By the time the film was finally placed in the cans and sent off to Santa Barbara for a sneak preview, it had cost $2,800,000. Cohn himself had chosen the location because he figured that too many people would know about the picture if it were shown in Los Angeles – and any unfortunate reactions from the audience would get too wide a public on the grapevine.

As it was, everyone who was anyone did find out – and was at the Santa Barbara theatre which had the legend on its marquee, 'Major Hollywood Preview Tonite'.

Al arrived with Erle and confessed it was like a Winter Garden opening all over again. There were butterflies as big as dragons in his stomach.

He sat with Erle on one side of him and Harry Cohn on the other. All the time, his legs kept shaking so violently that a man sitting in front complained. 'I feel as though I've been hit by an earthquake,' said Jolson – and rushed out to the toilet at the rear of the theatre.

Cohn sent a young executive, Jonie Taps, to see how Al was getting on. Al said he was fine and would watch the film from the back of the house. But every time he heard his own voice he put his hand to his mouth and rushed back to the toilet. He saw the rest of the picture between the men's room and the manager's office – where he was persuaded to lie down halfway through the film.

The picture was still running when Harry Cohn decided to cut the 'Sonny Boy' number. But apart from that, he knew that he had a winner. He thumped Jolson on the back and said, 'It's great, Al.'

Erle rushed to the back of the theatre to give her husband a big kiss. And that seemed to be the most important thing of all. She could, at last, see how great he not only had been, but was still.

As the audience were filling in their comment cards on the way out of the cinema, Jolson hung back behind a pillar and listened to the things some of them were saying to each other. There was one that he would never forget, 'What a pity. . .' said a little old lady as she blinked her eyes in the strong glare of the foyer lights, 'what a pity that he isn't alive to see it.'

Fourteen

There's a Rainbow Round My Shoulder

WHEN JOLSON HAD BEEN seriously ill after the operation on his lung just over a year before work on the picture started, the Associated Press had circulated to their subscribers a full biographical obituary. The obituary to his career had been written and published many times in the years before that.

Suddenly, though, the ghost was walking, dancing and singing. Reports of his imminent death had been grossly exaggerated.

But there was nobody, absolutely nobody, who could have predicted the amount of life that was injected into Jolson's system by this new hypodermic of a picture – or the extent to which it was to jab the entertainment industry out of its own fondly-held convictions. It was to prove beyond a shadow of a doubt that the kids were not always content with syrupy crooning and that the robust Jolson voice was just what they needed.

The impact of the picture and of Jolson were really felt when it opened at a world première at Radio City Music Hall, New York – without Larry Parks; the story at that time was that he couldn't afford the fare, although that seems unlikely on reflection. Columbia didn't see the importance of getting him to the East Coast until several days later.

But the word that Jolson was back had spread among the film colony in Hollywood and Beverly Hills as soon as the curtain was down that night.

They knew it by instinct and they sensed that Jolson

himself had that instinct, too. From the moment he saw 'The End' flash on to the screen, he was his old self again, behaving in the same old Jolsonesque way.

He was so excited by it all when people saw *The Jolson Story* for the first time that he put his arms around Stephen Longstreet who had written the screenplay and said, 'Steve, I'm gonna give you a present to show how much I appreciate what you did.'

Longstreet had visions of cars, gold watches, expensive furniture flashing before his eyes. The next day, the gift arrived. It was a signed photograph inscribed 'To Steve – who took my life.'

'I hung it in the toilet,' Longstreet told me.

Al Jolson was now all of sixty-one. But he was behaving like a young kid who had just been plucked out of the second row of the chorus to receive the thunderous applause of an audience for the first time. As proud as he was to show Erle that he could be on top again, he was equally glad to show his fellow entertainers what he could still do.

The Hillcrest Country Club invited him to take part in their twenty-fifth anniversary benefit concert – and allowed him to top the bill at the very end.

Jack Benny was compère at this Jewish club on the West Coast. 'I'm appearing here as master of ceremonies tonight by virtue of the fact that Bob Hope is a gentile,' he quipped in a remark that has now become part of show business lore.

One by one he introduced Danny Kaye, Danny Thomas, Van Johnson, Frank Sinatra, Margaret O'Brien, Gene Kelly, Mickey Rooney, Red Skelton, Jose Iturbi, Xavia Cugat, Carmen Miranda and George Burns.

Finally, after four hours, came another ten violin players to augment the principal orchestra of the evening. They played the opening bars of 'Mammy' and Al Jolson in a smart newly-tailored dinner jacket bounced on to the stage as if he were at least forty years younger.

'Danny Kaye said he was a young man when he came here tonight,' Jolson gagged, 'and that he was old by the time he got on.

[254]

'Well, Jolie's case is different. When I got here I was an old man already.' As for his comeback, 'That was no comeback. Until now I just couldn't get a job.'

The show was expected to last no more than the four hours it had taken to reach Jolson. In the end, the proceedings – all in a huge marquee – lasted nearer six.

Eight-hundred people jammed in to hear Jolson sing, wisecrack and reminisce about the days when being an entertainer meant more than a mere ability to hold the microphone properly.

Half-way through his performance – although no one had really expected him to last that long – Jolson suddenly broke off to make a brief speech to the people out front.

'My biggest thrill is not seeing all you people here – but having my wife with me. All she knew about me as a performer was from my old scrapbooks or what Jack Benny and Groucho Marx told her. Tonight I've been showing off just to impress her.'

There were few more dry eyes left in the house at that moment than there would have been had he just sung 'Sonny Boy'. Jolson was back – and in charge.

The Hollywood papers were full of it the next day. They were even more keen now to anticipate the sort of success *The Jolson Story* was likely to have. They expressed their feeling that a really great entertainer was back in their midst and, what was more, the industry needed him. This was pleasing because they could have thought that it was simply for old time's sake – that Jolson was being received on a wave of nostalgia for the used-to-be.

A dinner in New York on 1 October 1946 – just nine days before the scheduled world première of the film – proved this new enthusiasm.

The Motion Picture Chapter of the American War Veterans Committee gave a testimonial banquet for Jolson at the plush Hotel Astor, with the proceedings broadcast from coast to coast. In Los Angeles, Bob Hope and George Jessel paid tribute to Jolson in between their own jokes and songs.

Eddie Cantor joined in from San Francisco to sing

'Toot-Toot-Tootsie', Dinah Shore dedicated to Jolson 'You Made Me Love You', Sinatra gave out with 'Rock A Bye Your Baby With A Dixie Melody', Hildegarde sang 'April Showers', Martha Raye was 'Waiting For The Robert E. Lee' and Perry Como performed 'By The Light Of The Silvery Moon'.

At the other end of the line in New York, the former Mayor of the City, James J. Walker, made his final public appearance – he was to die soon afterwards – when he introduced Jolson:

'We are gathered to pay tribute to Al Jolson,' he said. 'We are saluting a great showman – and New York loves great showmen. The man whose very name means Broadway. . .'

When Al came to the microphone there was more than just one lump in his throat.

A thousand people had packed the banqueting hall to hear him. They clapped, cheered and stood as James Walker announced, 'The hearts of the American Veterans Committee and the microphone are all yours.'

To Jolson it was quite clearly a tribute he had not expected – and he said as much. 'As a rule, ladies and gentlemen, I generally sing my speeches. I am not a talker . . . Up to about eight o'clock tonight, I did not know I was going to have a dinner. I knew they were making a testimonial but I treated it, I'm ashamed to say, as a joke. I couldn't believe it.

'I am at an age in life when people quit . . . but then at about a quarter to eight I started to get nervous. I said to my wife "I've got to get dressed." She said "What have you got to wear?" And I said "A blue suit and a tie." I got dressed and came over here.

'There won't be any singing from me. There's been a lot of singing tonight and I don't think I could follow it. . . As usual, I'm not lost for words . . . but tonight all I can say is to everyone from the bottom of my heart, thank you.'

Again it was a wonderful plug for *The Jolson Story*. But that was still an unknown quantity to most people. Jolson himself was at last being recognised as the man who had turned American entertainment into a national heritage – but not as a singer who could bring in the masses.

To launch the film, Harry Cohn wanted an album of songs

from the picture to be released on record. But that was much easier said than done. In those days no one conceived of using the actual film soundtracks on disc and it was still two years away from the birth of the LP. And, despite the Hillcrest benefit, despite the dinner at the Astor, no one thought that Al Jolson's voice was the kind that would set the juke boxes rocking.

Cohn set Jonie Taps on to the job. Taps had just done a deal with Cohn to join Columbia as head of the music department. He was an executive with Shapiro Bernstein, the music publishers, and was still working out his six-months' notice when Cohn phoned him with an SOS.

He needed some Jolson records and no one would market them. Columbia had no recording set-up of its own. Its namesake record company Columbia Graphaphone was unrelated and not interested. RCA Victor and the other labels had said 'No', too.

And Jack Kapp, head of Decca, was equally unimpressed. But Taps decided to keep pressing him – because he had Jolson's promise of ten per cent of the deal as his agent if he could swing it.

It seemed impossible to break through to Kapp. He had had the experience of Jolson's 'Swanee' and 'April Showers' combination of the previous year and was, at that time, thinking of getting the disc withdrawn from the catalogue. It was not doing so well!

What's more, he told Taps, 'Look, I've got Sophie Tucker, Harry Richman and Ted Lewis under contract – and I can't give them away. What do I need another one for? Crosby is the one who's making money for me now.'

Eli Oberstein of RCA seemed to weaken. A special showing of *The Jolson Story* was arranged to convince him. It convinced him, sure enough – that he should stay away from Jolson.

Meanwhile, Jack Kapp had been lured into the Columbia net once more.

'Come and see the picture,' Taps pleaded with him. 'Then you'll decide whether you're on to a good thing or not.'

Kapp said 'OK' and saw the picture. He left the viewing theatre in a daze.

'You make the pictures with Jolson,' Kapp told Cohn. 'I'll make his records.'

By the time *The Jolson Story* opened at Radio City on 10 October a deal had been signed for an album of ten records featuring songs from the picture. When the first royalties from Decca reached Jolson a month after the records' first release he discovered he had just earned himself $400,000.

The people who, despite torrential rain, were queuing for four blocks around the theatre, were buying Jolson's music to take home with them. So long before his success became obvious in other directions, Jolson on records had made a most stupendous comeback.

Morris Stoloff was there in the recording studios at Decca to give the Jolson numbers the same updated touch that he had provided on the film set.

He had done for Jolson what Nelson Riddle was to do for Sinatra ten years later. He had created the new Jolson sound.

So once again, Jolson's voice could be heard on Broadway – blaring from the speakers outside the string of record stores which then as now littered the theatre district. Before, they had lived on a diet of Crosby, Sinatra, Como and Dinah Shore. Now it seemed that all the shops were playing on their machines were Jolson records.

You could hear him singing 'Mammy' in one shop, 'Toot-Toot-Tootsie' in another, 'Swanee' next door and 'You Made Me Love You' two shops farther away. Everyone was buying Jolson.

Everyone should have been happy – but Jonie Taps wasn't. Jolson refused to give him the ten per cent he had promised him. He never forgot it and he has never forgiven the injustice of it.

'Instead, he tried to get Cohn to fire me before I started work,' he remembers. 'He thought I was proving too useful to Cohn and might prevent his getting near him himself. Cohn told him to leave the store alone!'

To Jolson himself the situation was little short of uncanny.

[258]

He literally did not know what had hit him. He would lie back on his hammock as it swung on the patio of his house, talk to Erle about the amazing change in his fortunes and feel completely unable to take it all in.

His house was once more plagued with sightseers. Day by day fan mail mounted.

But the fans were not the people who had seen him on Broadway or the ones who remembered seeing him on the screen with Ruby Keeler. This was a new generation of worshippers, the bobby soxers and their boyfriends who had run home excitedly screeching to their parents about this 'hep new singer Al Jolson'.

For all that, the excitement was in some ways an excitement with a ghost. Day by day as his rating in the music business hit new heights he could still walk through the streets unrecognised. The novelty of being wanted again was still too strong for that to begin to concern him. And he admitted more than once, 'I never liked the idea of having leaking fountain pens thrust in front of my face.'

To the average cinema fan he was a grey-haired version of Larry Parks – the star they were now reading so much about in the newspapers and magazines. Few of them had yet seen the picture. It was doing such hot business at Radio City that the four-block queues were there from seven o'clock in the morning. Not since *Gone with the Wind* had there been such enthusiasm.

On the air, day in, day out, the disc jockeys, too, joined in the Jolsonmania. The old 1945 version of 'April Showers' had been resurrected by Decca and made the 'A' side while 'Swanee' was relegated to 'B' status. In the first week of the new labelling it had sold more than twice as many copies as when it was first issued.

Not only was Al Jolson achieving enormous success and beating his younger successors at their own game, but they were also joining him on the field. Bing Crosby recorded 'April Showers' and 'The Anniversary Song' – as did many other crooners.

Jolson's own definitive version sold a million copies in a

month – a Jolson tune on the hit parade being bought by people who had never even heard his name weeks earlier.

In Britain, too, 'April Showers' was one of the really big hits of the year. But 'The Anniversary Song' was to be the success of successes. For five weeks it was on top of the hit parade calculated by the British music industry. Everybody seemed to be singing it on BBC radio and on the fledgling British television service too. But it was the Jolson recording that was being aired more than any other.

At home in California Jolson sat back, read his mail, played his new records and developed signs of a second childhood. He no longer walked anywhere – he ran.

When he answered the telephone, he didn't merely say 'Hello', he sang it – usually to the tune of 'Mammy'. He took up swimming. He had always been keen on a morning dip, but now he did it seriously, usually clad in a pair of bright orange trunks.

His doctor had told him that swimming was the perfect cure for ill-health and old age. They were the two things Jolson feared most and he took the doctor's advice. Every morning he swam two lengths of the pool.

He also made up his mind that ice cream was good for his voice. From the moment he started making records again he devoured two dishes of this 'health food' every night before going to bed.

The Press reported that Al was once more raising money for charity, and there was no cause that seemed more pressing to him than the Jews who had crawled out of the concentration camps of Europe.

At a United Jewish Appeal luncheon organised at the Hotel Astor in July 1947 he saw the target set by the Greater New York division of the appeal reached – to the tune of $1,750,000. 'Although Governments of the world are callous and indifferent to the fate of 1,500,000 Jews of Europe, we in America must rally our maximum resources to prevent the victims of Nazi persecution losing hope,' he said. Despite criticisms of Jolson being remote from his own people, he had always responded to causes like that. (In 1922 he had beaten eighty rivals by giving $50,000 to the relief of Latvian Jews.)

In Denver, Jolson was presented with the Rose Award – named after Major General Maurice Rose – 'for services to the Forces in the War.'

New success brought new assessments of his wealth. Jolson, everyone said, was in the money again. What was more, *The Jolson Story* was building up a unique form of fan loyalty.

By the 1980s, there were people who could report seeing it as many as 200 times. When the picture was re-released in 70mm widescreen and stereophonic sound in 1969, Margaret Hinxman wrote in the London *Sunday Telegraph,* 'The *Jolson Story* is a mere twenty-three years old and as it is revived and reframed in 70mm, I wouldn't begin to predict how it will affect a younger film-going generation.

'But I loved it then and I love it now, every last sentimental showbiz cliché, every over-sung song. I know it so well that I can recite the throbbing dialogue; anticipate the exact bar of "Goodbye My Bluebell" when little Asa's voice breaks: judge the stop on which Jolson's future wife – Ruby Keeler in real life but a pseudonymous hoofer in the film – fumbled her dance routine on a Ziegfeld opening night; and spot the brief appearance in long shot of the real Jolson singing "Swanee".

'Though I can never justify my devotion to it as an act of critical sense, I still think its prime virtue – a passionate, exuberant affection for its cocky subject – is more valuable to a film than we're inclined to allow. And how right was Larry Parks who played Jolson, miming the songs while the entertainer contributed his own voice.'

That said all that had to be said then and twenty-three years before. *The Jolson Story*'s recipe was an international appeal. It had schmaltz but there was meat to go with it, too. And the meatiest part of the lot was Jolson's voice.

In Britain in 1946 Jolson was barely even a memory to most people. Few of his earlier films had done well in the country. So *The Jolson Story* provided a discovery that outmatched even the impact it had had in America.

It was bringing him a new fortune. But it wasn't that which gave him new life. He was not simply working again – but was now wanted as he had never been before.

Even so, he felt he had a duty to be thrifty without being stingy. The only socks he ever wore were those Erle knitted for him. He had even been known to break into his wife's conversations with other women when he discovered extravagances in the home.

On one occasion Erle told Mrs Morris Stoloff that she had managed to get hold of a new consignment of nylons – in the days when they were almost more precious than gold.

Al broke in, 'But baby, I told you I could get them for you wholesale!'

By the end of 1947 it became more than obvious that Jolson was back to stay. It wasn't just the nostalgia for the past as some critics had suggested. Nor was it a case of the boys returning from the front line, glad to welcome the man who had cheered them up when things were hot. And most important of all, he knew now that *The Jolson Story* wasn't going to be a ten-minute wonder. Al had now added to the records he made of *The Jolson Story* hits.

It was ironic to think that the man, who months before couldn't give his services away for nothing on radio, was now the hottest property on the air – without a show of his own.

Some idea of the effect Al Jolson was having on radio audiences was seen at three o'clock on the morning of 27 October 1946 – seventeen days after *The Jolson Story*'s première. Al was invited to take part in a chat show for night owls – the Barry Gray programme on WOR-Mutual. He was expected to talk for up to half an hour about his long career and his reactions to the picture. He brought Harry Akst along with him for the ride, found him a piano and, as his old friend played, sang some of his favourite tunes from the picture. He finally went off the air eighty minutes later.

The reaction to this programme, which finished before most of New York was awake, was astonishing. The next day the networks were knocking on his door – but Jolson played it cool.

He decided to confine himself to guest appearances. He had got out of the habit of driving himself hard on his own show and was still reluctant to repeat the 'bum joke' experiences of the thirties.

But this was a new Jolson and the networks realised it. In January 1947 he was the guest star on Bing Crosby's *Philco Radio Time*. He was not just outstandingly good on that show – he was as brilliant as he had been on Broadway. All his old reserve had left him. He was bubbling over with confidence – knowing that anything Crosby could do he could do better.

Crosby knew it, too. As an experiment, they did their very first duet together – 'April Showers', followed it with 'Ma Blushin' Rosie' and left the audience in the studio shouting for more.

Philco liked it too – and signed Al for four more shows that year at $10,000 each.

He appeared on the Crosby show two weeks in succession and the ratings were higher than they had ever been before. If neither of them had been successful as solo artists, they could there and then have established themselves as the perfect comedy and singing team.

Even the commercial for Philco radios in which the two clowned – to words and music by Jimmy Van Heusen and Johnny Burke – brought the house down in the studio. They could do nothing wrong and Jolson himself had never been funnier. 'What's that badge on your lapel?' Crosby asked him on one of his first appearances, 'That's what you get for seeing *The Jolson Story* 100 times,' quipped Al.

Columbia Pictures liked that. A publicity campaign was introduced offering real badges – for people who had seen the picture ten times. The badges were gone almost as quickly as they were manufactured.

Eddie Cantor, his arch rival of the old days, invited him on to his own radio programme. They dueted 'Toot-Toot-Tootsie' together, Al sang 'Ida' as a dedication to Cantor's wife, and as the programme ended was told by his host, 'Thank you Al – you're still the World's Greatest Entertainer.'

Al took the hint. The next time he appeared on the Crosby

show he was wearing another badge bearing the letters AJTWGE. 'What's that Al?' asked Crosby. 'That, son, says, "Al Jolson – the World's Greatest Entertainer".'

He was now showing a new side to his character. The man who had been condemned for so long as cruel and uncharitable was generosity itself to the man who had done so much to fashion his new career, Morris Stoloff.

When first he had an invitation to appear on the Crosby show, Jolson asked to be allowed to use Stoloff as his musical director. The producers ruled this out. Crosby had always worked with John Scott Trotter and it wouldn't be right to drop him just for Jolson.

'But I need him for my arrangements,' Al countered. 'Well,' they told him, 'bring him along as an adviser.'

'Al did,' Stoloff told me 'I went to every session and never did a thing.

'But you ought to have seen those cheques he gave me. I've never known a man more generous. I did absolutely nothing.'

Al's last 1947 Crosby show was in December – eight months after the one before. When the May show ended, Crosby's agents had tried to sign Al up for another ten programmes that autumn. But the two singers couldn't agree terms.

One report said that Bing and Al were at least $1,000 apart on what Jolson's guest appearance fee should be. Another stressed a more likely reason for the row, 'Bing did not enjoy the publicity over the fact that his rating went up on the show whenever Al was the guest.'

That was the *New York Times*'s view of the situation. But Bing's brother Everett denied the rift and Al's Press team said there had been hopes for a deal – but it had never come off. It was to be two years before Al appeared again on the Crosby programme although Bing was to join him on his.

Bing had wondered at the very beginning of their association how the live studio audiences would take to Al appearing as himself. He thought they would be too amazed at the difference between Larry Parks on the screen and

Jolson's real appearance. But it never seemed to matter. They loved Jolson as he was – and of course the Crosby-Jolson team.

Decca cashed in on the situation. Both artists were under contract to the label and they issued a new version of one of the numbers Al and Bing had sung on the Philco show – 'Alexander's Ragtime Band' and backed it with a novel version of 'The Spaniard That Blighted My Life'. Stoloff did the orchestrations for this. It was Jolson's way of showing how much he appreciated the value of the balding musician who had begun his professional life as a violinist.

However it was to be the only commercial recording Jolson and Crosby made together. Contractual difficulties prevented more. But even in the 1980s pirated recordings of their radio duets still delight those able to acquire them.

Al continued to make records. But it was radio that really looked interesting. The *New York Times* commented, 'Thanks to radio, some of the brightest chapters in *The Jolson Story* seem to lie still ahead.'

Jack Benny, Amos 'n Andy, Edgar Bergen, Jimmy Durante – all featured Al as their guest star.

Bob Hope asked him when he appeared on his show, 'Tell me, Al, you're such a sensation on the radio now, why don't you get your own programme?'

'What,' Al tried to reply before being swamped by a hysterical round of applause and cheers. 'What?' Al tried again – and still the people out front wouldn't let him speak. Finally he managed it '. . .what – and be on the air only once a week?' This time the house collapsed. Al needed no more embarrassing coughs in a radio programme.

They were now his own jokes and he was master of the situation. If he didn't like a subject, he didn't bother with it. And everyone seemed delighted.

Jolson and Eddie Cantor hit it off again on the Cantor radio show – acting out a routine that Al devised himself. 'How much do you want?' Eddie asked him.

'Don't talk about money,' Al replied. 'Forget it.' But the day after the show, Cantor received a bill for $1,500 from Jolson's tailors. Al had charged him with the cost of six suits he was having made at $250 a time – it was to be his fee for the show.

Early in April 1947 Al did star in his own programme – a one-off feature in the Lux Radio Theatre series in which he was the narrator for a new version of the film, *Alexander's Ragtime Band.*

He followed this in June with a version of *The Jazz Singer* – hardly different from the one he did for Lux in the thirties except that, this time, his parents were played by Ludwig Donath and Tamara Shayne, the couple who played Papa and Mama Yoelson in *The Jolson Story.* It provided the touch of authenticity the public wanted. The programme did so well that copies were waxed on disc and issued to American Forces radio stations.

Jolson had now come to terms with radio in a way he never had before. In October 1947, he once more headed the bill on the *Kraft Music Hall* for NBC. He had taken over from Nelson Eddy who himself had succeeded Bing Crosby. He was again the host on the show he had founded all those years before.

Maurice Chevalier had been provisionally booked to take over from Eddy. But then came *The Jolson Story* – and Chevalier was politely told that Al had the job instead.

Time magazine saw the niceness of the situation.

In an article headed 'The Big Switcheroo' they recalled Jolson's own approach to Kraft soon after he heard Crosby was leaving the 'Hall':

'I told the sponsor I'm the guy who can do it,' he chuckled to the *Time* writer. 'And what did they say? "You're too old." So I says to myself? ''Al – forgive them. They don't know what they're doin'.'' But after *The Jolson Story* – they did the Big Switcheroo. . . "Please, Mr Jolson, don't sign with anyone else . . . sign here, please, please."

'Sign, ha! I didn't want to sign anything for nobody. So I tell 'em "All right – for $7,500 a week." They says "yes" and I almost drop dead.'

He came to terms for a four-year contract – doing thirty-nine shows a year.

There was to be a regular format – Al singing his old songs –

and with a few new ones sprinkled among them – a female vocalist and a new kind of stooge – Oscar Levant.

This brilliant pianist was regarded as one of the greatest living exponents of the work of George Gershwin and this provided an easy rapport with Jolson who naturally shared his enthusiasm. His caustic wit – he had been the star of the radio programme *Information Please* – rubbed up against Jolson more than once, and there were the occasional rows over the air. But they seemed to smooth things over most of the time.

He continually ribbed Jolson about his age. 'Don't tell me you weren't around when Teddy Roosevelt led the charge of San Juan Hill?' Levant would taunt him. Or he would say, 'Weren't you there when Tchaikovsky first played his piano concerto?' 'Of course not, Oscar,' Jolson replied, pretending to be hurt. 'I was on tour at the time!'

And there were always the celebrity guests. Not just singers like Bing Crosby and Dinah Shore, but also actors like Humphrey Bogart and Charles Laughton – who sang their own versions of 'Mammy' and 'Swanee'.

When Oscar Levant missed one programme, he was replaced by Yehudi Menuhin. Jolson was as much the confident bill topper with this sort of competition as he had been that night at the Metropolitan Opera when he followed Caruso.

There were seventy-two Jolson Kraft radio programmes. The last was broadcast on his supposed sixty-third birthday – 26 May 1949. The pattern hardly changed. He continued to sing the same songs – twice if he liked them particularly, throwing producers into a frenzy because most of the shows were live – and to tell the same sort of jokes. These often had something to do with cheese.

'I saw a wonderful film last night, Oscar,' he said on one programme. 'It was called *Cheese every Saturday*.'

'You mean *Chicken every Saturday*,' corrected Levant.

'Oscar,' Al added in mock disgust. 'You just failed the Kraft loyalty test.'

Radio was the medium for Jolson now. There was talk of

him starring in his own film, but he didn't appear to be interested.

The owner of New York's Roxy Theatre invited Jolson to appear live on the stage of his cinema. He wanted to do six shows a day – for $40,000 a week. Al turned him down. 'I don't need that sort of money – or to work that hard,' he replied.

Meanwhile, many of the biggest American stars were coming to the London Palladium – the only big variety theatre left in England. Danny Kaye, Jack Benny and Bob Hope were really drawing people in. The invitations rolled into Jolson's home, to Columbia Pictures and to NBC – 'Please come to the Palladium.'

Al replied, 'Everyone's a sensation there. I like to set records.'

The only live shows he wanted to do were benefit concerts and every time word got out that Jolson was to appear there was hardly room for the other people on the bill to get through the stage door.

When he sang for a benefit in honour of Bob Hope at the Hollywood Friars Club, he demanded a full orchestra and a runway through the makeshift theatre created for the occasion out of the main dining lounge. The Friars turned him down on the question of the runway and so Al had to content himself with removing the vase of flowers in front of him and using the table as a stage. It turned out to be the usual sort of Jolson performance.

Al Jolson was quite clearly happier now than he had ever been in his life. Erle and he, as far as everyone could see, were happy as a married couple and, although they had no children, it was quite startling to see how well they got on together.

He was proud of his pretty wife and liked to be photographed kissing her goodbye in the mornings before leaving for the studio date for Kraft.

When an ignorant waiter asked him what his daughter wanted to choose from the menu, he pulled the man's sleeve and told him, 'She's too young to be my daughter. That's my wife.'

[268]

Meanwhile, several journalists tried to contact Ruby Keeler to find out her views on the new Jolson success story. She constantly refused to comment. However, she did admit to one writer that she had not seen the film.

In 1948, Jolson donated the deeds of the $75,000 estate he owned in Mulholland Drive, Hollywood Hills, to the Cedars of Lebanon Hospital, while he and Erle went to live in Palm Springs. He said he was grateful for the good health he now enjoyed.

'I may not be alive in ten seconds,' he told a reporter at this time, 'but I feel better now than I have for twenty years.'

To prove the point, Erle and Al adopted a baby boy and called him Asa Junior. They had to wait months before the adoption agency approved them as prospective parents, but when Asa finally turned up, Al was a happy and proud father once again.

'Erle's crazy idea about kids,' he explained. 'Nuts about them – and so am I. I used to watch her with other people's kids. Why, I betcha if we hadn't found one of our own she'd be going into the baby-sitting business, just to be near kids,' he joked.

When there was no doubt that Asa would be theirs, the Jolsons converted a spare bedroom into a nursery – complete with a desert-air lamp to make sure that nothing could be wrong with the atmosphere.

'Look at him, honey, Just look at him,' Al would call to Erle. 'What a kid. What a sweetheart. Makes you want to sing or cry or something. He's just wrappin' those tiny fingers around my heart.'

And he planned the future expectantly. 'Gonna send him to a good school,' Al told reporters. 'But a hard one. Want no spoilin' of this boy. You can't always count on money. Sometimes I read the papers and I start singing. "I'd climb the highest mountain . . . and then jump off. . ."'

He was to continue to tell stories about Asa Junior till he died. In one of his last broadcasts with Crosby he joked about the boy's amazing progress in arithmetic.

'You mean he can count all the way to ten,' Bing asked. 'To

ten? Bing, don't be silly. He can go right up to the king.'

Although Jolson was now proving that he was once more a top man in entertainment, it pained him to be thought old – even if he continually joked about it. He began tinting his greying hair black. He had to wear glasses to read by and to walk down the street, too. Yet if he saw someone he knew approaching, he'd make sure that the spectacles were back in his pocket before anyone noticed. His head was also held noticeably high – as if to balance an invisible crown he believed was rightfully his.

At the Hillcrest Country Club he was his old brash self. He didn't bother to get his friends sturgeon any more. Just occasionally, though, he still felt unsure of himself when he was about to do a benefit at the club.

'Al, put on the blackface and you'll feel better,' Jack Benny told me he advised him on one occasion.

'Somehow,' he explained, looking back to those days, 'he could lose himself under that makeup.'

That, as much as anything, could have been the real reason for Jolson's reluctance to face 'real' live audiences after his comeback. 'I die every time I go on to a stage,' he confessed more than once. 'What's the use of my falling on my face now?'

But in the late 1940s he wasn't likely to fall on his face.

Early in 1948 he went to Washington, saw his step mother and his half brothers and sisters and just like old times, called into the White House. President Truman welcomed him as an old fan. 'I used to see you in Missouri,' he told him – and asked Al about the way he had managed to hold audiences spellbound over the years.

Jolson told him that he was at last thinking of retiring.

'I'll kiss sixty-two goodbye next May,' he said, only getting near to admitting his age. 'And I'm trying to find a way to quit.'

'Don't do it, Al,' the President told him. 'You might drop dead.'

So Jolson announced he was going to keep on singing – and introduced a number on the radio especially for Asa Junior – called 'Nearest Thing To Heaven'.

His records were selling everywhere, in Japan and

Germany as well as in the United States, Britain and Western Europe. His radio programme was doing so well that it was now getting higher ratings than any other. At the end of 1947 Jolson had been voted most popular male singer on the air – with Crosby coming second, Perry Como third and Sinatra fourth.

Everything Jolson recorded sold in tens of thousands. But in 1948 the musicians of America went on strike, and there were no orchestral backings for him. Decca got over that by recording two sides with the Mills Brothers and their guitar – 'Down Among The Sheltering Palms' and 'Is It True What They Say About Dixie?' and there were another two sides with a mixed chorus.

Jack Kapp of Decca was responsible for the last two. He was watching a televised rally at New York's Madison Square Garden celebrating the birth of the new State of Israel.

'Al, you should have seen it,' Kapp told him on the phone immediately after the broadcast. 'It was the most moving thing I've ever seen. They sang 'Hatikvah' – you know Israel's national anthem. Al, do me a favour, especially for me. Record it for us.'

Al recorded 'Hatikvah' and an adaptation of an old Jewish folk tune which he called 'Israel'. The royalties he donated to the United Jewish Appeal. 'It's the most wonderful thing I've ever sung,' he said. 'I've never been so proud to sing a song in my life.'

Jolson and *The Jolson Story* were so successful that Columbia made a decision that was absolutely unique for a film biography of its kind. They decided to film a sequel – and this time there was talk of Al playing himself.

Al thought it wise not to pursue this suggestion after a pretty girl had approached him with the greeting, 'Gee Mr Jolson, you're much better looking on the screen.'

He may not have had the girls stopping in their tracks when they saw him, but he still had full control over the people to whom he sang. At a party given by Morris Stoloff, Jolson sang his heart out. When he finished, the entire place

[271]

was in rapturous silence. Stoloff approached another of the guests to give a song of his own.

'I can't follow that,' replied Frank Sinatra – and walked away.

Fifteen

'N' Everything

JOLSON NOW HAD MORE friends than ever before in his life. There were the new generation of admirers for whom the sound of his voice provided a constant supply of magic. There were the show business people who clearly wanted to get near his renewed success in the hope that some of it might rub off on to them. And there were the old timers for whom he still represented all that was brash, all that was exciting and all that was pulsating about entertainment.

To them Al Jolson was the greatest thing that had ever happened. One man, a shirt manufacturer called Sammy Hamlin, used regularly to ring Jolson's California home from his own house in New York. All he'd say was 'Al, I love you – goodbye.' He'd follow Al around the country – sometimes sleeping on the steps of the singer's hotel all night so as not to miss Jolson's early start to the day.

Another devotee was a New York dentist, Sam Lubalin. If Jolson rang him from Los Angeles to say he had a toothache, Lubalin would cancel his appointments for two days and fly to California. For his devotion, Jolson gave him a small percentage of the profits of *The Jolson Story*.

In his own way Harry Cohn was just as devoted an admirer. Back in the days when *The Jolson Story* was still just an idea, it was his faith in the greatest entertainer he had ever seen which persuaded him to go ahead with the project and before long to do so with enthusiasm.

Now Cohn was walking through the studio corridors with a look of triumph about him. He had told all the doubters that he would succeed and now he was determined not to let anyone forget it.

And if *The Jolson Story* could succeed, so could a sequel. What is more he was willing to let the singer call the tune even more this time than for *The Jolson Story*. After all, it had been the soundtrack and Jolson's voice on that track which had been largely responsible for its triumph.

This time he felt he could afford to be magnanimous and if Al wanted to play himself – so be it.

He wasn't being very subtle. But nor was he betraying his real reason for the magnanimity. This was because there were rumours that Jolson was moving to MGM – and that he had agreed that Gene Kelly should play him this time.

However, predictably, Al was still slightly taken with the idea of playing himself and even did a test shot singing 'She's A Latin From Manhattan' to a group of soldiers. But now Jolson himself was the one to call a halt. Why risk sinking a ship that was very successfully floating along?

The Jolson Story had been full of illusions that had proved exceedingly profitable. Why try to shatter those illusions now?

Larry Parks had done wonders with *The Jolson Story*. Let the people, he thought, see the rest of that picture – as though they were picking up the tale where they had left it before going to buy a packet of popcorn.

'This kid Larry Parks plays me better than I play myself,' he said – and was only half joking.

In August 1949 the people saw the result. The preamble after the opening titles promised, rather pessimistically, 'The rest of the story of Jolson.' It was called *Jolson Sings Again* – as if he had ever really stopped. It began in the same nightclub where the earlier picture had ended. There was a quick flash of Parks miming to Jolson's 'Rockabye' and dissolving quickly into the search at home for his missing wife.

Conveniently, the night-club scene ended after Evelyn Keyes' departure and there was no need to call her back to complete her side of the story. Just as Ruby had left Jolson's life in the early 'forties, so Julie Benson had ceased to exist on the screen.

The plot went through Jolson's fallow period, through his triumphs in the war and his meeting with a young brunette nurse called Ellen Clark – Ruby Keeler had a new name in *The Jolson Story* so Erle Galbraith had to have one in the follow up.

Once more, Al mimed his songs on film – each demonstration take at Columbia prefaced by a clapper board. Once again, his enthusiasm occasionally got the better of him. He had to race to catch up with his own voice – a problem never obviously one Larry suffered with, as far as the audiences were concerned, anyway. At times, Al loved every minute of showing the assembled technicians what a great 'mover' he was. At sixty-four he was still managing to do the occasional dance step that was as much an impossibility for Larry Parks in *Jolson Sings Again* as it had been in *The Jolson Story*. But occasionally, it was apparent that Al was both bored and frustrated by this exercise. Wearing a sports jacket over a heavy sweater, he appeared thoroughly delighted when a take was over. The smile he had had on his face when singing, totally disappeared just as soon as the last note had left his throat – and he walked off, still on camera, before the orchestra had finished playing.

Barbara Hale played the new Mrs Jolson. She had the same drawling Southern accent as Erle, the same teasing of the man old enough to be her father, and the same addiction to knitting.

'This time she's really got to look like Erle,' Al told Sidney Buchman who was now officially writing and producing the picture.

For six weeks before filming began, Larry was working in front of his mirror, miming the songs in the movie for eight hours a day.

Barbara Hale has described to me making *Jolson Sings Again* as 'one long holiday – and about the best holiday I ever had. It was a blessed event.'

She was a young girl, barely into her twenties who had

made an occasional Columbia film before, but had never even approached a starring role until now. 'Max Arnow, the talent scout at Columbia, asked me if I could do a Southern accent. I said that I could – and showed them. The next thing I knew, I was being asked to play the part of Erle. I met her and we laughed over my attempts to talk the way she did – but perhaps not quite so broad. She was lovely. Later, she even let me have some clothes of hers that she no longer needed.'

As for Al, 'he was a darlin'. He was on the set quite a lot of the time and seemed to get on very well with Larry. I didn't have a lot to do with him, but he was very nice to everyone. I was in sheer awe of him. I was told I was going to meet him and just didn't know what to do. I sat down and when he came over to me to shake my hand, I was just crying.'

The film took a lot longer to complete than was expected. 'In the scene on the Jolson home patio, I was supposed to be sitting on a hammock knitting. Well, I decided that if I had to knit, it might as well be something useful. So I made my husband a sweater. The filming took so long that I had to keep folding my knitting under. But the time, we finished, that sweater was six feet long!'

Ludwig Donath played Cantor Yoelson again – this time, apart from the brief synagogue sequence, always without his skullcap – but Tamara Shayne's Mama Yoelson died just before Al's tour of the battle zones began.

There was the trauma of his losing part of a lung, and then the great triumph of *The Jolson Story* – with no less than ten minutes of extracts from the original picture. They were not only entertaining – there were advertising a picture that Columbia had every intention of reissuing.

Once more Parks was superb, once more Al's voice was magnificent. It wasn't really the same voice as before. This time, it was even deeper and slightly more nasal. The old man of about sixty-four was singing better than ever.

Strangely both Jonie Taps and Morris Stoloff had the same explanation for this, 'He was so much more confident now. He couldn't help sounding better.' And there were new

Jolson hits to go with the picture. 'Is It True What They Say About Dixie?' became as great a revival hit as 'April Showers' had been three years before. 'I Only Have Eyes For You' looked like rivalling 'The Anniversary Song' – though nothing could really succeed in doing that. It was the top musical film of 1949.

Within five years it was to have taken $5 million and be listed among the ten most successful films of all time. It wasn't the success that *The Jolson Story* had been – almost nothing could be. But it was successful enough for most people. And it kept Jolson on top. Nothing, it seemed, could make him slip now. Everyone appeared still to want him. There were more Bing Crosby radio programmes, more shows for Kraft. And now he started thinking seriously about the television offers that kept dropping on his doormat.

He and Larry Parks made frequent radio appearances together and when his shadow wasn't around, he joked about him on other people's shows.

'When I die,' he said with a roguish grin and chuckle, 'they'll bury Larry Parks.'

Jimmy Durante had Al as guest on his radio shows. 'Notice, Mr Jolson,' he called, 'I don't need a Larry Parks to play the black notes.'

As for Parks himself, a big row with Columbia Pictures robbed him of the sort of parts he wanted. He complained of being typecast. 'That's just what I am,' he told a columnist, 'a shadow.'

He was loaned to MGM for *Love Is better than Ever* with Elizabeth Taylor – and it was not only Miss Taylor's worst picture but almost the worst flop in that studio's history.

Jolson did not concern himself about Parks. He did not worry about Oscar Levant, who now was constantly grumbling about the Kraft show and its writers. 'It's all above their heads,' he told Jolson.

Al replied, 'When things went above our heads when I was with Dockstader, everyone ducked.'

As the money rolled in for the Broadway opening of *Jolson Sings Again,* and as he continued to draw a minimum of

$1,000 a week from Decca for his records – in addition to the royalties – so the pressure built up for new Jolson enterprise.

He was for once taking television seriously and CBS believed they had just the deal to satisfy him. But the money still wasn't right and he wanted time to think.

What he was really tempted to consider was getting back to the live audience once more. Somehow now he felt ready for it again. Once more he wanted to see the reaction on people's faces when he sang to them.

Columbia Pictures provided him with the answer to his dream. They asked if he would agree to make a tour of the East Coast, plugging *Jolson Sings Again*. It turned into a nation-wide tour – travelling by aeroplane, by train, by car.

Once again, there was the sound of Jolson in the flesh singing his great old songs. The man who had always known how to tailor his appeal to an audience hadn't lost any of his old wisdom. In the Chinese district of New York he sang 'My Yellow Jacket Girl', echoing days of *Honeymoon Express*, and adding a chorus of 'Chinatown My Chinatown' for good measure. In the Italian districts, he gave a sample of 'Come Back To Sorrento' and his impersonation of Caruso.

But it was in the Bronx and Brooklyn that Al Jolson really felt he had come home. To the bearded men in wide-brimmed Homburg hats and their wives in headscarves he sang again 'The Cantor For The Sabbath'. When he told them that his next song 'Hatikvah' had raised more than $100,000 for the United Jewish Appeal, the cry was 'Mazzeltov'.

He told them stories in Yiddish, traded recipes for gefilte fish and made certain that there would always be a Jewish following for *Jolson Sings Again*. The Yiddish Press made certain of it for him – with its own lavish praise of the new picture.

While in the mood, he ordered the William Morris agency to get busy on a tour of Israel – 'just as soon as I get this television thing settled'.

For the moment, he was consolidating what he already had. And what he was very big at still was making records.

[278]

Every time a Jolson 78 was pressed, it was snapped up in the shops and stores of every country where the biopics had played. Some discs were superb. Every Jolson sound on tunes like 'God's Country' and 'Remember Mother's Day' were sung as though he were still on the Winter Garden stage and still making love to that audience. But others were, frankly, disappointing. He recorded a whole set – later issued on LP – of Stephen Foster numbers. Apart from 'De Camptown Races' and 'Oh! Susanna', they were all very pedestrian – and sounded as though no great effort had been put into them, that they were made as though to fulfil a contract and for no other purpose. With television, he was sure he would do much better.

He was becoming more keen on television because it represented the sort of challenge he had never been able to turn down. But he was wary of the effect it had on performers. He knew that it was too intimate a medium for the kind of performance he personally gave. There were three or four sets in his own home – quite remarkable for those days – and he would watch them fascinated.

He saw a youngster on the screen one evening and threw up his hands. 'That fellow,' he said in disgust, 'proves that all you have to do to succeed on TV is to show up.'

But on another occasion, he sat glued to the screen long after the star had left and the show had dissolved into the commercials.

He had felt shattered watching Frankie Laine singing 'Mule Train'. It was the sort of frenzy he himself had employed. 'No wonder they call that kid the Al Jolson of 1949,' he murmured to Erle. 'He's good – darn good.' And he quite definitely didn't like admitting it.

Finally, he and CBS came to terms. He was going to lead a big television minstrel show and it was going to be one played with all the old ballyhoo, including the once familiar street parades.

Trade magazines featured full page advertisements of the new 'find' – a big hand seemingly clutched around the corner of the page and announcing, 'I'm coming.'

He was coming to the tune of more than a million dollars over the next three years. But he had other things on his mind before work on the series began.

He and Erle had adopted a baby girl as a sister for Asa Junior. They called her Alicia and they had big plans for the two children.

There were two film deals cooking, too. Harry Cohn was pressing Jolson to do a third picture with Larry Parks and it was near the signature stage. But first he wanted to work on the other deal – one in which he was definitely going to play himself.

Jerry Wald and Norman Krasna of RKO Radio Pictures wanted to present a full flag-waving picture about the work of the USO during the war, but it would be centred around Jolson. He was going to play Al Jolson because he was never able to play anyone else. But this time there would be no other stars to take the glory away from him. It was going to be a true story, but not a documentary. And there would be songs by the bundle.

Al was very excited about the picture which had a working title of *The Stars and Stripes Forever*. But just as production was about to get under way, a new title was agreed – *Let Me Sing*.

New tunes had been written to go with the standard numbers which inevitably had to fit into a Jolson picture of any kind, but it was Irving Berlin's song, which Al had first sung in *Mammy* and then used as the fitting prelude to *The Jolson Story*, which was going to be the title theme.

The trade Press announced that Jolson would begin work on the film just as soon as he had finished a whirlwind tour of eight Midwest one-nighters.

He posed for new pictures – at the piano with Wald and Krasna. And then came the doubts. Not because people wouldn't want to hear him any more – but because those publicity pictures told a story. Showbusiness folk who had kidded Jolson about his age now looked at them and felt a sense of shock. There was a worn look about him.

About this time, London *Daily Express* columnist Eve Perrick met Jolson at a party.

[280]

She wrote, 'From his voice, from the stories of his triumphant renaissance into the entertainment world after *The Jolson Story* and *Jolson Sings Again,* you imagined he was someone of whom you would say "Marvellous. He looks about fifty." Jolson looked all of his sixty-four or more years.'

But Al Jolson was not going to admit it, and there were always those ready to have a joke about his age. There were others who would joke about his money. Bob Hope told an audience who had expected to see Jolson at a benefit, 'He couldn't come tonight – because he couldn't get a sitter for the Bank of America.'

It did the Jolson ego good to hear those stories, although it was easy to see that he was more happy with jokes about his money than his age. It was quite obvious just by following him down the street that he was no longer a young man – but if he thought anyone recognised him, he would quicken his step and hold his head up high.

He was honoured as *Variety*'s Man of the Year and in November 1949 the Variety Club of Washington named him their Personality of the Year – that was the kind of praise he liked.

The presentation was made by Secretary of Defense Stephen T. Early – the man he had bombarded with requests to be allowed to sing to the Troops eight years earlier.

'This is presented to you in recognition of your outstanding contributions to the world of entertainment,' he said. 'The District of Columbia is happy to bring to the attention of its citizens the achievements of one of its own sons.'

Al replied 'Jolie's rarin' to go.'

Unlike those from RKO, the publicity pictures released by Decca and the radio networks were usually at least ten years old – or doctored to look that way.

The pictures he had around his house – lining the staircase and the landing upstairs – were of an earlier vintage and mostly of himself in blackface. As always, he could hide from reality that way.

But strangely he needed no camouflage to hide from the insurance companies. Early in 1949 he did the well-nigh impossible. At the age of (at least) sixty-three and after a rigorous medical check up, he took out $75,000 worth of life insurance.

By 1950, Al was seemingly more popular than ever. He had just recorded a number that once again had his name on the composer's credits – 'No Sad Songs For Me'. This, based on the title of a hit film of the time, was the result of collaboration with Harry Akst, the man responsible for another of his big sellers of this period 'Baby Face'.

In Britain Jolson had shown the way to another new business trend. His name was featured in the country's very first batch of long-playing records – with a selection from *Jolson Sings Again.*

When Al met Harry Truman again, he asked the President if he intended running for office once more. 'I don't know,' Truman told him. 'They may not want me again. Maybe I should run on the slogan "I need the job".'

Al told him of the time he had been to Key West, and was shown to the same room that the President had occupied there.

'It was a room with two beds and I spent the night jumping from bed to bed. But I never did figure out which one the President had slept in,' he said afterwards.

Jolson always liked talking to the great – or the men he believed to be great. At the same time, he generally had a word of encouragement for new people who were just starting out on their show business careers.

He made a transatlantic telephone call from his Palm Springs home to Jean Simmons in London – because, he told her, he believed her performance as Ophelia in the Laurence Olivier version of *Hamlet* was the most exciting thing he had seen in a non-musical film.

Jolson seeing *Hamlet?* The cynics squirmed and Jolson himself laughed at their reaction.

'I like to see a gal play romance and character parts,' he said. 'But then I haven't changed my style or my delivery for fifty years. It's your heart in it that matters.'

And he could have added 'your ego'. He said in that same

conversation that he thought Harry Lauder, W. C. Fields and himself were the only three really great showmen of his time.

Jean Simmons didn't disagree with him – and nor did anyone else in 1950. He told her about his new contract with CBS. But for once Al Jolson was not the confident extrovert the world had known. He had his doubts about the medium, he confessed. Television, he predicted, would never take the place of radio.

'Television is eating talent and swallowing it wholesale,' he said. 'You just can't get people to look at the same faces every week. But they'll listen to the same performer on the radio – unseen.'

In a way he was right – although he had no idea how radio itself would be swallowed equally wholesale by the same monster. But people don't see the same big entertainers as often on television as they once heard them on radio. Even those with weekly shows have much bigger holiday breaks – and many of the really big stars content themselves with the occasional 'spectacular'.

Television was worrying Jolson, but in the autumn of 1950 something happened to take his mind off the subject.

Al and Erle had spent the previous Christmas in Honolulu where there had been a typical Jolson show for the troops – some 12,000 of them. On the whole, it all looked very peaceful and there was little to say about it – except that it rekindled the magic candle inside Jolson that seemed to light up whenever he saw soldiers wanting to hear his voice.

The flags he saw being waved on his television screen late in the summer of 1950 were being carried by men who didn't look half as happy as the guys in Honolulu. They were in a far less happy place – Korea.

The United States had answered the call of the United Nations Security Council – meeting without the Soviet Union, and so without their veto, too – and had gone to fight the North Koreans.

Al never even gave the idea of 'My country right or wrong' a thought. As far as Jolson was concerned, his country was always right.

[283]

He rang the White House again, 'I'm gonna go to Korea,' he told a startled official on the phone. 'No one seems to know anything about the USO, and it's up to President Truman to get me there.'

He was promised that President Truman and General MacArthur, who had taken command of the Korean front, would get to hear of his offer. But for four weeks there was nothing.

Finally, Louis Johnson, Secretary of Defense, sent Jolson a telegram. SORRY DELAY BUT REGRET NO FUNDS FOR ENTERTAINMENT STOP USO DISBANDED STOP.

The message was as much an assault on the Jolson sense of patriotism as the actual crossing of the 38th Parallel had been.

'What are they talkin' about,' he thundered. 'Funds! Who needs funds! I got my own mazzuma ain't I? I'll pay myself. Comin' too, Harry?'

Harry Akst, his right arm in the World War, was with him when the challenging wire from Washington arrived. 'No, Jolie,' he said. 'I've had enough – and so have you.' He didn't think Jolson should make a trip of that kind.

Al tried not to worry about the refusal. 'OK,' he said. 'I'll get someone else.'

Abe Lastfogel of the William Morris agency followed the matter through. The next day he rang Akst and requested that he change his mind. 'I want you to go, Harry,' he said. 'Al wants you to go.'

'If he wants me to go so badly, why didn't he ask me himself?' From Lastfogel there was no answer. Two days later he put the same point to Jolson himself. 'Because you're beautiful,' he told him.

In the thirty-odd years the two men had been together, Akst said he had never known Jolson to ask for anything.

Akst telephoned Erle to tell her he was going along with Al for the ride. 'It's Next Town Reilly again,' he said – recalling the character they had known on the racetrack circuit. Reilly was always losing, but optimistically certain that in the 'next town everything would be all right'.

Jolson was moving on to yet another 'next town'.

Erle was in tears when the military car called at their Palm Springs house to take her husband to the airport. She and Asa Junior came along for the ride – in which Al was all dressed up for his new part.

He wore a ski cap, a hunting jacket and a pair of riding boots left over from the second act of *Hold on to your Hats*.

As they boarded the plane, Asa Junior called out, 'Daddy. Are you going to 'Okio?'

'Okio it was. Tokyo, where Al had vowed to sing 'Mammy' in the shadow of Hirohito's palace five years before, was to be the headquarters from which he would work – but on the precise understanding that he would take no outside engagements while there.

'Just imagine,' he laughed, 'outside engagements!' 'That means we mustn't play at the Loew Theatre, Pusan.'

Al laughed till it hurt – and hurt it did. He had to have eighteen shots of antibiotics and vaccine before the military authorities allowed him on their plane. It all proved much too painful to sit down.

Despite the discomfort, Al Jolson was like a little boy facing a new adventure. He looked very pleased with himself indeed.

But when the two veteran entertainers arrived in Tokyo, he wasn't feeling quite so happy. There had been an overnight stop at Wake Island after the Stratocruiser developed engine trouble and the only place the two men, singer and accompanist, could sleep was in a double bunk in a very cold, very damp hut. Both arrived in Tokyo suffering from streaming colds and irritating coughs, caught, Erle was to say, from an officer they had met on the plane.

Just as they checked into their hotel, Al went down to the reception desk and asked for the nearest hospital. He was directed to an Army dispensary where he was immediately ordered to lie down.

'What are you here for, Mr Jolson?' asked the young doctor who was examining him.

'To sing,' said Al and he croaked a few lines of 'Mammy' to prove it.

'I'm afraid you won't be able to sing for weeks. Take it very easy. You're not a young man, you know.'

That was the one thing Al did know – but also the very thing he didn't want to be reminded about. It was the same old challenge.

'I gotta sing, son – so don't give me any of your nonsense.'

He was obviously going to be a difficult patient. The doctor gave Al a towel to put over his head and a bowl of steaming menthol to put under his nose – and ordered him to inhale for thirty minutes. Jolson came out of the tent after the thirty minutes and promised to repeat the dose every hour for the next week.

But what was he going to do, now that he had come all that way to Tokyo? 'What da ya think I can do?' he taunted Harry Akst. 'What da ya think I can do? Sing that's what – if only my voice wasn't so rusty. Perhaps I'll just tell a few jokes.'

A staff car came to his hotel to take him to the military hospital in the heart of the Japanese capital. 'Just gonna tell your guys a few jokes,' he told the commanding officer who came to meet him at the door. 'My pipes are a bit bad. Hope they understand.'

'Of course, Mr Jolson,' said the CO. 'Of course, they'll understand.'

But Jolson could see the look on the face of the base commander – and the hospital was regarded as a base by everyone in it – to know that it wasn't really going to be enough.

'Look, Harry,' said Al as he was being escorted down the hospital corridor. 'I'll just sing 'em one song. Then it won't seem so bad. After all, look what some of these guys have got. Not just a little cold.'

There was an uproarious clamour as Jolson entered the big hospital waiting hall which was being turned into a temporary theatre. There were cheers. There were whistles and there was the distinct thump of wooden crutches on the tiled floor.

Harry Akst played the opening bars of 'Mammy' and Al picked it up on the chorus. He coughed – but ordered Akst to

[286]

play 'Swanee', and then 'April Showers'. Also 'Some
Enchanted Evening' and 'Bali Hai' – the hit songs from *South
Pacific.*

He sang for nearly an hour, joked for twenty minutes more,
then apologised for having to go. But he didn't go straight
back to the hotel. His driver had to drop him off at the
dispensary first, for another dose of menthol.

The next day there was another hospital stop – and a new
dose of steam inhalation to follow.

Jolson always had the people waiting to hear him sing and
there was always a song specially for them. But there were
occasions when he had to work harder than others.

At Iwokuni, just before Al and Harry took off for Korea, he
had trouble getting through to his audience. In fact, half of
what should have been his audience weren't even there.

'Where are these guys?' Jolson asked between songs –
looking hurt but feeling positively crushed. That sort of thing
had not happened to him for a long time. One man out front
struck up enough courage to tell him.

'It's our Wing Commander,' he said in a broad Australian
accent. 'He didn't come back from Korea today.'

That was all Al had to hear. He left the platform, walked out
into the airfield and pushed the men outside into the mess hall.
'Now,' he said, 'you gotta hear me. The CO had warned that
you'll all be in trouble if you don't listen to my songs. Now
what'll it be?'

Once finished, Jolson rushed back to the dispensary for
more inhalations. But now they weren't doing him as much
good as before. The next day Al, Harry and the 'purple latrine
on wheels' – Akst's piano – were loaded on a plane for the
Korean city of Pusan.

At Eighth Army headquarters, Jolson was introduced to the
commanding General, Walton Walker. He sang his heart out
in Pusan – entertaining thousands of men in a swimming pool.
'I don't feel so good,' he told them. 'But maybe after listening
to me, you'll feel worse!'

The Jolson-Akst show, moved on to Chinghai, Miryang and
Masan – while the continuous sound of rifle fire interjected

itself between the bars of his song.

'If they don't like my show why don't these guys go away?' Jolson joked – and brought the house down quicker than the North Koreans could manage.

In a hospital ward, a nurse caught a soldier bandaged from head to foot applauding wildly while his hands were supposed to be suspended in traction.

'Don't do that,' she scolded. 'That could be very dangerous for you.'

'I don't care,' answered the soldier, 'this guy's good.'

But there was no menthol in the hospital for Jolson. Now he had to be content with a gargle of antiseptic solution. It really wasn't enough.

'Al's going on nothing but nerve now,' said Harry. At times, he was so exhausted he had hardly enough energy to use the gargle. But he had enough to feel angry. Jolson had been the first entertainer to come to Korea, but it was obvious that the other stars were taking their time in following him.

A tired and very shaken Al Jolson came on the short wave from Pusan to talk to Louella Parsons live on her Los Angeles radio show. He told her, 'You know, honey, I performed for fighting men on battle fronts all over the world in World War Two. But there's never been anything to compare with this. This is no border line skirmish. This is war with all the hell, death and destruction that only war can bring.

'I'd like to see some of you Senators and Congressmen come over here and live under the horrible conditions these kids – and believe me, they are just kids – are living under. They'd find out that this Korean thing is the worst ever. The mud, the stench, the filth everywhere are unbelievable.'

Then he added something right from the heart. It was a typical Jolson statement, 'Just the same, Louella, I wouldn't change what I've done and trade it for a million dollars.

'Louella, listen honey, I want you to do me a big favour – and don't fail me on this – tell all the Bob Hopes, Jack Bennys, Bing Crosbys, Tony Martins, Eddie Cantors, Danny Thomases, George Jessels and all the others, "If you don't come to Korea to entertain these kids immediately, and do your part you'll be sorry for the rest of your lives – and I mean that.'''

No Jolson message got through louder or clearer – despite the static line. 'Oh what a ham I am,' he added for good measure.

Before Al had left Korea, the first USO troupe had arrived. But before they came, there were more Jolson concerts, more songs and more coughs.

General Douglas MacArthur, not yet in disgrace with President Truman for wanting to extend the conflict into China, invited Al to his home. While waiting for the General to arrive, Mrs MacArthur entertained Al and Harry with small talk about her family, and got round to Jolson's singing. '"Sonny Boy" was always my favourite,' she said.

That was enough. Cough or no cough, Al motioned Harry to the piano in the MacArthur lounge – and sang 'Sonny Boy' specially for his hostess.

The General entered the room while Al was still singing. He spent the next two hours talking to him about the fighting, about life back home and about Jolson's singing. When he left, Al told reporters, 'I think the General is one of the greatest men there is.'

That evening a military policeman arrived at Jolson's hotel – with a brown envelope. Al opened it with fumbling fingers. He was quite clearly more excited than he had been for a long time.

Inside was a large photograph. It bore the inscription, 'To Al Jolson with gratitude and admiration. Douglas Mac-Arthur, Japan 1950.'

On Al's last night in Tokyo before returning home, Brigadier General Paul Kelly gave him a surprise dinner – complete with geisha girls. But they were not the usual sort of geishas. They had been specially trained to sing 'April Showers' – the song he had sung for the last time in Korea the day before.

Jolson said he was feeling better now. But Harry thought otherwise. It was just another form of self-deception on Al's part to prime himself for his reunion with Erle.

[289]

At the airport he was bubbling with jokes. His face was still deeply suntanned. On the aircraft he chatted ten to the dozen with newspapermen, all anxious for a story on how he had managed in Korea after forty-two shows.

Every time the stewardess came round with the drinks, Al put his hand in his pocket and pulled out a couple of dollar bills. Through the whole journey to Hawaii, he paid for the drinks and refused to allow anyone else to spend a thing.

He talked as fast as the words would come out. 'They're the greatest guys the world has even seen – and Mrs MacArthur, would you believe it, she's a baseball fan. Keeps talking about batting averages. Imagine!'

The plane arrived at Hawaii two hours too late to catch the connecting flight to Los Angeles. 'Never mind,' said Al. 'We'll go to the Royal Hawaiian. And I'm paying – I paid my own way out to Korea, didn't I? So this won't make too much difference.'

Jolson had found himself an audience again. He could afford to be generous, it is true. But now he wanted to be. In September 1950, he felt he had a lot to be thankful for and he didn't want anyone even to have to buy him a glass of whisky. It was Jolson's party.

'Forty-two shows, eh, Jolie?' asked one newspaperman. 'Whatda ya mean forty-two shows? *142*, ain't it?'

Whether it was or not, Harry Akst had to agree that it had certainly seemed like 142.

On the journey one of the Stratocruiser's engines failed. The plane limped back to Hawaii – with Jolson still telling stories about his life, about Broadway, about Hollywood and Korea.

'I wouldn't take a penny or a million dollars for the chance to sing for those guys. Believe me, 150 shows just wasn't enough.'

By the time the plan landed at Los Angeles the next day, Jolson had done 160 shows in Korea – and one reporter said he had told him he did 165. It didn't matter. In the forty-two shows that the records at the Pentagon detail, Al Jolson sang not just his heart out – but every inch of his flesh and spirit, too.

If he had never sung anywhere in his life before arriving in Tokyo a fortnight earlier, his mark would have been made on show business just by making that one trip across the Pacific.

Erle was waiting for Al at the airport. With her was little Asa. Al gave them both a great big hug and handed Asa a sombrero he had picked up in his travels. With a cigarette in his mouth, he posed for the expected pictures.

But the interviews he gave soon after his return were totally unexpected. 'I'm gonna check with my accounts to make sure I've paid enough income tax,' he told the newsmen.

But the real shock was what he said next. 'I'm not interested in anything. I'm really two shakes ahead of a fit. My pulse is fast, I don't sleep good. So I think I'll go up some place, maybe Palm Springs or Arrowhead, I don't know. Maybe a week will do it – if I can sleep.

'And I'm a little nervous.'

'What of the future?' he was asked. 'Well, the Morris Agency want me to do a television around Thanksgiving but I want them to find me somethin' to do for nothing.

'One of the first things I've got to do is to go round to Columbia, to tell Harry Cohn that maybe I won't do a third picture.' It sounded ominous. It was.

Still wearing his overalls with an Air Force badge on the pockets, he showed Erle and the boy into their car and drove away to Palm Springs. He didn't rest. He spoke on the telephone, met friends and 'danced around'. But he looked tired and ill. He was now perhaps three shakes ahead of that fit.

But there was a promise he had to fulfil before thinking about resting. His records were still being played on the radio every hour of the day and Bing Crosby had begged him to appear on his show. Crosby didn't really need Jolson – but he wanted to be the one who was officially to welcome him back to the United States and the homegrown brand of show-business.

The show was being aired in San Francisco.

On 23 October 1950, Al kissed Erle and Asa Junior goodbye, got in his car and drove to Los Angeles Airport. The San Francisco flight was held up ready for the arrival of his party – Al himself, Harry Akst, Eppy and Martin Fried.

Sixteen

When I Leave the World Behind

THE CAR WHICH HAD been waiting at San Francisco's International Airport took less than half an hour to complete the journey along the winding coastline to Downtown San Francisco.

Up and down the hills, alongside the rattling cable cars, to Union Square and the St Francis Hotel – the place where the world's greatest celebrities always stayed when visiting the Golden Gate City.

Al jumped out of the car, rolled his eyes for the cameraman, patted the usher on the back and walked into the lobby.

'What ya want to do, Harry?' Al asked Akst as soon as they got to their room.

'Well, maybe we should discuss the show.'

'Sure, but let's go down to Fisherman's Wharf first and have some of that seafood everyone talks about. Haven't been in 'Frisco for a long time.'

It was as though he were expecting a new earthquake. And in a way he was.

Outside the hotel there was a car waiting for the party. But Al decided to sweat out his fatigue in the hotel's Turkish bath before doing anything else. After the steam session, Al said he felt tired, but very refreshed – and ordered his cronies to get themselves ready. He bounced out of the lobby and into the car, with Eppy and Akst following.

Martin Fried stayed behind because he wanted to work on the musical arrangements for the Crosby show while they were still in his mind. He had a new version of 'I'm Just Wild

About Harry' dedicated to President Truman, that he wanted to try out on the piano.

At the Wharf Al ate a hearty supper – clam chowder, prawns and all the things his doctors, his father and his religion warned him against. He ended up with the more acceptable sole.

At one stage during the meal Al seemed to be searching for a belch that wouldn't come. But he passed off the momentary feeling of flatulence. He had had the same feeling a week earlier – only then it had been much worse.

He and Akst had been to a boxing match at the Olympic Stadium in Los Angeles, to see Enrique Bolanos and 'Little Duke' Dukison scrapping. Just as the fight had reached its climax, Al put his hand to his chest.

'What's the matter Al?' his old friend asked. 'I should never have had that Spanish food on the way here,' Al said looking decidedly pasty. 'I can't resist the stuff – but it always has the same effect.'

Akst drove him back to Beverly Hills. Erle was waiting for him at her mother's house.

'Make him see a doctor, honey,' Akst advised and left.

The next day, the Jolsons went to a doctor. He advised Al to start taking it easy. 'No more Koreas, Mr Jolson,' he said. 'Your heart isn't quite the same as it used to be.'

Jolson panicked. 'What da ya mean, it ain't the same?' he growled in the aggressive tone he had always adopted when faced with an unpleasant fact. 'I'm gonna 'Frisco next week to appear with Bing and I'm gonna make a couple of films.'

'Do all the films and the radio shows you want to do,' said the doctor. 'But no more Koreas.'

Al promptly went to two more doctors – and heard the same advice.

He could not help but think of that advice now as he sat in the restaurant overlooking the bay and the bridge. But there was a lot of satisfaction in being there. People were coming up to him, shaking his hand, telling him how great he was on the stage, on the films and how much they admired his work in Korea.

On the journey back to the hotel, through the Chinatown he had sung about so many times, Al was happily content with his lot. 'They like me, don't they?' he said to Akst. 'Yep. Jolson still has them in his mind.'

Back in his room, Al undressed and put on a bathrobe. Martin Fried was writing a letter and wasn't in the mood to discuss the show the next day.

'Let's play some gin rummy,' said Jolson. It was the sort of command his friends were delighted to accept.

They played two games – and Al won them both. 'Another game, Al?' asked Eppy and got the cards out to deal afresh.

'No,' said Jolson. 'I'm feeling a bit tired. Think I'll just have a lie down.' He looked at Martin Fried, who was already standing up. 'Do Jolie a favour, will you,' he called. 'Go, call room service and get me some bicarbonate of soda.'

Fried dialled room service and went back to the game – or at least intended going back to the game. Instead, he went in to see Al, who was now lying on his small single bed. Jolson looked pale and Fried decided to make another call – to the house doctor.

'There are two,' said the operator. 'But both are out on calls. Would you like the nurse?'

'Yes,' said Fried. 'And ask her to hurry.' Nurse Anne Murchison was there in moments.

Al knew what was going on. But made no protest.

'I heard about a doctor here called Kerr,' he called out. 'Why not get him?'

Akst took a long time to find the doctor – he wasn't listed in the telephone directory. But the hotel nurse knew him and found the number. She took Al's pulse and told him it was nothing to worry about. 'I really think it's just indigestion,' she said. 'But try Dr Kerr.'

The doctor, later to become professor of medicine at the University of California, wasn't very happy about being called.

'It'll take me some time to get there,' he said.

'But this is for Al Jolson,' said Akst.

'Al Jolson? Is he in San Francisco? All right, I'll be straight down. But until I get there, call the house physician again.'

Meanwhile Jolson himself had picked up an extension. 'Don't worry, Doc,' he said, 'I don't want to read in the papers tomorrow that Al Jolson called a big shot doctor out for a dose of indigestion.'

But Dr Kerr detected a note of distress in the singer's voice.

'Don't worry, Mr Jolson. I'm coming. You don't worry about the papers. I won't tell anyone.'

When he arrived at the room at the St Francis, Dr Walter Bech, the house physician, was already there with the patient. He heard Al joke, 'You know, President Truman only had an hour with General MacArthur. I had two.'

Dr Kerr, meanwhile, told Al how much he had always admired him. 'I saw you in London in 1929,' he said.

The doctor went into the bathroom to wash his hands and Anne Murchison took a look at the patient.

'Don't worry, Mr Jolson,' she said. 'You're going to be all right.'

'All right?' said Al. 'Who yer kiddin'? I've got no pulse.'

The two doctors went to the bedside. 'Pull up some chairs,' Al ordered them, lifting his head. 'I've got some stories to tell you.'

Al reached for his pulse again just as Eppy, Harry Akst and Martin Fried joined him at the bedside.

Again he seemed to be pulling himself up. 'Well boys,' he said faintly. 'This is it . . . I'm going.'

The men around the bed looked at each other. Dr Kerr reached for Jolson's pulse. There wasn't one. Dr Bech put his stethoscope to the patient's chest. It was quiet.

Jolson had gone. The greatest entertainer the world had ever known was dead. No applause for his final exit. But tears and curtains.

Seventeen

You Ain't Heard Nothing Yet

THE NEWS OF AL JOLSON'S death hit the front pages of newspapers throughout the world.

In his own city of Los Angeles the *Times* brought out a special Extra edition with three-inch banner headlines, 'AL JOLSON DIES – Heart attack Claims Famed Jazz Singer in SF Hotel.'

The *New York World Telegram* printed a simple cartoon. There was just a pair of white gloves outstretched – with the caption 'The song is ended.'

But what the *World Telegram* did not know that day in October 1950 was that the song was by no means ended. Just as Al Jolson's body was being taken into Temple Israel on Hollywood Boulevard to lie in state for a couple of hours, stores throughout the United States, Canada, Britain and down under in Australia and New Zealand, too, reported an unprecedented demand for Jolson records.

Al Jolson's fans were anticipating a rush to grab every Jolson disc before they were sold out. If those people had known that it would take thirty years before a single Jolson record would be deleted from the catalogue they might not have rushed quite so frantically.

Jolson films were shown on television screens. Cinemas throughout the world had Jolson seasons. In October 1950 there was just the instant feeling of sadness. A real grief had hit the people who had been paying money to see and hear him almost as much as it had struck his contemporaries in show business.

[296]

Women jostled each other to get vantage points in the boulevard outside the temple. Men, women and children filed in a single line to view his body in the open coffin.

It was a fitting end for a king. He wore a blue suit with the Jewish prayer shawl draped around his shoulders. In his lapel was the ribbon of an Italian decoration he had been awarded for his work in entertaining the troops during the war – a unique gesture by a formerly enemy country.

When the funeral service began, it was plain that America's great showmen had come to pay homage. Jack Benny and George Burns were among the pall bearers. So were Eddie Cantor and George Jessel. Larry Parks was one of the principal mourners together with Harry Cohn, Sidney Skolsky, William Demarest and Louis B. Meyer.

Erle, who had collapsed on hearing the news of Al's death – she was knitting a pair of socks when Dr Kerr got on the line – had to be helped into the temple by her brother, still an Army sergeant.

Harry Jolson was at the service and so were his half brothers. Harry said that the past was forgiven but not forgotten. It was an obvious statement. No one who had ever heard a Jolson record could forget the experience. The bitter hatred that Harry had for Al at times couldn't blind him to the impact his younger brother had made. The jealousy that he and many of the people who had maligned the Jolson name had felt could not cover up the admiration they had for the way he could dominate both the audience and the business.

When Jessel finished his eulogy, he whispered 'Goodbye, Al' and walked to the coffin. He did not then realise how much Jolson was to haunt him in the years to come. In the late 1950s George Jessel was invited to appear before the Queen and the Queen Mother for the annual Royal Variety Performance at the London Palladium. 'I had the great honour to dance with the Queen Mother and it was during that dance that I realised their mistake. They thought they had invited Jolson to appear before them and not me. They didn't know he was dead.'

The people who still buy Jolson records and who hear

them regularly on their transistor radios could be forgiven for not knowing it either.

When Jessel entertained troops in Vietnam in 1971 the constant request was for him to sing Jolson songs. For even twenty-one years after the original's death there was still a demand for an imitator.

When Al died, a British newspaper columnist said that even in that act of death Jolson had shown a trooper's timing. He had gone while still on top, before old age and ill health had sapped him of the zest he needed for living.

Daily *Variety* put it more poetically. 'An institution and an era of the show business stopped breathing Monday night in a St Francis hotel suite in San Francisco. A legend now begins to live.

'Al Jolson, the greatest musical comedy star of his time and perhaps of all time, died at the age of sixty-four. The end came suddenly and dramatically. It came at the height of his career, with the cheers of the GIs in Korea fresh in his ears – and a new fabulous picture contract to afford him sweet knowledge that he was still a top star. . .

'He had a record to be envied, both for his war work and as a star. He hit the top in every medium he tried and was already considering television when he died. There is no question among showmen that Jolie would have been great in television, too.'

It was just part of the Jolson heritage – rather different from the one he used to sing about so frequently in the Irving Berlin ballad 'When I Leave The World Behind'. Halfway through the song, he would speak the main chorus, 'I'll leave the sunshine to the flowers, I'll leave the songbirds to the blind. I'll leave the moon above to those in love, when I leave the world behind . . .'

Jack Benny once commented at a benefit concert at which both he and Jolson were featured, 'How do you like that Jolson,' he said, 'he's worth at least $8 million and what does he leave us? Moonbeams!'

In the end Jolson's published will showed he was worth $3,236,000 – practically all of which went to charity. It was to be equally divided between Jewish, Catholic and Protestant institutions with $300,000 of it being devoted to the college education of poor boys and girls.

He had made private arrangements for Erle and the children. She had a $1,000,000 trust fund with a $3,000 weekly allowance. Within months the estate was said to be worth an additional $30,000, the result of dividend interest at the end of the financial year. Erle received this additional amount when Harry Jolson contested the will. He received $10,000 – and let reporters know he would have liked more. But he, too, was to die in the early 1950s.

Their step mother received nothing in the Jolson will. She was dying and her son George kept her 'Aisekla's' death a secret till the end.

Harry Akst and Lou Epstein – the ever-devoted Eppy – were left nothing more than their memories. Al had made it clear that he considered he had looked after them more than enough when he was alive. A lawyer who had been given a ring by Erle soon after Al's death offered it to Eppy as a consolation memento. He said thanks, but he would be content with his memories.

But Jolson himself lives on in these memories as well as in legend and in voice. When Asa Junior was ten years old he was handed the keys to a vault in a Hollywood bank. It contained a real hidden treasure – the tapes of the Jolson radio shows, many of which were soon to be transcribed on to discs by the Decca company and to become bestsellers in their own right, long after his death.

In the annals of his country, the name Al Jolson stands high as a hero. General George Marshall, then Secretary of Defense, pinned on the breast of Asa Junior America's highest decoration – the Medal of Merit, awarded posthumously to Al. The citation read that Jolson had given his life in Korea just as any serving man on the battlefield.

For tourists, Al Jolson is remembered in a towering marble monument at Hollywood's Hillside Memorial Park. Travellers see it glinting in the sun during the day and at night floodlit on their journeys to Los Angeles' main airport.

The memorial was Erle's idea – shortly before she married film producer Norman Krasner and went off to live in Switzerland.

The greatest memorial of all, however, was a record spinning at 33.3 revolutions per minute or a film being projected in a cinema or on a machine in a television studio. For the people who enjoyed Al Jolson in life would continue to do so for as long as they had the chance.

Eighteen

That Haunting Melody

No ONE CAN BE positive about Al Jolson's birthdate. It most
certainly was not 25 May – although that day in late spring
had a lovely feel about it. Just as assuredly it was not 1886,
although when he first started telling people that was the
year in which he was born, it made him seem youthful with a
long future ahead of him. But that was the way things were
done. As a matter of principle, Hollywood studios would take
years off stars' ages. In the generations that have passed
since Asa Yoelson became Al Jolson and wrote out the
details for his own fanciful birth certificate, friends have
remembered his own stories about how he came to adopt the
date.

He told them he had invented the year as well as the
month because he never knew for sure when it was that he
was born. George Jessel, never a dedicated uncritical Jolson
fan, told me he remembered Al saying he had taken off a
year from his real age. Ignoring the fact that in Korea, Al
looked a great deal older than his official sixty-four years, it is
fair to assume that he was born before 1886. Taking Jessel's
story – repeated to me by a number of other contemporaries
over the years – in this case on face value, it can be assumed
that Al Jolson was born at least a hundred years ago,
probably in 1885.

What is beyond doubt is that he made an almost unbelievable impact on the century that followed the events in
Srednicke, as Cossacks rampaged around the tiny, ignorant
self-effacing community there.

The Yoelsons' connection with Srednicke didn't end with the family's emigration to the United States. There were still distant relatives in residence there – until the village itself was virtually wiped off the face of the earth in the holocaust, a time when its most celebrated son was entertaining troops of another nation continents away. (What was left of Srednicke is now the Lithuanian Republic town of Seredzius.)

We know now that this was the mere dawn of a new career for Al Jolson, a new discovery for a generation of kids who are now grandfathers. Any one of the young men in uniform cheered by Jolson singing 'Swanee' or 'April Showers' in a dusty wind-blown gun site or in a mud-clogged tank depot could have told you they were watching the most exciting performer any of them had ever known. What none of them could have imagined was that forty-three years after he had called out to a group of lonely soldiers in Glasgow, 'My name's Jolson and I sing – do you want to hear me?' there would still be people who would shout, 'Yes'.

When Al died in 1950, he had pretty well set a record, among all the others he had scooped up. Few top entertainers had been at the top in show business as long as he. In the years that followed, others would eclipse him in mere longevity. Across the sea, his much-admired contemporary Maurice Chevalier would go on singing for another twenty years. In his own country, mere children like Frank Sinatra would be legends in their own lifetime – a cliché virtually coined for Jolson himself – thirty years later. Bob Hope would be fêted by his President on his eightieth birthday, still actively performing. Fred Astaire, still hale and hearty at eighty-five would be courted as the greatest dancer of all time – and still available for work in character roles on film.

And the one survivor of the Jolson clique, George Burns would at the age of eighty-eight in 1984 still be the master of perfect timing, still the darling of the cabaret circuit and the TV chat show – and telling readers of his latest book that sex at his age was perfectly reasonable – 'just as long as you don't inhale'.

The difference is that Jolson has been dead since 1950 and almost thirty-five years after his death, his name still conjures up an image of a small man in blackface and white gloves who got down on one knee and sang songs that are still being played and hummed wherever popular music is heard.

The difference is that almost thirty-five years after his death, a set of long-playing records of Jolson songs would be advertised on British television and reach halfway up the week's bestseller charts – with Jolson himself singing them. That week, it was ten places higher than the newly-released John Lennon album.

The difference is that thirty-five years after his death, Jolson is known to a generation for whom the names of Cantor, Jessel, Tucker, and all the other sensations of his age are not merely names, but totally forgotten by all but a few stragglers of their age and a handful of aficionados of that period in show business history. It is a fact that Jolson records outsell those of Bing Crosby – who died some twenty-seven years after Al and who made more discs than anyone in show business history.

In 1977, America remembered the Jolson legacy with a special screening of *The Jazz Singer* at the Academy of Motion Picture Arts and Sciences. It commemorated the fiftieth anniversary of the coming of sound. At the same time, the Post Office issued a new stamp.

The Jolson generation has now almost totally disappeared along with its principal idol.

In 1978, Al's most devoted fan, Jack L. Warner died.

Five years later, he was followed by George Jessel. Shortly after Al's death, Jessel had called on Erle and asked her if he could have a pair of her husband's shoes – an immensely symbolic gesture. She made some excuse. Erle knew what Jessel secretly knew himself – neither he nor any other entertainer could possibly fill those shoes.

He was to tell me himself: 'Jolson was a no-good son-of-a-bitch, but he was the greatest entertainer I've ever seen.'

No one else had come along to keep the title of the World's

Greatest Entertainer – although both Danny Kaye and Sammy Davis, Jnr were, in their time, to have laid claim to it.

When Jolson died, a writer declared that he had left behind 'an industry in sackcloth'. But what was principally left behind was the image – and the influence. In the United States, a singer called Eddie Fisher had come and gone claiming that Al Jolson was the man he admired most and on whom he would have liked to have modelled himself. Tom Jones said the same thing – as did Frankie Vaughan. Even Larry Adler was to say that he played the mouth organ the way that he did because of Al Jolson.

In Britain, the Jolson Society is one of the most active fan clubs in existence – the BBC's view, despite the remaining legend of the Beatles, the posthumous tributes to Elvis Presley and the adoring kids of the rock generation. Every year, some 200 people gather for a Jolson teach-in where they discuss the impact of this man on the world's entertainment scene.

Members gather from as far away as New Zealand, the United States and Canada as well as from France and Holland and almost every big town in Britain. Among their number are barristers, senior clergymen, doctors and people from practically every other walk of life. They watch Jolson films, listen to Jolson records, transcription discs from his radio show and speculate on what might have been.

Larry Parks is now dead, too. When this book was first researched, I tried to contact Parks. 'Larry doesn't want to co-operate,' I was told by his agent. 'He says he's been living in Jolson's shadow ever since the pictures and he's had enough.'

It was one of my profoundest regrets – both that I had not seen him in the 'flesh' and that he felt that way. In 1983, his widow Betty Garrett told me: 'But that just wasn't true. Larry always said he was tremendously grateful for those two films. He used to say, "How can you not be grateful for a part seen by a hundred million people"?'

What Al Jolson undeniably had was impact. The impact was in making other entertainers want to be like him and in persuading listeners that he was the kind of performer they would give anything to hear again.

In the early 1980s there were serious plans for a Broadway musical based on the Jolson story. In 1984, the London Palladium was the scene of a Jolson tribute – in light – entertainment terms a phenomenon never experienced before.

When *The Jolson Story* was run on British television in 1982, the television companies reported soaring ratings – and Columbia was bombarded with demands to make the picture and its sequel available for video. The fact that they have been reluctant to agree says that they still believe, after all these years, that there is still a future for the movies in other media.

Jolson's greatest contribution of all was the voice that, to quote Morris Stoloff, 'still gives the chills'. But what he did, too, was to prove that entertainers could be inovative as well as entertaining. If Jolson were alive and active in the 1980s, he would be telling Stephen Spielberg how the newly-revived 3-D film needed him singing in quadrophonic sound – because that would be the only way he could appear to be dancing up and down the runway that would project from the screen. He would also be negotiating with Marvin Hamlisch for a new Broadway show which he would be planning to take on a world tour before going to Hollywood, where he ran his own studio. His records would long ago have appeared on compact disc and there isn't the slightest doubt he would be making the most exciting videos to go before the cameras.

Las Vegas would have hailed him as a bigger money spinner than the gaming tables. His best shows would have long before been established as the year's top spectaculars.

As for today's stars, he would say they had a few things going for them. He would have enjoyed being photographed with Sinatra before he started – by his lights – going downhill, would appreciate being coupled with Barbra Streisand and Neil Diamond. But he wouldn't have liked appearing on the same bills with them.

He would have been as intolerant of critics and newspapermen as ever in the past. He wouldn't have liked to hear the imitators. He would have not merely sat in the box office of theatres where he played – he would have gone on television to plug the shows and then argued with anyone who disagreed.

If Barbara Hale could tell me in 1983 that she regarded the making of *Jolson Sings Again* 'the biggest holiday of my life', it was a memory tinged with a certain amount of pathos. She was one of the last living links with the two biopics (Evelyn Keyes is the only other surviving star of the movies.)

In 1983, William Demarest followed Ludwig Donath, Bill Goodwin, Myron McCormick and Larry himself – all of them remembering to their death beds, Al Jolson as the reason for some of their most notable film roles. Tamara Shayne died in 1983 too – on 23 October, the thirty-third anniversary of Al's own passing.

'Eppy' and Harry Akst had long since died, too.

Sidney Skolsky, Alfred E. Green, Sidney Buchman, Morris Stoloff have all died. Gordon Jenkins, who conducted most of Jolson's last recordings, died in 1984. There are still a few living links with his own early movies and Broadway shows –Don Ameche and Alice Faye are still in fine fettle, for instance. But they are a diminishing band.

George Burns told me in 1983 that he was 'the only one left at the table'. But when he did meet up with other members of the Hillcrest Country Club who had memories stretching back before 1950, Jolson is the only one they all want to talk about.

'Al Jolson,' Burns said, 'was undoubtedly the greatest entertainer of them all.' Which you may have heard before.

The most aged of the Hillcrest set no longer complain about Jolson doing them out of their sturgeon or beating them to the final spot on a benefit bill. Most of them would give their not inconsiderable fortunes for just one more chance of seeing that slightly corpulent figure roll his eyes, throw out his arms and call 'You ain't heard nothin' yet.'

For they all know – as anyone who ever saw him knows – that they'll never see or hear his like again. As one white-haired showman put it, 'Jolson? Its been a very long time. But I still miss him.'

Index